Norton

Stedman

Gilder

Curtis

A Genteel Endeavor

John Tomsich

A Genteel Endeavor

*American Culture and Politics
in the Gilded Age*

Stanford University Press
Stanford, California

1971

228654

Stanford University Press
Stanford, California
© 1971 by the Board of Trustees of the
Leland Stanford Junior University
Printed in the United States of America
ISBN 0-8047-0762-6
LC 75-119503

Acknowledgments

This book began as a University of Wisconsin dissertation directed by Merle Curti. I am so profoundly in his debt for understanding and assistance of every sort that I would like to dedicate this book to him.

I owe thanks also to fellow graduate students at Wisconsin, especially John C. Livingston and R. J. Wilson. William R. Taylor and Loren Baritz gave the completed dissertation a suitably critical reading, but one that encouraged me to persist in trying to make it into a book. Since then, I have been assisted in my research by Sharon K. Coleman, Peter W. French, and Bradley Kent Carter.

For their permission to quote from previously unpublished materials, I gratefully acknowledge the Library of the American Academy of Arts and Letters; the Boston Public Library; the Columbia University Library; the Houghton Library, Harvard University; the Princeton University Library; the Collection of American Literature at the Yale University Library; the Richard Watson Gilder Papers, Manuscript Division, the New York Public Library, Astor, Lenox and Tilden Foundations.

Selections from John Richie Schultz's *The Unpublished Letters of Bayard Taylor in the Huntington Library* have been reprinted with the permission of the Henry E. Huntington Library and Art Gallery, San Marino, California. The University of Pennsylvania Press has authorized my quotations from George Henry Boker's *Sonnets*. Both the University of Pennsylvania Press and the Union League of Philadelphia have kindly agreed to the reproduction of the photograph of Boker that appears herein.

I wish to thank the staffs of the Central Library of the Library Association of Portland, Oregon, and of the Reed College Library who aided in the final stages of preparing this book. The F. L. Griffin Fund of Reed College paid for the typing of the manuscript.

J.T.

Contents

A Genteel Endeavor

Introduction: A Genteel Tradition

THE "Genteel Tradition" was an epithet already rich in connotations at its birth. Once coined by the philosopher Santayana in 1911, it so successfully answered to the diverse prejudices of a generation that its meaning could not be contained within the limits of Santayana's intentions.

Not that those intentions were narrow. In his famous address "The Genteel Tradition in American Philosophy" Santayana attacked the entire tradition of philosophical idealism. That broader attack was forgotten, however, in the flurry of attention drawn by Santayana's eloquent indictment of American culture.

America . . . is a country with two mentalities, one a survival of the beliefs and standards of the fathers, the other an expression of the instincts, practice, and discoveries of the younger generations. In all the higher things of the mind—in religion, in literature, in the moral emotions—it is the hereditary spirit that still prevails. . . . The truth is that one-half of the American mind, that not occupied intensely in practical affairs, has remained, I will not say high-and-dry, but slightly becalmed; it has floated gently in the back-water, while, alongside, in invention and industry and social organization the other half of the mind was leaping down a sort of Niagara Rapids. This division may be found symbolized in American architecture: a neat reproduction of the colonial mansion—with some modern comforts introduced surreptitiously—stands beside the sky-scraper. The American Will inhabits the sky-scraper; the American Intellect inhabits the colonial mansion. The one is the sphere of the American man; the other, at least predominantly, of the American woman. The one is all aggressive enterprise; the other is all genteel tradition.[1]

On poetry, the most genteel of America's cultural activities, Santayana was even more devastating. It was "simple, sweet, humane, Protestant literature, grandmotherly in that sedate, spectacled wonder with which it gazed at this terrible world and said how beautiful and how interesting it all was."[2]

For a rebellious generation of intellectuals, Santayana's choice of the word *genteel* to describe their enemies was exactly right. Before the middle of the nineteenth century, *genteel* had been a term of praise. Introduced into English as *gentle* (from the French *gentil*) in the thirteenth century, it was applied to the gentry. It was readopted into English in the sixteenth century and acquired its present spelling.[3] Its usage, especially in America, was gradually broadened. Noah Webster's influential *American Dictionary* (1851) omitted its original reference to an economic class, defining the word as polite, well-bred, easy and graceful in manner, decorous, refined. Forty years later the *Century Dictionary*, while retaining Webster's definitions, noted a new meaning, fastidious pride in refinement and family position.

At about mid-century in England the usage of *genteel* became derogatory. The shift occurred somewhat later in America, but already in 1859, world-traveler Bayard Taylor employed the term in the depreciatory sense that it would commonly carry later. In describing a formal ball in Germany, Taylor suggested that if his reader preferred, as he did, "the grotesque, the curious, and the comic, to the stupid and the proper, we will leave the genteel society to simper and dance in the banquet-hall, and accompany the peasants to their penny-shows."[4] Taylor was describing Europe, not America; abroad he was always bolder. Whitman, on the other hand, whom no one accused of gentility, was not reluctant to apply the term closer to home. In *Democratic Vistas* (1871) he anticipated the charges Santayana would bring against American poets, among them Taylor. "Do you call those genteel little creatures American poets?" he asked. "Do you term that perpetual, pistareen, paste-pot work, Ameri-

can art, American drama, taste, verse?"[5] Instead of a real literature, he continued, we have

> a parcel of dandies and ennuyées, dapper little gentlemen from
> abroad, who flood us with their thin sentiment of parlors, parasols,
> piano songs, tinkling rhymes, the five-hundredth importation—or
> whimpering and crying about something, chasing one aborted con-
> ceit after another, and forever occupied in dyspeptic amours with
> dyspeptic women.[6]

Neither in Whitman's sense nor in Santayana's did the term
genteel very precisely describe Taylor or his friends. It would
be more accurate to say that gentility as a public face masked the
group's profound pessimism not only about the future of poetry
in America, but about American society in general. The twentieth-century critics who followed Santayana, however, were less
interested in understanding the past than in creating a new and
vital future. They were in no doubt about what had to be ex-
orcised from American life to make that future possible, and
they seized on Santayana's phrase, the Genteel Tradition, to describe it. To Van Wyck Brooks, the Genteel Tradition meant
the nineteenth-century respectable culture that had inhibited the
development of a natural, realistic American literature.[7] It meant
the same to H. L. Mencken, who muddied the debate by describing most American literary figures—especially his genteel
enemies—as Puritans.[8] Besides the literary radicals, a group of
political liberals led by Vernon Parrington found their own use
for *gentility*, which they defined as an irresponsible indifference
to the political and economic needs of the people.[9]

Despite their different focuses, the literary and political reformers of early-twentieth-century America fought a common
enemy. After 1920 they moved apart, but it was to their common
theme that Sinclair Lewis spoke on receiving the Nobel Prize
for Literature in 1930. Responding to complaints from Henry
Van Dyke, a well-known New York minister, diplomat, and
sometime academician, that he was an inappropriate choice for
the honor, Lewis launched a broadside against America's established cultural institutions. There were so few writers of note
in the American Academy of Arts and Letters that the Academy
"does not represent literary America of today—it represents

only Henry Wadsworth Longfellow." The universities were as bad; wherever established culture held sway, Americans feared any literature that did not glorify America.[10]

Lewis neglected to tell the Swedish Academy about certain cultural developments in America—new publishing houses hospitable to the new literature, experimental little magazines, a more sophisticated reading audience—which had largely nullified the effects of the institutions he attacked. In the year that Lewis received the Nobel Prize, there was a stir in American intellectual circles over the New Humanism of Irving Babbitt, Paul Elmer More, and their handful of followers. But it was brief. This latest manifestation of the Genteel Tradition distinguished itself chiefly as an intellectual exercise. By 1930, contrary to Lewis's diagnosis, the institutions that had supported and unified the traditional genteel culture had lost their force. In its newer forms American culture moved decisively toward a more pluralistic pattern.

It is difficult to say when this trend became evident, but the reputation of the Genteel Tradition was skidding after 1900 not only among its critics but among its friends as well. There were those like Van Dyke and Hamilton Wright Mabie, Van Dyke's best friend and author of a trilogy of books on culture, who continued to champion the old-fashioned literary ideals. Others, including English professors George E. Woodberry and Barrett Wendell, defended the ideals but found that their predecessors in the tradition had not accomplished much. Woodberry's *Literary Memoirs of the Nineteenth Century* had a few appreciative lines for the critic Edmund Clarence Stedman, but came close to calling Bayard Taylor a hack.[11] Wendell's *Literary History of America* barely mentioned Taylor's circle, and was as harsh on Taylor as Woodberry's book.[12]

Whatever its reputation may have been, however, genteel culture did exert a significant and pervasive influence in America from the Civil War until about 1910. If that influence was never as unchallengeable as Brooks or Mencken believed, it was nonetheless real. Malcolm Cowley recalled in 1936 that his generation of literary radicals considered genteel culture more oppressive than its English counterpart. In reaction to the lawlessness and corruption of the Civil War years and to the financial crises of the post-War years, Cowley wrote, a generation of reformers emerged who turned their energies to the defense of the

middle-class home and its presiding spirit, the pure young girl. The reformers tried to keep them both unsullied by ignoring or denying the brutalities of business life. Every cultural object that entered the home was supposed to express the highest ideals and aspirations. Every book or magazine intended to appear on the center table in the parlor was kept as innocent as milk. American women of all ages, especially the unmarried ones, had suddenly become more than earthly creatures; they were presented as milk-white angels of art and compassion and culture. "It is the 'young girl' and the family center table," Frank Norris complained in the 1890's, "that determine the standard of the American short story.[13]

Applying these narrow standards to American culture were a group of men who represented older values threatened by the rise of the city, who were Protestant in religion and English or North European in ancestry. The institutions they directed, Cowley said, constituted a formidable array of literary power and status. There were the quality magazines—*Harper's Monthly, The Century, The Atlantic Monthly, The North American Review*—the major publishing firms, the major Eastern universities, the most influential social clubs, and the American Academy of Arts and Letters. To win the recognition of this conglomerate, an author need only appear in the pages of the *Century*. But to do that, as one editor advised Edith Wharton, one must avoid certain topics—"religion, love, politics, alcohol or fairies."[14] Authors who disregarded the advice, if they were not independently wealthy, had the odds stacked heavily against them.

The leaders of genteel culture, of course, saw things quite differently. They did not deny that they tailored literature for middle-class standards. Thomas Bailey Aldrich granted that the *Saturday Press*, of which he was an associate editor in the late 1850's, addressed itself primarily to the wives and daughters of the aspiring middle classes; it never offended anyone, he said.[15] Richard Watson Gilder, editor of the *Century*, was never apologetic about the purity of American literature. In reply to an English jibe that Americans were prudes, Gilder said, "It may be that this accusation is well-founded. If so, we can only say that this is the price we pay for being, on the whole, the decentest nation on the face of the globe."[16]

Gilder, born in 1844, was the youngest of the genteel circle. Since his career developed after the Civil War, he missed that "unfriendly time" for authors that his older friends had lived through.[17] His friends knew, as he did not, that the New England Brahmins had won esteem for their writing, but very little else. Except for Longfellow, whose first dozen volumes of poetry sold 155,000 copies between 1839 and 1864, literature as a paying vocation could barely be said to have existed before the War. Hawthorne's *The House of the Seven Gables* sold only 6,500 copies its first year.[18] It was not at all surprising to Taylor in 1877 that Emerson had not received his first decent royalties until he was nearly sixty; that Bryant, then eighty-three, had never been able to buy even a modest house from all his earnings; that Irving was seventy before he could support himself.[19] The drama critic William Winter has written of his astonishment at the great success of Harriet Beecher Stowe's *Uncle Tom's Cabin*; it was so popular that it was sold from baskets, like apples, by streetboys.[20]

Beginning with those early days, the genteel circle considered their success, or lack of it, an index of the national cultural level. They consistently pictured themselves as heroes, almost missionaries, in the cause of culture. Before the Civil War, their aim was to establish literature, properly understood, as a legitimate vocation. After it, they tried to hold to the standards they had gained against the pressures of what they believed to be a steadily declining public taste. They could scarcely have agreed with their critics that they had inhibited the development of literature in America. On the contrary, they would have insisted, in a land hostile to culture, they had created and nourished it. They had transformed the individual and isolated pursuit of literature into a public and institutionalized profession that would have amazed their predecessors. If the transformation had not brought them the success they sought, it was because America was too immature for serious literature before the Civil

War and too corrupt for it afterward. Had any of the genteel circle lived to hear Santayana, they would have been shocked. They were accustomed to criticism from corrupt politicians or gauche businessmen or literary barbarians who scribbled dialect poetry. But to be accused in one of the institutions of culture by one of the spokesmen for culture of inhibiting culture would have left them speechless.

This book is not an attempt to defend the Genteel Tradition against its critics. It is an attempt to reconstruct and explain a part of that tradition through the lives and thought of eight men who worked within it. These men, all but forgotten now, were among the most eminent figures in respectable American culture in their day. They are the poet, Richard Henry Stoddard; the poet, novelist, and short-story writer, Thomas Bailey Aldrich; the poet and playwright, George Henry Boker; the poet, novelist, playwright, and world-traveler, Bayard Taylor; the editor of *Harper's Weekly* and crusader for civil service reform, George William Curtis; the specialist in late medieval literature and architecture, Charles Eliot Norton; the editor of the *Century*, Richard Watson Gilder; and the critic, Edmund Clarence Stedman. These men constitute an identifiable group. The ideas they held in common formed the basis for an extensive correspondence and in some cases for very close friendships. All eight men were born on the Eastern seaboard and lived their lives there. All of them except Stoddard lived comfortably. The oldest of them was born in 1823. The youngest was born in 1844 and died in 1909. The span of years chosen for this book coincides with their years of greatest productivity and influence.

Why concentrate on these men? Critics of the Genteel Tradition would have included them within a much broader group. Why omit Howells, for example? Sinclair Lewis's speech did not: "Mr. Howells was one of the gentlest, sweetest, and most honest of men, but he had the code of a pious old maid whose greatest delight was to have tea at the vicarage."[21] Yet Howells and his fellow novelists Henry James and Mark Twain, as realists, offered a crucial threat not only to traditional literature but to the very art of poetry. Seen from the later vantage point of naturalists like Frank Norris, Theodore Dreiser, or Jack London, Howells looked all too genteel, but such hindsight entirely obscures the difference felt in the 1880's and 1890's between the idealists' defense of poetry and the realists' call for fiction. The undertones of the debate, as we shall see later, involved far more than literature.

But if poetic idealism is a crucial defining trait for the genteel circle, why omit Santayana's colleague at Harvard, Josiah Royce, whose philosophical idealism was a good example of what Santayana meant when he condemned the Genteel Tradition? It is true that the two varieties of idealism are logically related, but the genteel authors treated in this book were hostile to all philosophical systems, including Royce's. The group, moreover, moved steadily away from religious conceptions of the universe. Most of them became agnostics and Norton eventually repudiated any kind of teleological thinking. It was the loss of religion, above all, that brought despair to the group, and reduced its mission to little more than a concern with manners.

If these eight men comprise an inner circle of Santayana's Genteel Tradition, as I would argue, it was a circle very much in the public view. Literary historians describing the Gilded Age write as if James and Howells and Emily Dickinson, not the genteel authors they fail to mention, were the recognized writers of their day. Measured by the worth of their contribution to literature, the genteel authors deserve the oblivion they have suffered.[22] Contemporary sources, however, reveal quite a different picture. In 1884 the New York *Critic* polled its readers about their favorite authors. Curtis placed sixth and Aldrich seventh; both were ahead of Henry James and Mark Twain.[23] A similar list published by the Harvard *Crimson* put Curtis first and Aldrich second.[24] Aldrich's biographer says that he was considered the equal of Howells and Twain and ranked favorably with Longfellow, Lowell, and Whittier.[25]

It is impossible to know how accurate these estimates are, but they do highlight something that has been almost completely forgotten: the extent to which the genteel authors occupied center stage in American culture between the Civil War and World War I. In their day, they were far more consequential than certain of their contemporaries who have subsequently been classified as great. They were the ones—Gilder and Aldrich and Stoddard and most of the rest at one time or another—who sat in day-by-day control of what passed into the hands of America's better-informed readers. It is their attitudes and values, carefully drawn for a large, but not too large, audience, that shaped cultural life in Victorian America.

As a group, they were bound by extraordinarily close personal relationships. The nucleus of the group was formed in New York in 1848 when Taylor, Stoddard, and Boker met. In 1848, anxious about the fate of some verse he had sent to the *Union Magazine*, Stoddard went to see Taylor, who was its acting editor. Poetry made them instant friends. "We never spent a night together without talking about it," Stoddard wrote, "and without reading the poems we had written since our last meeting." They imagined themselves, in their weekly sessions in Taylor's attic rooms, as the twins of Shelley and Keats.[26]

In these meetings they were soon joined by Boker, the third member of their "Trinity," as the *New York Knickerbocker* dubbed it.[27] The son of a very wealthy Philadelphia family, Boker had graduated from Princeton and had married and traveled abroad by the time he met Taylor and Stoddard. When *The Lesson of Life*, his first volume of poems, appeared in 1848, Taylor reviewed it critically for the *Tribune*. The two men met at the home of T. B. Read and became friends. Boker met Stoddard through Taylor. Boker sold poems for Stoddard and Taylor and got friendly notices for them in the Philadelphia magazines. His lifelong friendship with Taylor was intense; he felt an "almost feminine tenderness" for him. Throughout their lives they reserved a "Bayard's room" and a "George's room" at each other's homes.[28] In the 1850's, after Stoddard's marriage, his home was a regular gathering-place for the Trinity, although Boker hated to travel and came to New York only to see the theatre and his friends.[29] Or the group would gather at the home of Fitz James O'Brien to eat oysters, smoke cigars, and hold races in which the object was to compose the fastest parodies of poets whose names they drew from a hat. Taylor called their New York meetings "The Shrine of Genius."[30] In their early days, as always, Boker lent his friends money. Even after Stoddard secured an appointment to the New York Customs House in 1853 through a letter from Hawthorne, he often needed financial help. He was able to reciprocate in part by looking over Boker's books in manuscript and praising them in print. Taylor did his share, too; in 1856 he persuaded Ticknor and Fields to publish Boker's *Plays and Poems.*[31]

At about this time Aldrich was introduced to the circle,[32] probably by Nathaniel Parker Willis, editor of the *Evening Mirror* and the *Home Journal*, and initiator of the vogue of travel literature from which Taylor was profiting. Aldrich's wife had very mixed feelings the first time she called at the Stoddards'. Their flat, the Century Club, and Pfaff's Beer Cellar were New York's three centers for literary society. The Stoddards' guests were always eminent—authors, actors, artists, musicians, professors, journalists, and critics. "It was rather a solemn thing" to belong to that circle, she said. "The new member entered its (to him) inhospitable door with somewhat the same feelings that would have represented his complex mind had it been the portal of a church."[33] Aldrich himself often found the atmosphere too stuffy. After he became associate editor of the *Saturday Press*, then headed by Henry Clapp, the "King of Bohemia" who presided over the raillery and serious talk at Pfaff's, he occasionally dropped in at the beer cellar instead. Criticism was not muffled there as it was at the Taylors' and Stoddards'.[34] Whitman told Aldrich, "I like your *tinkles*: I like them very well."[35]

In 1865 Aldrich married, with Taylor writing a sonnet for the wedding, and began, on *Every Saturday*, a series of editorships that took him back to Boston for the rest of his life. It was just as well; he had never liked New York society. Later, he repeatedly denied that he had ever been a Bohemian. Even in his newfound respectability, Aldrich did not break with his New York friends, but after his move to Boston he saw much less of them.

He left at the right time. Relationships in the genteel circle were troubled for a while. In 1865 Ticknor and Fields published Aldrich in its prestigious Blue and Gold series. Taylor had appeared in the same series the year before, but Stoddard remained little known. The friends, of course, did not draw unflattering comparisons, and they tried to avoid reminding Stoddard of his continuing poverty. In private, though, they complained that he did not pay his debts to them. They were especially upset by his book reviews, which Stoddard took seriously. His refusal to write the usual puffery of book reviews in those days, and his attempt to treat even his friends objectively, struck them as madness. "The difference between you and me," Stoddard wrote to Taylor, "is that you think a man should not be criticized much, at any rate not to his disadvantage, *after* he has made a certain reputation, while I hold the exact contrary. The reputation of no artist is saved, in my eyes, when he writes badly."[36]

The bonds of friendship, however, persisted through these irritations. The genial influence of the group's newest member, Stedman, helped.[37] Like most of the others in the group, Stedman had begun his career as a journalist. After various unsuccessful attempts to run newspapers of his own, he took a job on the *Tribune*. He met his fellow staff member, Taylor, whose family was then living with the Stoddards. At his first dinner with them, he met Boker, and Aldrich soon thereafter.[38] He had followed the poetry of the group since his editing days on the *Mountain County Herald* in Connecticut, when he had reprinted their work without paying royalties, a common practice in the absence of copyright laws.[39] When Taylor opened Cedarcroft in 1860, Stedman and the rest of the group were guests. Later that year, Stoddard helped Stedman find a publisher for his first book, *Poems, Lyrical and Idyllic*.[40] As Stoddard's friendship with Taylor and Aldrich cooled, he turned increasingly to Stedman. Stedman himself in later years considered Aldrich his closest friend, although they lived in different cities.[41] When Stedman's anthology of Victorian poets appeared, Aldrich wrote to say that his selections would have been the same.[42] He probably meant exactly that. The genteel poets not only thought alike; they thought in the same language. In 1872 Taylor compared one of his poems with one of Stedman's and found three identical expressions.[43]

After the Civil War the last poet of the group, Gilder, was admitted to it. Gilder got his first job in journalism on the

Newark Daily Advertiser through the influence of Stedman's aunt. At about that time he also had several of his poems published in *Harper's Weekly,* then edited by Curtis. He later met Curtis, and they became allies in the cause of good government. On a visit to his mother in Newark in the late 1860's, Stedman met Gilder. They became close friends, and Gilder presided at the memorial ceremony after Stedman's death.[44] As editor of the *Century* magazine, Gilder saw to it that most of Stedman's poems and criticism appeared there first.[45] In 1874, Gilder married Helena de Kay, an artist studying at the Cooper Institute in New York. For years afterward, their home was a center for younger artists and actors like John La Farge, Augustus St. Gaudens, Stanford White, and Joseph Jefferson. Their unhappiness with the conservative Academy of Fine Arts led them to sponsor a rival exhibition and in 1877 to found, in their home, the Society of American Artists.[46] In 1875 on his first trip to Cambridge, Gilder met Norton, probably Aldrich, and the surviving New England Brahmins.[47] He enjoyed the excursion, especially the political talk with Norton, but he could not appreciate Boston. Gilder, like most of his friends, was a New Yorker.

Norton was emphatically not a New Yorker. From an old New England family, Norton was the son of Andrews Norton, often called the Unitarian Pope.[48] Returning from a trip to India by way of Europe, Norton met Curtis in Paris in 1850. Fresh from his own travels in Egypt, Curtis was on his way home to write *Nile Notes,* the book that brought him his first reputation.[49] When Norton returned to Cambridge, he took Curtis around with Longfellow and Lowell to bachelor suppers and fancy balls.[50] Curtis was attractive and charming, and quite at home in Norton's company. He too had colonial ancestors and wealthy and respected parents. And he had lived for four years at New England's intellectual center, first as a boarder at Brook Farm and then in Concord. When he met Norton, he was finishing a leisurely four-year tour of Europe and the Near East. In the 1850's he published two books based on his travels, a novel and a collection of essays, and he began to write for the *Tribune.* In 1853 he turned to writing for and eventually to editing magazines, a field he remained in until his death.

Norton for a time was as deeply engaged in journalism as Curtis. In 1857 he began writing for the *Atlantic Monthly*, recently begun under the editorship of his good friend James Russell Lowell. During the Civil War he became so concerned that Northern readers be exposed to sound opinions about the conflict that he agreed, with Lowell, to accept the editorship of the *North American Review* from 1864 to 1868. In that journal, since 1815 the sounding board for New England letters and scholarship, Norton published most of his significant political writing.

In 1864 Norton bought a summer home in the quiet village of Ashfield, Massachusetts, which the Curtises occupied for three years while Norton was in Europe. On Norton's return Curtis bought his own place in Ashfield, and thereafter both men and their families enjoyed regular summers there. Curtis worked in the morning and rode with his wife or walked with Norton in the afternoon. The two men were greatly respected in Ashfield, though the farmers ridiculed Norton's aesthetic preference for stone walls instead of barbed wire fences. The cows weren't aesthetic, they insisted; they just climbed over the walls.[51] Both men were active in village affairs, especially the annual dinners for the Ashfield Academy begun in 1879. Norton presided at these occasions, which were actually fund-raising picnics addressed by nationally known literary and political figures. If what was heard was Mugwump oratory, that was fine with Norton and Curtis. Civil service reform, tariff reform, Negro education, and anti-imperialism were causes that they championed.[52] Curtis met Aldrich at the Ashfield dinners, and thereafter they regularly exchanged books.[53] Curtis had met Taylor earlier, in the 1850's, after Curtis's return from Egypt. Some ten years later Taylor brought Curtis some tobacco from his own travels so the two could reminisce about the Near East. They did just that at a dinner at Longfellow's and succeeded in boring their host.[54]

Besides privately entertaining each other, the genteel band gathered at the same cultural and social clubs. At the Author's Club, founded at Gilder's home, or at the Century Club they could be expected for the dinners and elaborate receptions offered to visiting cultural luminaries. Before the clubs became too large and too diversified in their membership after 1900, they were among the fundamental institutions of genteel culture.[55] The publisher Henry Holt described them as society's most important institutions outside the home.[56] William D. O'Connor, a close friend of Curtis, had a different view:

> They go to their scratch-my-elbow club . . . and they read each other their little essays and their less verses; and they call each other gods and geniuses; and they concoct their epigrams and epithets, and arrange who shall be written up, and who down, and police Parnassus generally.[57]

The aim of the clubs, like Gilder's aim on the *Century*, was to elevate the tone of American civilization.[58] They attempted to accomplish this, not by furnishing centers for literary work, but by providing places for literary fellowship. After 1900, too big for the intimacy that had marked the burlesques and satires of their monthly dinner parties, the clubs declined in cultural importance.

Before 1900 the clubs were always an adjunct to the world of publishing. It was that world in which the relationships of the genteel authors were clustered. As a description of it, the word *genteel* is strikingly appropriate. When the term was reintroduced into English in the sixteenth and seventeenth centuries, it was probably used by the new commercial middle class, who were not gentry, to distinguish themselves from the commoners. The very word *genteel*, therefore, is intimately bound up with defining and defending status. During the Industrial Revolution in England, before the term became derogatory, it was used by the established classes to describe what the new wealthy were not. In nineteenth-century America, where there were no sharp class lines, status worries were probably deeper than in Europe. Geographical and social mobility undercut family and class continuity. They also, however, made it possible for more people to aspire to positions of high status. In colonial days, status had been conferred by occupation and family standing. In the nineteenth century, formerly respected professions like the ministry, medicine, and the law actually declined in social standing. The educational system, moreover, had not begun to serve its twentieth-century function as a ladder of social mobility. Institutions of higher education were stagnant or declining at mid-century and did not revive until the age of the university in the 1880's. Money, of course, brought position as it always had, but at no time in American history did it seem so necessary to dignify money with manners, tastes, and associations.

This civilizing function, from the 1840's until about the turn of the century, was assumed by women and by the publishing world that catered to them. The division of labor drawn by industrialism allotted to women what Santayana called the higher things of the mind. The social patterns of work, child-raising, and education that supported this development are well known. America, however, added its own emphasis to the general pattern: because children, especially unmarried girls, were much freer participants in adult society than, for example, in France, the cultural objects entering the American home were all too often designed for them.[59] After the 1880's America's concern for what reached its young merged with its fear of the uneducated immigrants who were entering the country from Southern and Eastern Europe.

The drive for status and the feminization of culture both operated with particular force in publishing. In the absence of other effective media for national cultural instruction, the printed word was given the task. Logically, women should have staffed the press and the publishing houses themselves. But primary responsibilities in the home kept all but a few from doing so, although many became authors as an avocation. Many more still, by what they bought and read and by their letters to male editors and publishers, enforced what became known as the genteel standard. In a day when newspapers and magazines were often owned by book publishers, as they were in nineteenth-century America, especially before the Civil War, the influence of these women was very great. It was most evident on the magazines. But because the magazinists—the term was created to describe the genteel journalists and their friends—served their apprenticeships on newspapers and had their books published first as magazine serials, there is a common complexion to at least that part of the publishing world in which they worked.[60] Almost interchangeably, authors, editors, and publishers exemplified the values that their audiences expected from them.

The new generation of magazinists were the first recognizable group of American writers to make their living by writing. Their appearance signified a new kind of literary vocation with a common career pattern and common standards and values. These common qualities defined the professionalization of literature in America.

Typically, aspirants to a literary vocation were obliged to serve their apprenticeships on newspapers like the *New York Tribune* that were open to young writers. Sometimes, as Stedman and Gilder did, the hopeful author had to begin much lower in the publishing world. Gilder's daughter recalled that while he ran the *Newark Daily Advertiser*, he "wrote editorials and locals, solicited advertising, set a little type, occasionally helped make up the form, wheeled it down the street to the pressroom, and before going to bed in the morning, superintended the sale of the paper by the newsboys."[61] With a little newspaper experience, a man could easily move to editing one of the many short-lived magazines, survive its death, and move on to another, as Aldrich did several times. Even with his own reputation as an author established, the man of letters might not relinquish his relationship with the more prestigious journals. From 1881 to 1890 Aldrich edited the *Atlantic Monthly*. His fame as an author and his financial success were already secure, but he knew that there was scarcely a more influential position in American letters than the *Atlantic* editorship. All of the members of the genteel group spent part of their early writing careers in or near the world of magazine-writing and magazine-editing.

In the 1840's and 1850's the magazines were beginning to reveal the pattern that they would hold to throughout the century.[62] Although many magazines had the briefest of lives, publishing began to be a profitable business. *Harper's Monthly* worked out a successful formula to appeal to its predominantly female subscribers: English fiction, biography, travel accounts, and a generous use of illustrations. The *Atlantic Monthly* was more literary and *Scribner's* (later *The Century*) more political, but the three were typical of the nineteenth-century quality magazine—slow in pace and serious in tone, uninterested in contemporary matters and deferential to the interests and tastes of its upper-middle-class readers.

After the Civil War, magazines were able to quadruple their audience to over a million readers without altering their content except to include more advertising and more illustration. The number of periodicals quadrupled, too. Besides the quality magazines and other magazines of general interest whose contributors were less distinguished, there were innumerable specialized periodicals—religious, reformist, agricultural, medical, legal, comic, juvenile, educational and business.[63] The quality magazines attracted and held their new readers by entering the now acceptable field of American fiction and by using many superb woodcuts and halftone photographs. The circulation of *Harper's Monthly* after the War exceeded 100,000; *Harper's Weekly* was about at that level except when Thomas Nast's cartoons of the Tweed ring tripled circulation. The *Century* had 200,000 readers in 1885. In the 1890's with lower postal rates, technological improvements in printing, and reduced paper costs brought about by a depression, a new class of ten-cent magazines (the quality monthlies sold for thirty-five cents) emerged. Faced with this new competition, but not wishing to expand the reading audience, the quality magazines found it necessary to include more contemporary materials. With this one adjustment, they survived much as they had been almost until World War I.

During this half-century, a golden age for magazines, the position of the magazine-writer also improved substantially. In 1877 the *National Republic* was able to report that magazine-writing now drew a living wage and was a profession of trained experts.[64] It is estimated that in 1888 five thousand journalists earned their living writing for magazines.[65] Editors, of course, received much more; Gilder was paid $10,000 by the *Century* in 1890[66] at a time when non-farm laborers earned around $500 a year. Besides their salaries, writers also could expect that their names would become known as signed articles became more common. And with the passage of the International

Copyright Law in 1891, American authors were recognized as being capable of full competition in the market. The publishers of cheap reprints, even the house of Harper, had resisted an international agreement since the 1850's with the argument that it would raise the price of good literature in America. When American authors became as widely read in England as English authors in America, however, it was in the interest of authors and publishers on both sides of the Atlantic to modernize their procedures.

In the fight to win passage of the copyright bill, Gilder and several of his friends were vitally involved. Henry Holt said later that Gilder was one of four or five men who were to be credited with getting the law passed.[67] He often lobbied in Congress and at the White House, where his good friend President Cleveland favored the bill. When the engravers threatened to tack on an amendment that would have killed the bill, Gilder threatened them with "the indignation of the world." A compromise was reached.[68] George Haven Putnam said the law, which almost all the prominent publishers wanted, passed only because it was agreed that all copyrighted works had to be printed in the United States.[69]

Modernizing the publishing industry was not easy. As standard procedures for payment of royalties and merchandising of books developed, some of the established publishers saw evidence that their industry was becoming commercialized. Henry Holt lamented the disappearance of "Courtesy of the Trade," by which most American publishers voluntarily paid English authors for advance sheets of their new books and respected the copyright of the American publisher who made such arrangements first. Holt was especially disturbed by the appearance of literary agents who shopped around among publishers. He wanted authors to be friends, not clients.[70]

Holt was particularly insistent on the point, but there is ample evidence that the commercialization of the literary profession did substantially alter the traditional relationship of author and publisher. Throughout most of the nineteenth century, publishers deliberately blurred the differences between themselves and authors. James T. Fields, the famous publisher of New

England's great literary figures, may serve as an example.[71] His wife's biography of him is strikingly similar to any number of nineteenth-century biographies of nineteenth-century authors. There is the same literary gossip, the same travel to the same places, the same genial account of social life. The similarity in content and tone is undoubtedly a function of the pervasive influence of the nineteenth-century life-and-letters genre; it would be unfair to say that authors and publishers were as much alike as their biographies. Yet the role of the man of letters, for which the biographical form of the life-and-letters was well suited, could and did encompass both authors and publishers.

It is not that all publishers wrote fiction and poetry or that all authors acted as editors, although both occurred frequently, but that they appear to have shared to a remarkable degree a common set of values. Publishing was a business, of course, but almost to a man the major publishers resisted the notion (how much they resisted the practice is another question) of setting a price upon literature. In 1904 Gilder expressed the traditional view to the poet George E. Woodberry: "What bothers me is the system of business competition as applied to the literary world....Why should I have to be a party to putting money values on intellectual and soul outcome?"[72]

The nineteenth-century publisher persistently distinguished himself from the rest of the business world.[73] He complained continually about the unprofitability of his enterprises. He believed that his own business and its practices, unlike those of the monopoly capitalist, were ethical. When self-interest operated, it was disciplined by decent restraint. Knowingly or unknowingly, he flattered himself in these views, for there were economic reasons why the publishing industry would not have lent itself to monopoly control even had its leaders been less scrupulous than they were. Yet publishing was not so competitive as it might have been. And it is true that, since they were certain to lose money, many literary volumes, especially poetry, would never have appeared in print but for the personal enthusiasm of their publishers.

James T. Fields, the famous publisher of New England's great writers, was especially well known for his conviction that a publisher was obliged to support good literature. He was in fact the closest American counterpart of the literary patron. He merely paid his authors for their work, and did not offer them long-term support as aristocrats had done for centuries. Yet he performed one of the patron's most essential services to the artist—he was a knowledgeable and sympathetic audience. From the days of his bookstore at the Old Corner in Boston, Fields was at the center of New England literary culture. Authors gathered at his place of business, they flocked to his dinners, and they were taken on private excursions to meet one or another of the Brahmins.

Curtis's account of life at the Old Corner is marred by its conventionally over-appreciative tone, but it does suggest the flavor of life at the Old Corner and Fields' role in sustaining it.

The annals of publishing and the traditions of publishers in this country will always mention the little Corner Bookstore in Boston ... and those who recall it in other days will always remember the curtained desk at which poet and philosopher and historian and divine, and the doubting, timid young author, were sure to see the bright face and to hear the hearty welcome of James T. Fields. What a crowded, busy shop it was, with the shelves full of books, and piles of books upon the counters and tables, and loiterers tasting them with their eyes, and turning the glossy new pages—loiterers at whom you looked curiously, suspecting them to be makers of books as well as readers. You knew that you might be seeing there in the flesh and in common clothes the famous men and women whose genius and skill made the old world a new world for every one upon whom their spell lay. Suddenly, from behind the green curtain, came a ripple of laughter, then a burst, a chorus; gay voices of two or three or more, but always of one—the one who sat at the desk and whose place was behind the curtain, the literary partner of the house, the friend of the celebrated circle which has made the Boston of the middle of this century as justly renowned as the Edinburgh of the close of the last century....

And it was the work of one man. Fields was the *genius loci*. Fields, with his gentle spirit, his generous and ready sympathy, his love of letters and of literary men, his fine taste, his delightful humor, his business tact and skill, drew, as a magnet draws its own, every kind of man, the shy and the elusive as well as the gay men of the world and the self-possessed favorites of the people. It was his pride to have so many of the American worthies upon his list of authors, to place there if he could the English poets and 'belles-lettres' writers, and then to call them all personal friends.[74]

Fields' role of literary intermediary may not have been as fruitful for literary careers as the more direct route of newspaper journalism and magazine-writing. A sleighing party from the Old Corner to James Russell Lowell's home was less directly useful than the friendship of Nathaniel Parker Willis and access to his *Home Journal,* otherwise known as the "incubator" of young poets.[75] But the encouragement conveyed by a simple chat with Lowell was enormous. It was an encouragement given openly and freely. Even the most famous Brahmins made themselves available to almost anyone with the slightest pretensions to a literary career. They demonstrated their interest in their visitors by entering into scholarly and critical discussions with them. For very young aspiring writers, as Taylor was when he met Lowell, the conversation was both flattering and informative. With the journals themselves offering little valuable criticism until after the Civil War, even an exchange of definitions of poetry was something not to be missed. Moreover, the Brahmins occasionally offered more tangible services. In the yet preprofessional world of magazine-writing, where personal relationships meant everything, a note from one of them might bring a literary position or, if that was unavailable, government work. Stoddard's appointment as a New York customs official and Taylor's and Boker's diplomatic appointments were secured in this way.

For all the geniality and even the usefulness of publisher–author relations, however, they had their unfortunate side. The very eagerness with which publishers vied for the status of patron and man of letters explains in part their indifference and even hostility to improving their own business practices. A more efficient publishing industry might or might not have created a larger audience and larger payments for authors. But the "Courtesy of the Trade" that made it unthinkable for publishers to approach an author unless they knew he was discontented with his existing arrangements almost certainly lessened competition for manuscripts and probably lowered their price. The

entire publishing industry was slow to take advantage of technological improvements and of the possibilities for a larger
market opened up by modern advertising and merchandising
techniques. Publishers divested themselves of bookselling before
the Civil War and gave little assistance to the book-selling industry, which remained disorganized throughout the century.
The publishers' interest, before 1900, was heavily concentrated
on finding and producing a quality product, not on selling it.
Their identification with the artist was dominant.

It was especially dominant in Boston. As publishing concentrated in the New York houses and New England saw its
hegemony slip away, however, its continued insistence on quality took on a defensive note. The *Atlantic Monthly* of the 1880's
under Aldrich has been described as the best-edited journal in
the English-speaking world.[76] It was also among the more timid.
Aldrich refused to open its pages to the more controversial
political and economic issues of the day. He also barred articles
on religion. As an unintended symbol of his own remoteness
from the world, he corked up the speaking-tube that was his
only link with the outside. In peace and quiet, as one of the more
lugubrious of the gossipy accounts of nineteenth-century authors reported, he was able to look down on "a quiet old grave-
yard, like those of St. Paul's and Trinity in New York."[77]

Aldrich was an editor, not a publisher, it is true. And even
among his circle, his cheerfulness seldom rose above irony. He
is supposed to have discovered his vocation as a poet while reading Longfellow and mourning the death of a friend; the poem
that made him famous, "The Ballad of Babie Bell," is a lachry-
mose account of the death of an infant. For New England, the
conjunction of death and poetry seemed normal enough.[78] Aldrich could see the fortunes of his region declining as her great
men died.

But in prosperous New York, too, the same note was sounded.
The shadow of gloom hung over much of that friendly world
of authors and publishers, especially in the parasitical genre of
literary recollections. Adoring peeks into the homes of poets
and clammy descriptions of their desks, their pens, their bric-a-

brac, abounded.[79] William Winter, a close friend of Aldrich and a prolific gossip about the holy world of books, perfectly exemplified the kind of hack that the man of letters became in the late nineteenth century.[80] More a devotee than a journalist, Winter served up delectable bits about his relic-hunting (a bit of Poe's coffin, a glass used by Dickens) and bemoaned the loss of reverence for literature and its makers. Gone were the great days of hero-worship; no longer would girls gather, as around Dickens in Boston, "to furtively cut bits of fur from his seal-skin overcoat."[81] Winter could not forget the coat; his eye for the trivial was unerring.

Winter was neither an editor nor a publisher. But he was both a parasite on the world of authors, and a product of it. Far more nostalgic and melancholy than any of the genteel group, he was nevertheless only a banal exaggeration of them. All of them, authors, editors, and publishers, derived their primary professional satisfaction from their association with an art that conferred status. By itself, status might have been as good an incentive for art as any other. But as the century moved on, the genteel author, editor, and publisher used his status as a weapon against the broadening of culture. Winter's maunderings through the cemetery of literature are indicative of the lack of confidence with which the group regarded the future.

It was from that lack of confidence that their genteel endeavor sprang. Before the Civil War, as they successfully embarked on the careers they had chosen, the genteel authors moved to free American art from the political and moral assertions that had marred the work of the Brahmins. Their early endeavor was to win recognition for the idea that aesthetic criteria, and those alone, were relevant for art. The art of the beautiful was the credo of their youth, and remained their credo always. Yet from the beginning their art diverged less than they believed it did from traditional New England culture. There were differences indeed; Lowell especially was sensitive to them. But although they chafed impatiently at the restraints imposed by their elders, the genteel authors did not disrupt the continuity of culture in America.

After the Civil War, as social change assumed threatening proportions, the genteel endeavor became distinctly conservative. Its tool was culture, but its motivation was fear. The very idea of respectable culture was the creation of the genteel authors. It was they who forged that peculiar complex of the intellectual, the aesthetic, and the spiritual into a tool for enlightening and civilizing the middle classes. The Brahmins, of course, had left a legacy of culture of their own, but not until the genteel authors softened its moralism, made its scholarship more genial, and defined it as a measure of status did culture exert its major influence. There was another difference between the two generations. Pious as well as learned men, the Brahmins thought of character as a manifestation of inner qualities. They were men of decorum not only in public, but in private. The genteel authors, by contrast, sharply distinguished the public and the private. Gilder, according to Whitman's own statement, was hospitable to him even when his reputation was at its lowest; opening the *Century* to his poetry was another matter.[82] Boker candidly told his friends not to read the reviews he wrote, and was both honest and amused about the discrepancy between his love sonnets and his sexual conduct.

For all of the group, the genteel endeavor was to create a culture for the public. That fact in itself betrayed the purpose of genteel culture. Its emphasis upon manners, propriety, tradition, called attention to form, not substance. Its deepest motive was seldom rich scholarship or profound art; overwhelmingly its aim was didactic. Just as much as the popular women's magazines that first appeared in the period, genteel culture was committed to the mission of teaching men how to behave. Above all it was a reflexive culture, a culture thrown up in defense against the mobility of America; against the ease with which men came to America, moved around, and moved up. For the American masses, whether native-born or immigrant, genteel culture offered nothing at all. For the middle and upper classes, however, whose alliance it was designed to cement, it offered one clear set of standards to govern public behavior. In the long run the alliance proved untenable; the concept of a unified culture was reduced to a shambles in the twentieth century as men talked of highbrow, lowbrow, and middlebrow cultures.

Nevertheless, genteel culture did register some achievements. The occasional verse so characteristic of the period was uninteresting, but its magazine illustrations and short stories were excellent. Serialized fiction, too, although it hampered the development of new forms for the novel, nevertheless served to introduce the best American writers to a wide audience. It seems to have acted to span the age of transition, as Stedman often called it, between the day when poetry was written for a few and the day when novels sold to the many. And in its didactic capacity, genteel culture unmistakably raised the level of literary criticism and scholarship in America. Usually its achievements in these areas were derivative of English and German sources, but Norton's studies of Dante and of medieval and Renaissance architecture, Taylor's translation of *Faust*, and Stedman's uncompleted researches into the Sicilian idyllists were praiseworthy. They were a register of the continuing vitality of the New England tradition.

As America's publishing center migrated from Boston to New York, however, the vocation of literature was defined in new ways. It became a paying profession with intricate institutional arrangements for bringing authors together both on and off the job. The Brahmins saw one another socially, of course, but the multiplicity of professional and personal relationships that bound the genteel circle together were not a feature of Boston. Lowell complained that his fellow Bostonians had only two notions of hospitality: "a dinner with people you never saw before nor ever wish to see again, and a drive in Mount Auburn cemetery."[83] The salons of the Stoddards and Gilders were a world away. New York, too, saw an almost incredible proliferation of newspapers and magazines, filled, as the years passed, with a new, crisp, journalistic prose that contrasted with the heaviness that even Norton fussed about in the *North American Review*.[84]

There were losses as well as gains in the new journalism. In its eagerness to cultivate *American* letters, it encouraged young authors, like Taylor, to write too much and too rapidly. He may have been justified in complaining about unfriendly readers, but his editors and publishers were not critical enough. They took the respectable for the good; in an age of conflicting literary ideals, it was easier to recognize. The professionalization of literature did not mean an immediate gain in quality. The process was shaped by the genteel endeavor, whose standards were more likely to constrain than to vivify.

Playing at Escape

IT IS ironic that the genteel poets were described by their critics as Puritans; nothing would have offended them more. From the first, they defined their literary ideals in reaction to the New England Brahmins, especially Lowell, who exemplified for them the cold hand of the Puritan past. They wanted a literature more inclined to self-expression than self-restraint. In poetry they wanted an end of teaching, whether moral or political, and a beginning of pleasure. Their program was the romantic program of the day; their city, New York, was its center.

Their popular spokesman in the two decades before the Civil War was Bayard Taylor. Born in the small Quaker town of Kennett Square, Pennsylvania, in 1825, Taylor keyed his early career to an escape from its stifling values. He was apprenticed at 17 as a printer on a country newspaper. Rufus Mott Griswold, editor of *Graham's Magazine*, noticed his poems in the *Saturday Evening Post* and secured a publisher for his first book of verse, *Ximena* (1844), which brought him enough money to buy out of his apprenticeship. He then persuaded the publishers of two New York newspapers to give him a small advance for a series of European travel sketches. His collected articles, published as *Views Afoot* when he was only twenty-one, were an instant success. The book, which went through twenty editions in a decade, established him successfully in New York journalism and gained him a national reputation.[1] His reputation later hounded him. At first, however, he loved the role of world traveler and shrewdly profited from it. By 1860 he was the author of nine travel accounts and five books of poetry on travel themes. His books and lectures had brought him enough to build a $15,000 home.

Taylor was a celebrity on the lecture circuit. Through the *New York Tribune*, which he said was read almost as often as the Bible in western America, readers were familiar with his travels. Crowds came wherever he spoke.[2] Women were carried out fainting in the middle of his talks; young girls punctuated his words with breathless whispers. Even at small country towns, he could ask $50 a lecture, because people came in their wagons from twenty miles around to hear him. They carried him from place to place in triumph, put him up at the best hotels, and stared at him in awestruck silence. A few of his listeners were disappointed at his youth, but many more cared little for that. Dressed occasionally in Arab costume, Taylor was a handsome performer. Stoddard described him as "tall, erect, active-looking, and manly, with an aquiline nose, bright, loving eyes, and the dark, ringleted hair with which we endow, in ideal, the head of poets." His appeal was not confined to women. In 1854 Indiana State College made him a temporary Professor of History to enable him to talk in College Hall. His schedule forced him to postpone the event for a year. The College let him keep the title until then.

In 1859 Taylor returned to Kennett Square to build his home, Cedarcroft. It was not a return that pleased his neighbors. In contrast to their ways, Taylor bought a large tract of land and built a house patterned after the manor houses of eighteenth-century England. He aptly called it a castle. A large two-story structure of brick and stone surmounted by a tall, square tower, Cedarcroft had spacious windows, broad verandas and walls two feet thick. The rooms were paneled in wood, and the oak and black walnut mantelpieces were emblazoned with the coat of arms of the Taylor family, a simple crest, as Taylor told Boker, "a lion rampant, holding a scallop-shell in his paws, and three of the same shells on the shield." Taylor was proud of the landscape. He cut few trees to build his house and planted more than he cut. After he moved into Cedarcroft in 1860, he kept a close eye on his orchards and vegetable garden. Introduced to Latakia tobacco in Egypt, he raised a few of the plants at Cedarcroft.

Life was pleasant at first. Taylor avoided his neighbors and entertained his New York friends. There were delightful summer picnics, such as one to which he invited the Stedmans. A day at the Brandywine was interrupted by a herd of cattle that backed the party down to the river. Uncertain about whether the animals intended to charge or not, Taylor and Stedman considered carrying the women across the stream on their backs. That proved unnecessary when Stedman mounted a leading steer; Taylor, "like a sacrifical priest, took hold of one of the horns, and swinging his staff, led the astonished animal and his rider about in triumphal procession." The episode was of course commemorated in a sonnet.

After the Civil War, Cedarcroft was a constant source of trouble. Taylor had to fight off repeated attempts to cut a road through the grounds. And the estate was expensive and difficult to run. By 1870 he was willing to rent the place. "I am tired of having to do with blacksmiths, millers, threshers, harvest hands, hydraulic rams, and all the endless minor interests of life in the country," he complained to his mother. "In short, my attempt to combine farming and literature is a dead failure, and I have been carrying it on now for several years ... out of stubborn unwillingness to admit that I was mistaken." His neighbors, too, continued to plague him. They had disliked his pretentiousness from the start. He never joined the Quakers who dominated the town and he refused to bow to their prejudices. He openly served liquor at Cedarcroft and entertained visitors who drank it. It was not to justify this practice, but to set clear the right relationship between art and reform that Taylor, in exasperation, appeared at one of the local Quaker conventions. His skills as a lecturer aided him little. His argument, that reform was all right for reformers, but not for artists, persuaded no one. Cedarcroft was a burden to Taylor for the rest of his life; he could neither sell nor lease it.[3]

New, more serious problems emerged, too. Before the Civil

War, his worries had had less to do with money than with reputation. His first poetry was often described as imitative, especially by English reviewers. His response, in 1852, to such a critical notice in the *Westminster Review* was to think up six new poems in two days. "This convinced me that the faculty was not dead," he wrote Boker, "but only sleeping, and I shall never doubt it more. If God gives me life and health I shall prove that I am something better than a mere traveller,—a reputation which the world is now trying to force upon me."[4] The third member of the Trinity, Stoddard, had doubts, however. In 1855 he wrote to Fields, Taylor's publisher, that most of Taylor's poems missed the mark. Of one poem Stoddard said he could find no verbal fault with it, but it left no marked impression on his mind. "It seems *built*; it wants simplicity; it is more artificial than natural. The artifice of rhetoric is a second nature with Bayard."[5] Taylor's own letters to Fields express his constant anxiety over his reputation. There are implications also that he thought Fields was not aggressive enough in promoting his serious work. But he was careful not to displease the publisher. Fields was a friend and one whose literary judgment he respected.

After the Civil War, although his most pressing worries were financial, Taylor continued to be concerned with his reputation. Indeed, his need for reassurance increased as his income declined. In 1859 he had had a very profitable lecture tour of California; he actually lost money on a similar tour there in 1870. It shocked him that lecturing had fallen on bad times. The wealthy had found other things to do, his wife explained, and others turned increasingly to newspapers. The lecture circuit audiences had lost interest in pre-War political and religious causes, and the fad of travel accounts was over. People now demanded music and drama.[6]

Taylor viewed these events as ominous.

We have fallen on evil times. I think it will be ten years before either literature or art will be as popular and profitable as they were ten years ago. With all the splendid patriotism which the war called forth, we cannot escape its consequences. The people have become materialized, their culture is temporarily disturbed because not well grounded, the very best of the younger generation are lost, the rage for mere diversion and intellectual excitement taints the public taste,—and so nothing is left to us artists but to possess our souls in patience until the better time comes.[7]

If he were in England or Germany, he would withdraw into creative seclusion. But in America that meant only stagnation. "The creative natures are few and far apart," he said, "and they need all the development, all the comfort, all the encouragement which comes of association. There is not even an appreciative class in the country, and the lack of this will pull down an artist whenever he tries to rise."[8] What taste remained was being ground away on the one side by moralists like Josiah Holland, editor of *Scribner's Monthly,* and on the other by humorists like Josh Billings.[9]

In 1866 when *The Picture of St. John* appeared, Taylor received kind words from Longfellow. His reply was an outpouring of thanks and a statement of new directions:

Let me say that nearly everything which I have published, up to last year, seems to me more or less crude and unsatisfactory. My former works are simply so many phases of an education which circumstances have compelled me to acquire in the sight of the public. I had, in fact, very little early education except that of travel; I began to publish (it was inevitable) much too soon; and moreover, I am descended from two hundred years of Quaker farmers, whose transmitted slowness of maturity I have hardly yet overcome. The artistic sense was long dormant, and is only at present becoming fairly active: I am, perhaps, ten years behind a man who has had more favorable antecedents and opportunities. . . . I shall try to do better things in the future, taking a new departure from this point. There is still time, with life and health, to atone for the imperfections of the past.[10]

In the next few years, Taylor's time was consumed in his translation of Goethe's *Faust*. There existed few satisfactory English translations of Part I and none of the entire work in the original meter. Taylor tried to demonstrate the unity of the two parts of *Faust*, a notion not common at the time. He was extremely anxious about the critical reception of the translation. Nine-tenths of the reading public, he wrote Fields, had made up its mind about his abilities before the War. "I have given up my old audience," he said, "and have not yet obtained a new one."[11] The book was suitably praised, except in Boston's *North American Review*, which convinced him anew of its partiality for New Englanders. Despite its indifference, however, Taylor's translation soon became the best-known and most frequently recommended English version. It lacked the richness and depth of the original, but its scholarship was good for the day.[12] As poetry, its faithful rendering of the German meter made for more inversions than normally appear in English.[13] Yet Taylor had reason for pride; his *Faust* deserves to be classified with New England's other great translations—Longfellow's *Dante*, Bryant's *Homer*, Norton's *Vita Nuova*, and Cranch's *Virgil*.[14] He now resolved upon a double biography of Goethe and Schiller. He had earned very little from *Faust* and expected little from the biography, but he hoped finally to be rid of his reputation as traveler and to be ranked with the Brahmins.

A symbolic episode in 1876 proved that he was indeed their heir, but not their equal. As plans were formulated for the centennial of the Declaration of Independence, the commission in charge of the celebration at Philadelphia applied in turn to Longfellow, Lowell, Holmes, and Bryant to deliver a national ode. Age and indisposition brought refusals from them all. Taylor was next consulted and, though he knew where he stood in line, he accepted. He was cheered by popular applause for his poem, which he himself delivered.[15] It was a later critic who called it "one of the greatest failures in the history of American literature."[16]

In recognition of his knowledge of German literature, Taylor was appointed minister to Germany in 1878. A huge testimonial dinner at Delmonico's in New York saw him off. Just before he left, President Grant told him he hoped he would stay in Germany until his biography of Goethe and Schiller was finished. Grant said he had read Taylor's translation of *Faust* twice with great interest and instructed him not to allow his official duties to prevent him from completing the biography.[17] Illness, not duties, intervened. After less than a year in Germany, he died from what was diagnosed as liver disease and dropsy. Perhaps his biographer, who said he was worn out and broken,[18] was more accurate.

Most of Taylor's adult life had been spent in a futile attempt to overcome his early reputation as a traveling journalist. It haunted him to the day of his death. Perhaps if he had found after the War a new literary mode that struck the popular fancy, he would have lost less of his youthful romanticism than he did. But post-War literary trends threatened him deeply; he could neither understand nor sympathize with them. He turned from his age in disgust and wrote for a future that forgot him.

The genteel endeavor was nevertheless rooted in Taylor's early aims. He retreated from those aims, but the readers of his generation remembered him always as the venturesome boy of *Views Afoot*. Their judgment of him was better than his own. His real influence on American literature lay in the work he later despised. It was there that he helped to emancipate literature from the hold of religion and politics.

Taylor's travel books made no attempt to disguise his displeasure with American religion. He often offended his readers, but there was nothing remarkable in his religious opinions. The Deists and the Unitarians had been fighting orthodoxy long enough so that Taylor and his friends did not have to agonize over the issue or defend themselves; they simply *felt* their objections to repressive religion, and that was sufficient. An early poem by Taylor, "In Articulo Mortis," is representative. The poet asks his father why he exercised his

> Iron creed that drove your child,
> Sore with the scourging of its rigid laws,
> To the alluring license of the world?
> Why did you crush the healthy joys that craved
> Growth in a liberal air, the motions free
> That leap along the bounding pulse of Youth
> And pluck delight in the fresh fields of Time,
> Building your stern religion round the dreams
> That fill, self-born, the morning sleep of Life,
> And give us courage for its day of Toil?
> Had you not hedged each simple joy with sin,

And from the guileless blooms of Nature driven
My steps, to falter on your arid wastes
Of harshest duty, I had never looked
To Sin for joy, nor plunged amid the rank
Dense overgrowths of Pleasure, which conceal
Her soundless quicksands; had you turned the tide
Of warm, impetuous blood, that beat so strong
In every vein, to mingle with the streams
Of manly actions, I had spent its force
In watering many a pleasant field of life
With fertilizing increase; but you set
Your unrelenting dogmas in its path,
Locked the dark barrier with a cruel hand,
And thought the fierce rebellion you provoked
By tyranny against my nature's law,
The evidence of Hell![19]

The poem was typical; its objections to orthodoxy were not theological so much as humanitarian. The stiffness and narrowness that even Norton found in Puritanism were the basis of the group's objections. Perhaps it was the Quaker atmosphere in the town of Kennett Square that bred Taylor's hatred of asceticism. He thought it had become such a pervasive social force that people had forgotten how to live. At Oberlin College in Ohio, one of Taylor's lecture stops in 1860, they had certainly forgotten: he wrote to his wife that the students "live on bread and mush, and study theology and dyspepsia. Girls are forbidden to ride on horseback, and recite Latin grammar instead. After the yearly commencement, there are numbers of marriages—whether necessary or not, I can't say. To sum up, it is a very moral, righteous and disagreeable place."[20]

No form of the religious life ever appealed to Taylor or to his friends. The enormous undertaking by American Protestants to support foreign missions all over the world did not impress him. He never denied that the extension of Christianity was a good thing, but the self-sacrifice demanded of missionaries conflicted with his own notions of the good life. In 1853 he was ready to dismiss "the whole Missionary system from beginning to end" as "an enormous waste of time, talent and money...."[21] One of the few preachers he ever praised was a German pastor, who, after he performed a marriage, danced with the bridesmaid.

There was no asceticism in German theology, Taylor observed. The "great, warm, mellow, merry heart" of Luther, not his inkstand, put the Devil to flight.[22]

After the Civil War Taylor gave religion some close attention in three long plays, but before the War he seems to have had almost no theology at all. His friends Boker and Stoddard were explicit as early as 1850 in rejecting Christianity altogether.[23] The initial break for all of them seems to have been almost painless. They found Puritanism emotionally repugnant and that was that. They never explained why they dismissed religion so easily, but Transcendentalism probably had more to do with it than they would ever admit.

Anyone who seeks to establish a Transcendental influence on the genteel writers, in fact, must deal with their active hostility toward the movement. Except for Curtis, who lived at Brook Farm for a time and who helped Thoreau build his cabin at Walden Pond, the group invested the word *Transcendentalism* with connotations ranging from vaguely unpleasant to foolish.[24] It soon becomes evident, however, that the group's understanding of the philosophy was confused.

For Norton, the son of Andrews Norton, a Unitarian minister and arch-enemy of Transcendentalism, the issue was simple. In 1880, Norton ridiculed the Concord Summer School of Philosophy at which Emerson was scheduled to speak and of which "the potato-and-apple Evangelist," Alcott, was high priest. "The teaching is marvelous; and the intuitionists have it all their own way, and the contradictoriness of the intuitions of the different sages is the supreme test and evidence of their truth. Is not truth polygonal? Are not the ego and the non-ego resolvable in the last analysis into a single affirmation? You know the kind from of old."[25]

Norton never betrayed any taste for the intuitionism he saw in Transcendentalism; he called himself a Benthamite rationalist in his early days, and he remained one always. He did, however, take religion more seriously than the Taylor-Boker-Stoddard circle did, and he escaped their shallowness. But Norton's opinion is not representative; his friends maintained the opposite view that Transcendentalism was not intuitionist enough.

Curtis, in a letter written after his departure from Brook

Farm, said that he was too much of an individualist for the life there. "I live only for myself," he wrote, "and in proportion to my own growth, so I benefit others. As Fourier seems to me to have postponed his life, in finding out how to live, so I often felt it was with Mr. Ripley. Besides, I feel that our evils are entirely individual, not social. . . . That there is a slave on my plantation or a servant in my kitchen is no evil; but that the slave and servant should be unwilling to be so, that is the difficulty." Curtis found, too, a painful "lack of heroism" in the Brook Farm undertaking. He laughed heartily "at our absorbing charities and meetings, upon which we waste our health and grow thin." He was prepared to answer the "distressing plea for the rights of the oppressed, and the 'all-men-born-to-be-equal' with a smiling strength, which assures us therein lies the wealth and the equality which we are trying to manufacture out of such materials as association, organization of society, copartnership, no wages, and the like. . . . The love which alone can make your Phalanx beautiful, also renders it unnecessary."[26] The parallel with Emerson is clear: Brook Farm would not help either of them discover his true self. Yet in his later life Curtis chided his generation for foolishly confusing some of the "ludicrous aspects" of Transcendentalism with its "chief and only signs."[27]

Taylor's poem, "My Mission," is a good expression of this confusion.

> Every spirit has its mission, say the transcendental crew:
> "This is mine," they cry; "Eureka! this purpose I pursue;
> For, behold, a god hath called me, and his service I shall do!
>
> "Brother, seek thy calling likewise, thou wert destined for the
>   same;
> Sloth is sin, and toil is worship, and the soul demands an aim;
> Who neglects the ordination, he shall not escape the blame."
>
> O my ears are dinned and wearied with the clatter of the school:
> Life to them is geometric, and they act by line and rule—
> If there be no other wisdom, better far to be a fool!
>
> Better far the honest nature, in its narrow path content,
> Taking, with a child's acceptance, whatsoever may be sent,
> Than the introverted vision, seeing Self pre-eminent.

For the spirit's proper freedom by itself may be destroyed,
Wasting, like the young Narcissus, o'er its image in the void;
Even virtue is not virtue, when too consciously enjoyed.

I am sick of canting prophets, self-elected kings that reign
Over herds of silly subjects, of their new allegiance vain:
Preaching labor, preaching duty, preaching love with lips
    profane.

With the holiest things they tamper, and the noblest they
    degrade,—
Making Life an institution, making Destiny a trade;
But the honest vice is better than the saintship they parade.[28]

Taylor's major theme is that the Transcendental "crew" are too intellectual, too geometric, in their approach to life. It should be noted, however, that there is an undertone of worry about the "introverted vision" and the "Self pre-eminent" that will become increasingly important. This worry evokes his satire of the "Experience of the A. C." (Arcadian Community). The leader of the community, an avid food faddist, maintains that his instinct alone will tell him which foods are good. On impulse he is led to beer; he overindulges himself and gets absurdly drunk. One lesson is not enough for the group. It wrecks itself by following the "true and natural impulse" of each member to be utterly candid with each other. The holiday ends with the brethren hurling insults.[29]

There is no doubt that Taylor's intuitionism is more restrained than Emerson's, but because Taylor thought of the reformers of Brook Farm instead of Emerson when he spoke of Transcendentalism, he was able to accuse the Transcendentalists of making life into geometry. He was then able to see himself as an exponent of the truly instinctual and natural life, as his travel books show, without realizing how much more penetrating Emerson's vision was than his own.

Confusion of terms and misreading of Emerson notwithstanding, Transcendentalism opened the way for genteel liberalism. Had Stedman not balked at the same "systematic" quality that Taylor thought he saw in Transcendentalism, he might have understood his own religion better. One of Stoddard's best poems, "Carmen Naturae Triumphale," is a frank exposition of Emersonian religious doctrine. It has Emerson's naturism, his idealism, his primitivism, his attack on institutional religion. "My mind the Universe, the Universe my Mind!" Stoddard declares; the source of all truth and virtue is there.[30] But with the exception of Stoddard, the effect of Transcendentalism on the genteel figures was merely a liberating one. They used religious intuitionism to help them discard religious orthodoxy; for a long time they had virtually no theology at all and seemed content to let each man believe what he wished.

In pre–Civil War politics, the genteel circle took a stance of Emersonian individualism not only against organized reform but against any kind of political life. At their coming of age they dedicated themselves to art—an art of individual genius. Because their prevailing point of view from their earliest years was individualistic, they tended to view organized religion and politics as obstacles to life. It was for that reason, above all, that Taylor attacked Puritanism in religion and "Transcendentalism" in politics. He believed that the two had combined in America to produce a stifling conformity. He granted that America enjoyed political freedom, while Europe still suffered under political despotism, but it seemed more important to him that Europe had social freedom and America did not. No one could live as he chose in America, and the artist was especially vulnerable to the stultifying effects of this "prescribed regimen."[31]

The "prescribed regimen" was oppressive enough in life, but it was unbearable in literature. In their earliest works and criticism, the genteel generation hinted at an independence of the literary standards that had dominated New England. Because of the adulation still enjoyed by the Brahmins, the genteel authors treated them with reverence in public, but criticized them in private with a sharpness that verged on sarcasm. Wishing to be poets, they took their models from England, especially Shelley, Keats, and Tennyson, and not from America. Their agreement was firm on one principle: art must concern itself with the search for beauty for its own sake. Not understanding this, the Brahmins had not understood art. Lowell's verse, with its moral and political preachments, was a frequently cited example.

As the travel literature of the genteel authors began to appear in the 1840's and 1850's, Lowell wrote to caution the youngsters against their naughtiness and sensualism. Prostitutes were no proper theme for literature, Lowell thought; nor was the excessively rich celebration of the Arab lands.[32] Lowell might have served as a spokesman for the authors' families. Curtis deliberately did not send an advance copy of his *Nile Notes* to his father, because he knew what his reaction would be. The elder Curtis did not like his son's attention to Egyptian dancing girls, but George argued that they occupied no more space in his book than they did on his voyage. Only the "affected and self-conscious exaggeration of the moral sense," George wrote, made for alarm. The truth of the "essentially sensuous, luxurious, languid and sense-satisfied spirit of Eastern life" would provoke only those who were forever suspecting evil.[33] Stedman's opinion was that public approval of the novel with a purpose was downright unwholesome. It was "agin nature" to "teach the gospel of *old-maidism* and *morbid self-abnegation*."[34]

It seemed essential to the genteel authors in 1850 to assert the independence of art and morals. Later, when realism entered the American novel and Swinburne's school of sensuous poetry gained acclaim in England, the ethical function of art could not be dismissed so easily. Then, genteel opinion back-tracked considerably. But in 1850 moral emancipation seemed primary; moral assertion could wait. Inclined as they were, and convinced, with Taylor, of American conformity, the genteel authors could only look abroad, away from their own land and their own time. In that very year, Boker summed it up in a letter to Stoddard: "Get out of your age as far as you can."[35]

Boker and Stoddard, and Taylor as well, had good reason to know that they were setting themselves against the trend toward literary nationalism that had provoked a full-scale debate among American intellectuals in the 1830's and 1840's. They were for a time friends of Rufus Griswold, one of the foremost American anthologists, and a spokesman for Americanism in literature.

But even in 1844 the genteel circle felt that the cultural resources of America were too thin for great art. Transcendentalism never persuaded them that American nature would be a sufficient inspiration to art.

In 1859 Hawthorne's preface to *The Marble Faun* expressed his dissatisfactions with the American scene. Three years earlier, in *Lotus-Eating*, Curtis anticipated the charge. "The moment you travel in America the victory of Europe is sure," he wrote. America had no mountains like the Alps, no lakes as lovely as European lakes. It had "few rivers of any romantic association, no quaint cities, no picturesque costume and customs, no pictures or buildings. We have none of the charms that follow long history. We have only vast and unimproved extent, and the interest with which the possible grandeur of a mysterious future may invest it." The "*Idea*" of Western rivers and lakes or grass or forest was "as impressive and much less wearisome than the actual sight of them." The American artist went to Europe not only because of its social atmosphere, but also because of "the positive want of the picturesque in American scenery and life."[36]

Apparently American readers agreed with Curtis; they found his and his friend Taylor's picturesque accounts of their foreign travels very appealing. Both men established themselves as literary figures by the success of their travel books, the best of which dealt with Egypt. The pre-eminence of Taylor is clear, however. He traveled so widely, published so much, and lectured about his travels so often that by 1860 he had laid sound claim to the title of The American Traveler. He was also the only spokesman for genteel culture who was able to command a wide, popular audience. Only before the Civil War and in travel literature did genteel culture find a means for bridging what later became an unbridgeable chasm between the refined and the popular.

Taylor's travel books are not impressive. They have too much of the merely picturesque in them. Taylor was a passable reporter of foreign scenery, art and architecture, and customs. But even with these subjects, his best, he did not look closely or deeply enough. The relationships between time, place, and culture that good travel literature (Emerson's *English Traits*, for example) seeks to establish were relationships that escaped Taylor. He did not really *see* where he was, or understand the people there. He was content to enter, as his wife later wrote, "with a certain athletic joy upon the task of making literature, not a stick or a crutch, but a horse on which he proposed to ride hard into prosperity."[37] Intending all the while, one might add, to use his profits to build a great house at Kennett Square.

Yet, for all its limitations, the travel literature of Taylor and Curtis does have vitality. Taylor's narrative stance was marked by a cosmopolitanism that enabled him to give to sacrosanct topics a light treatment that would otherwise have been viewed as almost immoral and certainly ill-mannered. He advocated no breaches of conduct, but he used strange customs to provoke the righteous. Taylor's trip to Moscow, for example, provided him with an opportunity to praise the state-supported foundling hospital and to attack Americans who would ostracize unwed mothers. "It is a great mistake to suppose that the moral tone of Society can only be preserved by making desperate outcasts of all who sin," he wrote. "We should remember that a morality which is uncharitable, cruel, and Pharisaic, inevitably breeds a secret immorality." Then, to illustrate the lesson, he continued, "The Spartan holiness of the New England pilgrims was followed by a shocking prevalence of unnatural vice, which diminished in proportion as their iron discipline was relaxed."[38]

Even when Taylor was not so indignant, his laconic descriptions of a morality that contradicted America's carried their point. In *A Journey to Central Africa* he described how certain Arab tribes reserved to their married women every fourth day for their own use. If a woman loved someone better than her husband, she could invite her lover in for the day and oblige her spouse to retire. Taylor observed noncommittally that "no reproach whatever attached to the woman, on account of this temporary connection."[39] Middle-Eastern morality, like Middle-Eastern climate and Middle-Eastern indolence, appealed to Taylor so much that although many of its people seemed to be liars and thieves, he found this "a slight drawback only."[40]

Although Taylor was emotionally drawn to the Middle East —which he called simply the East—it was not the Arabs but

the Swedes who were his ideal natural men. Of them, he noted
an inverse relationship between manners and morals, that as
the one was strict, the other was not. "The very freedom of
manners (of the Swedes)," he said, "is here the evident stamp
of their purity." He described how Swedish girls "with the
frankest unconsciousness of impropriety" went in and out of
his bedroom while he dressed.[41] At a Lapland steam bath, he
discovered that a girl was in charge, but undaunted, he un-
dressed and took his bath. To have hesitated, he commented,
would have been "an indignity to the honest, simple-hearted
virtuous girl."[42]

Taylor never did approve of stiff society. And in this youthful and optimistic period in their lives, all of the genteel authors
except Norton believed that America was too much restrained
by its manners as well as by its morals. Taylor could be amused
by Bostonian primness. "The genuine Bostonian," he wrote, "is
the most complacent of mortals. With his clean shirt on, and
his umbrella under his arm, he sits upon his pedestal of Quincy
granite, and reads his mild, unexceptionable newspaper. He be-
lieves in Judge Story and Daniel Webster, reads the poems of
Hannah Gould and George Lunt, votes for Bell and Everett,
and hopes he will go to Paris when he dies." But Taylor was
always suspicious of excessive propriety: "I have sometimes
wondered whether all the Bostonians postpone their Parisian
delights until after death. Is there nothing volcanic under this
cold lava? No indulgence in improprieties, all the more attractive, because secret?"[43]

It was difficult to discard the "conventional masks of Society,"
Taylor recognized. There were formal balls in Berlin as well as
Boston. But one could, if one wished, leave polite society and
steal off with the peasants into the night.[44] To steal off, to escape
the restraints of civilized society; that was the deepest motive
in genteel travel literature. The escape was far from complete,
however, but rather more like a tourist's holiday. One flirted
with the exotic, but never confronted it. If one dreaded a return
to the city and bemoaned the curse of civilization, the protests
carried all the force of any protests that close a holiday. It had
been long enough, really; one could not (or dare not) live a

holiday. Meekly, as Taylor himself put it, he would hold out his wrists for the handcuffs of civilization.[45]

But if that was the foreordained close of a genteel travel book, the holiday itself was worth attention, and Taylor made a lark of it. He delighted in foreign disguise. In Khartoum he passed as a prince (or so he said), in India as a Maharajah. In Persia he wore a tarboosh, smoked a native pipe, and sneaked into the holiest mosques with perfect impunity.[46] Taylor was explicit that he was on a journey of escape, and for that purpose Europe could not compare with the East. "I came to bury myself in its heart," he wrote, "to escape from everything that could remind me of the toil and confusion of the bewildering world...."[47]

In the East, he felt free from all the restrictions of civilization. "I never before experienced such a thorough deliverance from all the petty annoyances of travel in other lands, such perfect contentment of spirit, such entire abandonment to the best influences of nature. Every day opens with a *jubilate*, and closes with a thanksgiving."[48] In a poem written in 1860, he compared this to a baptism, from which he, like Adam, emerged into "fresh immortal Edens."[49] For the other genteel authors as well as Taylor, the East was Lotus-land. There one capitulated to the philosophy of Bishop Berkeley, Curtis wrote, and the world dissolved in light.[50] Reality was suspended; one became as a pearl in a shell, balanced on the rippling sea, and fanned by sweet winds.[51] "I am content to lie," Stoddard declared, "Sipping, in summer hours/My wants from fading flowers,/An Epicurean till my wings are furled."[52]

Quietness, peace, languor are the hallmarks of this genteel version of the Arabian lands. Even when appreciation became more active, it remained an *idle* appreciation. The classic case is Taylor's chapter, "A Dissertation on Bathing and Bodies," in *The Lands of The Saracen*.[53] A lavishly detailed account of his visit to a public bath in Damascus, Taylor's chapter is one of the best he ever wrote. It is written from the viewpoint of a true believer at a religious ceremony. The bath attendant becomes a priest whose divinity is the human body. He carefully scrubs Taylor until "we slough the worn-out skin, and resume our infantile smoothness and fairness." At the climax of the bath comes the soaping. The attendant seizes Taylor "by the crown-tuft of hair upon our shaven head, he plants the foamy bunch of fibers full in our face. The world vanishes; sight, hearing, smell, taste (unless we open our mouth), and breathing are cut off; we have become nebulous. Although our eyes are shut, we seem to see a blank whiteness; and, feeling nothing but a soft fleeciness, we doubt whether we be not the Olympian cloud which visited Io. But the cloud clears away before strangulation begins, and the velvety mass descends upon the body." Another plunge, more rest, a cracking of the joints, and, at the end, "the slight languor left from the bath is gone, and an airy, delicate exhilaration, befitting the winged Mercury, takes its place." Finally, some foamy Arabian coffee, a glass of sherbet "cooled with the snows of Lebanon," a pipe, and a nap.

The languidness of the East was an antidote to the "Fiends of gold and work," but it also represented a sensuousness that was new to American letters. The poets of Longfellow's generation were more apprehensive than appreciative of sensual experience, but the genteel poets had their sympathies with Walter Pater. One cannot imagine Emerson or Lowell sampling hasheesh, as Taylor did, merely because of "that insatiable curiosity which leads me to prefer the acquisition of all lawful knowledge through the channels of my own personal experience, rather than in less satisfactory and less laborious ways."[54]

Taylor's curiosity about the Middle East was insatiable; he reveled in lush descriptions. Unmistakably his travels there were a high point in his life, and perhaps the closest he ever came to a debauch. But there is a conscious extravagance in all of Taylor's indulgence, and the note of didacticism is seldom missing. Americans could scarcely fail to see that Taylor's Epicureanism was intended as an object lesson. Philanthropy was one thing, and good enough for some, but as Taylor wrote in 1864, "My delight is in enjoyment, not renunciation . . . I know all this is gross, selfish, sensuous, mean, *devilish*, if you will—but how is it to be helped?"[55]

Taylor's Middle-Eastern adventures highlighted the passive, but he celebrated the active and vigorous, too. As a reaction against the "tyranny of public sentiment" in rural America,

Taylor said he felt the "irresistible spirit of adventure." He longed to "go into battle with an animal exultation, or dash on a steed of the prairies over some wilderness, or stand on the verge of a crag when "storm and rain are on the mountains."[56] More than once he lauded the "sensation of animal existence," and the "lusty joys of living and breathing."[57] Especially in California, Taylor found men who were men, men whose character was hardy, cordial, and blunt.[58]

In a lyceum lecture in 1855, "The Animal Man," Taylor argued that Americans had overemphasized the spiritual side of man and neglected the physical. He held fasting and other forms of self-denial to be a sin against nature and wondered how much political oppression, bitter theology, and individual cynicism and mistrust originated at that source. He emphasized the connection between physical and moral characteristics. Americans were deteriorating, he thought, because they worked too much and left too little time for play and rest.[59] Applying his own theories, Taylor became what his wife described as a physical cultist.[60]

But Taylor's assertion that the physical life was inherently good does not mean that he considered it also pre-eminently good. There were distinct limits to the virtues of the natural life. Taylor admitted this when he told his readers that he wished he could transfer the character and cultivation of European society directly into his American paradise, California. After an impassioned description of California in 1862, he made it clear that he would not live there. "It is *too new*," he said, "too recently fallen into the possession of man—too far away from the great centres of the world's life—too little touched, as yet, with the genial influences of Art and Taste...."[61]

In the great conflict between civilization and nature, there was no doubt which side was Taylor's. He wanted to relax civilization, but it never occurred to him to challenge it. The possibility of a real escape from civilization, which Melville at least toyed with in *Typee*, was never for Taylor. He shared the usual romantic feelings that life was superior to art, that primitive poets were superior to civilized poets. But the critical edge of these doctrines was blunt indeed in his hands. Civilization was too hurried, too busy, too materialistic, too decorous—those were the limits of his critique. He saw no necessary antithesis between civilization and nature, had no inkling that nature might be unbearable or frightening to civilization. Had his taste for the sensuous extended to the sensual, perhaps he might have known more. But there is no sex in Taylor's books, notwithstanding the mention of a prostitute or two. He luxuriates in sights and sounds and tastes and smells, but not usually (except for the chapter on bathing) in touches. Of course, his publishers and his reading public set up certain restrictions, but Melville's escapade in the South Seas was not seriously hampered by them. Taylor's restraints were ultimately his own. He appeared to show a cosmopolitan tolerance for exotic modes of life, but he never questioned his own moral standards.

Even his cosmopolitanism was more apparent than real. Foreign lands and peoples had their attractions, but even in Africa Taylor could not refrain from noting that the ancient Ethiopians had been of the Caucasian race. He found great significance in "the knowledge that the highest Civilization, in every age of the world, has been developed by the race to which we belong."[62] His preferences were not only with civilization against nature, but with Western civilization against the rest of the world. On a visit to India he was severely critical of the imperialism of the East India Company, but in the end he justified it as advancing the cause of civilization. He thought the Chinese beyond recovery.[63]

A final qualification must be written to the romanticism of young Taylor. From his earliest years, Taylor seems to have had some very grim views about the lot of mankind. Despite his religious liberalism, despite his almost total indifference to theology, he nevertheless retained the essentially Calvinistic notion that life is a battle. The devil had disappeared from the fray, but the cold, rough world had taken his place. In letters written when he was not yet out of his teens, Taylor warned himself to keep clear of the "morbid and unmanly feeling" of wanting to shrink from rough encounter with the world. "It will require time and resolution and the experience of pain," he wrote in 1848, "to familiarize myself with the world as it is, to expect and meet unmoved the thousand jarrings which pride and feeling have to endure."[64] But he looked forward, too, to his trial by fire: "I find that ... courage and self-denial will accomplish much in the world; and that this tossing about, during early life, but wins us the greater reward hereafter. That lofty, calm philosophy and heroic dignity of character which we admire so much in those who have passed the troubled morning was never attained without severe experience."[65]

Stedman also believed that the battle of life held a very definite lesson for the artist. In 1852, when he was only nineteen, Stedman wrote his mother:

I shall have no hesitation in telling you the wildest of my wildest hours. Nor am I—I trust—gloomy and misanthropic as I was when a boy,—taking narrow views of human nature, supposing myself the *only* unhappy person in the world, rolling my misery as a sweet morsel under my tongue. I have suffered—it is true. My childhood was very, very unhappy, but I humbly trust that it has had a good effect—that I have learned in suffering and have become more chastened and calm.

You have read "Wilhelm Meister," and you also know by experience, the education, the apprenticeship, which one of our temperament has to go through, before we can discern the undercurrent of life which moves through all things. Therefore I grow happier every day I grow older—though I have, perhaps, more practical trouble to encounter. I have learned by mingling with men and women, that every one has his sorrow; it is the common lot. . . . I am trying to make an objective character out of my subjective nature.[66]

Prior to the Civil War, relaxed and confident about their literary aims, the genteel authors did not share that distrust of the emotions that marked the Brahmins. From the beginning, however, their writing revealed a firm anti-intellectualism. Curtis, the most transcendental of the group, merely echoed Emerson's hostility toward systems and abstractions. But Taylor and Stedman expressed a much more thorough condemnation of the intellect. Both were convinced that any intellectual probing into the deepest mysteries of existence could not fail to be disillusioning. Taylor chided the German poet Schiller, for example, for not accepting life as it was, "with its stern truths and *relentless disenchantments.* . . ."[67]

Life was not to be puzzled over, but to be accepted. A sufficient therapy for thought was action. If thought persisted and confused the brain, the path to manliness was resolute silence. The walls of privacy would contain the troubling vapors. When Taylor's publisher issued an advertisement that made his *Poet's Journal* appear to be autobiographical, he was furious. He would not be "of the race who hawk their sorrows in the market-place," he said.[68] He worried lest the public misinterpret even his temporary lapses into subjectivity. In his *Rhymes of Travel*, he included a poem called "Impatience" whose theme was the difficulty of seeing through to happier times. He felt it necessary, however, to append a note to the poem: "This poem was written under the pressure of somewhat trying circumstances, and from the impulse of an impatient spirit. It has been retained for the lesson it bears to the author, rather than any poetic merit. That the feeling which it expresses is not habitual with him, is shown by the poem which succeeds it."[69] That poem was called "Aspiration."

There was a self-conscious hypocrisy in genteel "subjectivism" from the beginning. A two-edged taboo operated against intellectual inquiry if, as with theological questions, the results seemed likely to be disillusioning, and against emotionalism if it moved too close to sensuality. The taboo operated in public, especially through the standards of taste enforced by publishing houses and periodicals. The private self needed careful guarding; it was prone to fits of melancholy. And a beast lurked in the deepest shadows. Taylor consciously refrained from giving free rein to his one particular talent. "I am so condemnably thin-skinned," he wrote to Stedman in 1865, "that my cerebral productivity depends entirely on certain delicate conditions of the surface-nerves. The touch of dry sand or earth makes me shudder with horror; the smell of wild grape-blossoms inebriates me with an unspeakable sense of luxury; to feel velvet under my bare soles is a heavenly delight.... I have steadfastly turned my face away from the expression of sensation, because it is my strong (*i.e.*, weak) point."[70]

What was Taylor afraid of? One can dispose of the matter as both he and Stedman do, by saying that too free an expression of the emotions would interfere with their productivity as poets.

Even this, however, calls for an explanation. Surely they did not believe that emotions would simply take too much time and energy away from poetry. Taylor's and Stedman's descriptions of themselves as sensitive instruments for writing poetry suggest rather that excessive emotionalism (or intellectualism) would radically distort the proper functioning of the poetic process. The poet would go wild, and would produce nothing but insane babble.

Was the poet's vulnerability to excess unique to him? Not at all. The poet was but man writ large, as Emerson had observed. If the public pronouncements of the genteel authors were concerned with subjectivism in literature, their private remarks were as often directed to subjectivism in life. The dire consequences that subjectivism could have in the relationship between literature and life were spelled out in a letter by Curtis in 1854. An aspiring author had sent Curtis a review copy of a ghost story, which Curtis disliked extremely. He explained why to his friend, William Douglas O'Connor. Subjectivism, he said, was likely to make a writer "morbid,—too self-analytical and hence too self-conscious and unhappy. It is a tendency so strong that, wherever it shows itself, it ought to be resisted, and yet, when it shows itself, it is likely to be too strong to withstand. Poe undoubtedly weakened his mental and moral grasp by abandoning himself to this impulse." Carrying his argument a step further, Curtis called O'Connor's attention to a certain William North who had recently committed suicide. Curtis noted that in the first issue of *Putnam's*, North had published a story, "The Living Corpse." He was a victim of this "same tendency," Curtis wrote.[71]

But what made both unrestrained emotionalism and unrestrained intellectualism *morbid*? A Calvinist would have flatly called them sinful, but genteel culture was considerably removed from Calvinism. Or was Santayana right in suggesting that it was not? Eager to discard the Calvinistic measure of man—depravity—the genteel authors may have discarded less than they thought. Man was no longer depraved, to be sure, but if he did show what the Calvinists would have called evil inclinations, he was now described as morbid or diseased in mind or body or both. The Calvinist prejudices against impious inquiry or carnal behavior lived on more fully than the new generation recognized.

Yet the essence of Calvinism, which Santayana called the agonized conscience, had disappeared. The genteel authors were not complacent men, but they did not add fears of themselves to their profound misgivings about American culture. If they resolutely avoided probing their own mysteries it was not because they were tempted by hidden demons; there was no public or private indication that they were. In that sense, they had firm identities. They were what they had made themselves; they understood and accepted the compromises that that entailed. They did not question themselves, however much they questioned America, because, simply, it would not have been profitable. There was, they were certain, no alternative open to them.

Occasionally genteel pessimism was purely hypocritical. In England many eminent Victorians spurned inquiry because they feared that truth would breed the social disorder of revolution and atheism. Americans, too, feared these things, but the specter of revolution did not rear itself in America until the great strikes of the 1870's and 1880's, and as for American atheism, it was virtually invisible until the end of the nineteenth century. From a social standpoint, threats to the established order did not acquire intellectual significance until after the Civil War when immigration increased and industrialization was accelerated.

It was rather their lack of enthusiasm for the very endeavor to which they had committed themselves that underlay the earliest strands of genteel pessimism. Later, when they found more to criticize in American civilization, they became defenders of culture. Then, they forgot the romantic notes of freedom and self-expression sounded in Taylor's early work. They made a career, not a life, of art.

Home for the War

IN THE 1840's and 1850's the genteel artist aimed to get away from American life and politics. He sought subjects and settings that were universal, not American. After the Civil War, and particularly as the nineteenth century drew to a close, the impulse to escape reappeared. But, for a time, the War drew him home and committed him to his country.

Charles Eliot Norton best exemplified this commitment. More than any of his genteel friends, Norton retained throughout his life a devotion to the ideals of Brahmin New England. Norton believed in a life of public service; he believed that man ought to pursue the public good above his private gain; he believed in the values of family, of tradition, of cultivation. Norton was born into a wealthy and prominent family, and his training in the values of New England's professional elite was firm from the first. Like the Brahmins, he chose to enter literature rather than politics. After the demise of the Federalist Party in the first decade of the nineteenth century, the Brahmins—George Ticknor and James Russell Lowell are good examples—increasingly viewed literature as a substitute means for the dissemination of political and social ideals.[1] The didacticism of American literature in this period was a direct result of this view, a result deplored in the early writings of Bayard Taylor. Norton, however, did not share Taylor's opinion. He and Lowell saw eye to eye on the social functions of art, accepting the joint editorship of the *North American Review* during the Civil War for almost purely didactic reasons.

After Norton retired from the *Review*, he became America's first Professor of Fine Arts at Harvard, a position he held until 1897. His voluminous correspondence with Lowell and Curtis, his closest friends, for these later years shows that his political interests did not decline. But his teaching, which was tinged, if also embellished, with the decadent, overshadowed his earlier political role. His urbane attacks on Harvard's architecture were notorious. His biographer recounts a story, circulated at Harvard, that Norton had died and was about to enter heaven. "Suddenly he drew back and shaded his eyes: 'Oh! Oh! Oh! So Overdone! So garish! So Renaissance!' He decided to enter hell instead. But presently he returned, informing St. Peter, 'You are over-ornate here, but down there I found I was going to have to put in eternity looking at Appleton Chapel.' "[2]

As Norton's interest in literature and architecture deepened in the 1850's, he had begun to acquire a well-defined set of grievances against the state of civilization in America and an intellectual framework for explaining and judging them. He was much more critical of America, even in this early period, than Lowell. He worried over an excessively democratic spirit of innovation. He deplored the influence of uneducated immigrants; he was sympathetic with the aims of the Know-Nothing Party. He disliked urbanization and the selfish grasping after material prosperity that it seemed to evidence. And after his second major trip to Europe (1855–57), he found America ugly.[3] John Ruskin, whose acquaintance Norton had made in 1855, thought Norton's celebration of the Old World a little too unrestrained:

I can quite understand how, coming from a fresh, pure, and very ugly country like America, there may be a kind of thirst upon you for ruins and shadows which nothing can easily assuage; that after the scraped cleanliness and business and fussiness of it (America), mildew and mould may be meat and drink to you, and languor the best sort of life, and weeds a bewitchment . . . and the very sense of despair which there is about Rome must be helpful and balmy, after the over-hopefulness and getting-on-ness of America; and the very sense that nobody about you is taking any account of anything, but that all is going on into an unspoilt, unsummed, undistinguished heap of helplessness, must be a relief to you, coming out of that atmosphere of calculation.[4]

Norton was taken with the appearance and atmosphere of Europe from the first. The qualities he found or thought he found in Europe figured prominently in his architectural and literary studies and were conspicuous in his political and social criticism as well. At heart almost half an expatriate, Norton found Europe a source of virtues that could be recommended as curatives for the vices of America. His many trips to Europe, as well as his intimate friendships with Ruskin and Carlyle and many of the lesser Victorians, gave him something of an international perspective on American affairs. It bore some similarities to that of Henry James, later in the century. But Norton's internationalism was a typical style adopted by the conservative and cultured classes of his day. To use Europe as a standard for criticism of America implied for him—in this period, at least—only that Europe was temporarily superior. His deepest interest and his allegiance lay with America. Europe was an example for America. Norton did not describe Europe; he always spurned unnecessary attention to detail. His probing reached beneath mere reality to discover the ideals to which Europe gave testimony.

In European literature and architecture Norton found the ideals of an ultimately divine and universal order. That order, much more than a simple uniformity in Nature, extended itself into every area of human affairs. There were moral laws, laws for politics, and laws of beauty. All were *a priori* laws; Norton did not speculate about their origin and felt no need to prove their existence.[5] They were a basic determinant of his judicial and critical style. However much Norton loved art, his great concern was to inculcate correct principles. He did not appreciate; he taught. What interested him was to sort out the good from the bad, which meant the moral from the immoral. With a singlemindedness that was narrow indeed, he looked upon every object of art—cathedral, poem, or statue—as something to be assigned its proper rank. Ruskin understated the matter when he objected to the "chilly" tone of Norton's *Historical Studies of Church-Building in the Middle Ages*.[6]

Ruskin's objection was no stronger, perhaps, because he too believed in a universal divine order that revealed itself in aesthetic laws. He had invoked those laws repeatedly in the first two volumes of *Modern Painters*, appearing in the 1840's. When Norton first saw him in 1850, he looked on him with awe. *Modern Painters* had impressed him deeply; Norton's biographers described that work as the "clue and Key" to Norton's own aesthetics. Norton was not a pupil of Ruskin. With a grace not always characteristic of him, Ruskin even called Norton his "first real tutor."[7] But the aesthetic judgments of the two men usually agreed, and Norton always referred to Ruskin as a genius when discussing him with others.

They did differ importantly on religion. Ruskin's strict Evangelical upbringing, which he never fully cast off, contrasted sharply with Norton's early Unitarianism and later agnosticism. The contrast disappeared, however, when the two men confronted medieval European art. Neither could bear giving credit to an abhorrent theology. Thus both evaded the whole question of the relationship between Catholic theology and Catholic architecture. Ruskin found incipient Protestantism and Norton incipient democracy in the best of medieval art.

Though they both appealed to aesthetic laws, Norton need not have learned his aesthetics from Ruskin. In the America of Norton's youth, the canons of literary criticism retained the neoclassical emphasis on laws until a full generation after Romanticism had undermined those laws in Europe.[8] So far as the existence of laws of beauty, morals, and politics was concerned, there was no disagreement between Norton and his father. What was new to America in Ruskin was his notion that art was both the best expression of the spirit of a nation and the best means of judging it.

Norton accepted this proposition unreservedly. For him no further proof of the greatness of medieval civilization was necessary than to note the proximity in time of Dante in literature, Giotto in painting, and Gothic cathedrals in architecture. All three art forms gave perfect expression to the age and were parallel in structure. The artists who fashioned them did not merely happen to express their age; they believed more deeply than others in the medieval faith. Their belief gave the fundamental impetus as well as the basic form to their art.[9]

Norton never translated these generalizations into explicitly artistic terminology. There was an unbridged gap between his discussion of the forces that gave rise to great medieval art and the art itself. It was one thing to say, as he repeatedly did, that the best medieval art developed because of the integrity, simplicity, sincerity, naturalness, and faith of medieval artists. It was quite another thing to show how medieval art could be characterized by these qualities. His major book on medieval cathedrals, *Historical Studies of Church-Building in the Middle Ages: Venice, Siena, Florence*, was primarily a book about why cathedrals were built, not how they were built or what they looked like. There were no illustrations in the work.

Norton's letters reveal no more profound an interest in architecture itself than do his books. His interest focused on art as an expression of its age. It made no difference whether Norton was treating his favorite period, the Middle Ages, or its successor, the decadent Renaissance. He dismissed the latter as selfish, sensual, luxurious, materialistic—"purely immoral." His Harvard course in the history of the fine arts closed with the Renaissance; for him, there was no later art worthy of the name.[10]

Norton admired the Middle Ages because of the unity that Catholicism gave them. And despite the fact that medieval faith was indeed Catholic, it was not the Catholic Church but the Catholic faith that counted. Norton took pains to distinguish the two. Architecture that reflected the Church alone was Romanesque architecture; he ranked it as inferior. Gothic architecture, on the other hand, spoke for the faith of the people.[11]

How and why one style of religious architecture sprang from the Church alone and another from the people, Norton did not explain. For all his attention to the forces that generated art, Norton offered little about the mechanics of that generation. He observed a commercial and intellectual awakening in the tenth century, and he asserted that intellectual awakenings usually produce the moral awakenings that are essential to the production of great art.[12] But he did not believe that material developments in themselves would initiate such a chain of circumstances. More than any other single factor, he blamed materialism for the decline of art in the Renaissance and the decline of America in the Gilded Age. Apparently some wealth was necessary for art, but not too much. Apparently some liberty was also essential, but not so much as to breed the selfishness of the Renaissance or the Gilded Age. The genius of the Middle Ages lay in their appreciation of the proper degree of liberty and prosperity, and of the proper balance between this world and the next.

Partly because of what he ignored, Norton's art history is quite unconvincing. He could plead, as he did, that the documents necessary to prove his case had vanished, if enough of them ever had existed. That, however, could not justify his inferences. It was an appeal to *a priori* principles about the nature and function of art—which he nowhere spelled out—that underlay his generalizations. Even if he had recovered an abundance of documents he doubtless would have interpreted them to fit his preconceptions. The very dubiousness of his primary critical principle that the worth of art rested upon the moral character of the artist could only have led him astray.

Norton is unconvincing also because he hints that he himself is not sure of the truth of his most characteristic statement about medieval art—that it proceeded from a fervent popular religious faith. He did not doubt that medieval faith was fervent and popular, but the nature of that faith continued to worry him. The Middle Ages were too superstitious for Norton. They were too irrational, too much driven by fear. Worse yet, even the thirteenth century was much too materialistic. Norton knew very well that the same populace he glorified in his books believed quite literally in a material heaven as well as a material hell.[13] How, then, could the unworthy religious faith that Norton admitted he found at the height of medieval civilization have inspired the greatness of medieval architecture? Lightly enough, but with malice showing, Ruskin chided him: "To think that after all your work at Siena, you can still think that the races of men were made to do their best work *in heartily believing lies.*"[14]

When Norton left the Middle Ages and moved back in history to the other period he favored, classical Greece, the spirit of the times gave him less difficulty. He could give unqualified praise to Greece for its harmony, balance, sanity, moderation, temperance. The Greeks were the only race, Norton wrote, to incorporate into their conduct, as well as into their art, ultimate principles that could be universally applied. In the Middle Ages, religious faith directed conduct, but in ancient Greece, men were tutored by nature. The simplicity of life made all men artists and morally temperate citizens.[15] Since Norton was much better satisfied with Greece than with the Middle Ages, it is puzzling that he did not concentrate his architectural interests there. Probably he believed, like Stedman, that however enviable life might have been in fifth-century Greece, it was too essentially different from life in nineteenth-century America to be spoken of with authority. The thirteenth century was remote, too, but it fell on the familiar side of the dividing line of Christianity. The moderns could admire the ancients, but never truly understand them.

Whatever the period he dealt with, the structure of Norton's aesthetic ideas is clear. His art history preached one lesson—that a great nation, as measured by its art, owed its greatness to a homogeneous culture based upon common ideals maintained with conviction. The influence of these ideas, disseminated by Norton in his long teaching career and in countless articles, is most apparent in the work of the New Humanists Irving Babbitt and Paul Elmer More, but it touched other influential twentieth-century literary conservatives like T. S. Eliot and Allen Tate, too.[16] The importance of Norton's aesthetics, however, lies not in what he passed on to the twentieth century, but in what he expressed for the nineteenth. Like John Ruskin, his intellectual compatriot, Norton stood at the high-water mark of his century's commitment to the arts as the flower of a sound society. This mark was passed before the end of his teaching days, and Norton's lectures lost the bite they once had had.

Professor Norton lectured in Italian 4 this afternoon. The dear old man looks so mildly happy and benignant while he regrets everything in the age and the country—so contented, while he gently tells us it were better for us had we never been born in this degenerate and unlovely age."[17]

Yet through most of his life Norton's convictions about the relationship of art and society were as common in cultured circles
in America as Ruskin's were in England. Norton liked political
or religious verse no more than his genteel romantic friends did.
He agreed with them that artistic beauty was its own judge. In
their common reaction against the Brahmins, however, none of
them sought to render art truly independent of society; though
tempted by art for art's sake, they never succumbed fully to it.

Instead, the line from Taylor and Stoddard in the 1850's to
Norton in the 1890's represents a continuous attempt to elevate
the stature of the arts in America. The pre-War genteel poets
were the first to attempt to separate poetry from religion. In the
popular press their success was slight, but among reputable critics after the Civil War neither realists nor idealists questioned
the premise that the test of art was its execution. Norton capped
this premise with his view that the test of a civilization was its
art. In little more than fifty years, poetry and the arts in general had moved from fighting for the independence of their own
province to claiming the crown of civilization. The distance was
immense. Throughout it all, the genteel authors, no less than
their predecessors, presumed that there was *some* relationship
between art and society. They differed from the Brahmins in
their demand that the artist himself discover that relationship.
It was a demand, translated into other terms, for the legitimacy
and authority of the arts as professions. In telling the moralist
and the politician, as the genteel authors did, that art would look
after her own province, they were merely taking the first of the
steps that other professions, such as medicine, the ministry, and
law, had taken before them. In time, Norton's high claims for
the arts considerably surpassed those of other professions, but he
was flatly abandoned after 1900 by artists themselves. Some conservatives continued to accord to art the primacy that Norton
did, but the collapse of genteel aesthetics in America was as de-
cisive as the demise of Ruskinism in England.[18]

However, the aesthetics of Norton and Ruskin was both vital
enough and perfectly suited to shape the response of the genteel
group to the most important event in their lifetimes, the Civil
War. For a decade before the War, the genteel poets had looked

abroad to find their ideals and traveled abroad to satisfy them. Norton, not yet the internationalist he would become after the Civil War, had grumbled over his own misgivings about America—about democracy, immigration, urbanization. In his art history, Norton had repeatedly stressed the importance of the kind of unified culture present in the Middle Ages, but lacking in America. He even had premonitions that America was moving into her own Renaissance decline. When the Civil War burst on this scene of accumulating grievances that had nothing to do with it, Norton nevertheless looked to it for relief. For a time his hopes for a post-War cultural reform were so high that the War truly drew him home to America.

It drew his friends as well. All of them except Stoddard forgot for a time their youthful complaints about America and eagerly followed military developments. Stoddard kept his jobs as Inspector of Customs in New York and literary editor of the *New York World* during the 1860's. His wife needed support, for one thing, but Stoddard never favored the War; he voted Democratic throughout the period. Boker, who knew his opinions well, accused him of being a Copperhead. None of his friends understood why Stoddard opposed the War, and he did not explain. In his *Recollections* he said he managed to keep his friendships because "I never allow myself to dispute about such trifles as popular leaders and unpopular generals...."[19]

Of the other members of the genteel circle, three were active publicists for the Union cause, three served as war correspondents, and one, Gilder, enlisted in the ranks. The publicists, Norton, Curtis, and Boker, worked hardest of the group. Before the War, Norton had not shown much interest in the issue of slavery. Once the War began, however, and he could look to it for other benefits, his enthusiasm for abolition was strong. In 1863 he and Lowell became joint editors of the New England Loyal Publication Society, whose purpose was to enlighten and unify Northern opinion. Once or twice a week the Society printed about 1500 copies of broadsides containing original articles or reprints from newspapers. They were sent to loyal editors all over the country and widely republished. In 1864, as already mentioned, Norton and Lowell became joint editors of the *North American Review* and kept that journal on a staunch-ly unionist course until the end of the War.[20]

Norton's friend Curtis was a warmer advocate of the anti-slavery cause than he. He often spoke for the cause, beginning in the mid-1850's. Soon after John Brown was hanged for his raid on Harper's Ferry in 1859, Curtis was mobbed while giving an antislavery lecture in Philadelphia. Several hundred policemen and members of the junior Anti-Slavery Society armed with clubs beat off repeated attempts to storm the stage. Arson was averted only when the police chief announced that the rioters he had locked inside railroad cars on the ground floor of the hall would be left to the flames. Throughout the War, Curtis was busy with Republican politics in Staten Island, where he lived, and in the national organization. A delegate to the Republican convention in 1860, Curtis moved reconsideration and won pas-sage of the Giddings amendment adding the preamble of the Declaration of Independence (containing the "all men are cre-ated equal" clause) to the platform. After Curtis became politi-cal editor of *Harper's Weekly* in 1863, it became a forum for unionist sentiment. Few editors were better known or more re-spected; according to Curtis's biographer the influence of his wartime editorials was enormous.[21]

Unlike Norton or Curtis, Boker had never been involved in politics before the War. He was a Democrat, like Stoddard, but in 1860 for patriotic reasons he cast his ballot for Lincoln. He now threw himself into public affairs and became a leader in organizing the Union League of Philadelphia in 1862. He was the first secretary of the League and maintained that position until he resigned in 1871 to accept a post as minister to Turkey.[22]

Boker became one of the most prolific of the Civil War poets. From the beginning of the War, he thought the poet could exert a soothing and healing influence on the nation. He had not found a new function for poetry, however. His war poetry, like Taylor's and Stedman's, was inspired by the assumption that the Civil War had made America worthy of poetry.[23] In the Harvard Phi Beta Kappa address for 1865, Boker explained how the War had called him back from the past to the present: "The Past, unreal and far, / Loomed through the dusty vapors of our war,/And what was clear before my boyish glance/Lost, for the man, its old significance." In the same poem, Boker described the Civil War as without historical parallel in grandeur because it represented the first time that a nation had risen to right one of its own wrongs. America had recognized the eternal moral laws, and, in applying them, "wrought the work of Heaven."[24]

Even if America was newly worthy of poetry because she was unique in all history, she still might exemplify universal themes. Boker's war poems perfectly matched the abstraction of genteel political thinking about the War. Although they often celebrated actual persons and events, their real themes were universal heroics removed from time and place. As far as the genteel poets were concerned, the Civil War secured America's admission into the circle of nations possessing a stock of noble themes.[25]

That was enough to tempt Aldrich into seeing the War as an officer, though not as an enlisted man. He was appointed colonel in a New Hampshire regiment when the War broke out, but the commission never reached him and his friend Fitz James O'Brien went instead. The result, as Henry Clapp used to say, was that Aldrich was shot in O'Brien's shoulder. Next Aldrich tried for an appointment on a navy vessel, but that, too, came to nothing. In the fall of 1861 he spent a few weeks at the front with the Army of the Potomac as a correspondent for the *Tribune*; some of his poems and stories were based on the experience. From 1862 through the end of the War, he worked as an editor and continued his writing.[26] In 1864, worried about the possibility of being drafted, Aldrich wrote his wife that "I am not patriot enough to add one more life to the hundred thousands that have been thrown away in vain." If drafted, he said, he would pay $2,000 for a substitute. He was not drafted.[27]

Taylor was a more avid supporter of the War. When Curtis was mobbed in Philadelphia, Taylor was outraged; he insisted on lecturing there the very next week and did so under heavy police guard. In the spring of 1861, with rumors of war rampant, Kennett Square organized night patrols to defend itself against Confederate raiders reported just below the Maryland border.

Taylor equipped his with African swords and spears because he had nothing better. He flew the American flag from the tower of Cedarcroft and was pleased by the stoutness of his castle.[28]

After a brief term as war correspondent for the *Tribune*, Taylor went to Russia as secretary to the American minister in 1862. He needed the salary, $6,000 a year, and he hoped to explore the country. When the minister returned to Washington, Taylor was left as *chargé d'affaires*. He learned that England and France were attempting to enlist Russia in their effort to get a six-month armistice in the American War. To persuade the Russians that this would aid only the South, Taylor exceeded his diplomatic instructions and prepared a detailed confidential summary of Union revenues, military strength, and recent troop movements for their government. Secretary of State Seward, sensitive to the low opinion foreigners had of Northern strength, rebuked him mildly and made him inform the Russians that the document was not official. In 1863, the former minister to Russia was reappointed and Taylor returned home. He had expected to be dispatched on a special mission to Persia, which never materialized. When he arrived to protest the matter to Lincoln, the President was surprised to see him; he thought Taylor was in Persia. After that, Taylor paid little attention to the War.[29]

Stedman was the best known of the genteel correspondents. At the beginning of the War, he had been commissioned as a colonel, but he decided to remain in journalism. As a correspondent for the *New York World*, he spent more time at the front than any of his friends and rated the experience highly. It "lifted life out of the commonplace," he wrote later. His account of the defeat at Bull Run was the fullest and most graphic that appeared in Northern papers. It was the talk of New York for days and was reprinted as a pamphlet. He was no mere observer of the battle. His horse was shot from under him, but he managed to save the colors of the retreating Massachusetts Fifth.[30]

Stedman's mother could not see why he endangered himself. He did not expect to convince her, but he explained his reasons as both selfish and patriotic. The War offered him a chance for a "personal shaking-up and *rejuvenating*," a chance to express "the old, *healthy* love of *action*," he said. It also surprised him with his selflessness. "For the first time," he wrote, "the hackneyed stars-and-stripes have to me a significance.... For eight years I have cared *nothing* for politics—have been disgusted with American life and doings. Now, for the first time, I am proud of my country and my grand, heroic brethren." He expected the War to strengthen the American physique and chasten the American character. If he could throw literature aside, he said, the soldier's life would suit him fine. He could not, however, and when it appeared that the *World* would fail, he joined the United States Attorney-General's office as a clerk in the Pardon Bureau. In 1863 he resigned to enter banking and soon afterward opened his own New York brokerage office. He continued to follow the War closely and to express his gratitude for its renewal of his faith in America.[31]

Not a correspondent, but an enlistee, Gilder responded to active duty much as Stedman had. With his mother's permission, because he was only nineteen, Gilder was enrolled in the First Philadelphia Artillery in 1863. In his first engagement on the fringe of the Battle of Gettysburg, Gilder's squad were unable to fire their cannon. They dodged its mouth for weeks thereafter because none of them knew how to unload it without firing. This inconvenience and the hardship of living outdoors on short rations did not dull Gilder's enthusiasm for the War. He reproached his mother for her remorse in letting him go. "I know how hard it is for one to have so many to be anxious about," he wrote her, "but a great war does not occur in every generation...." "I am very glad I came a-soldiering this campaign. The disagreeables will not be so in the retrospect, and the acquisition of knowledge and experience in the subject military will amply make up for all of them. It is well, also, to know how it feels to have shells screaming and exploding around you, wounding men and killing horses." He noted these cruelties of war, but no more than for his friends do they figure in either his letters or his literature. In their personal experience, the War functioned like an adolescent testing ground.[32]

As a source of theory, however, the War offered a different testing ground. Norton was not alone in his conjectures about the moral and physical rejuvenation that would result from a period of national crisis. In the first years of the War, men as dissimilar as Emerson, Whitman, Francis Parkman, and Orestes Brownson all speculated optimistically.[33] Norton differed from them only in that he gave his primary attention to the general beneficial effects of the conflict. He did not just support the War, he celebrated it, because he saw in it a logic that would elevate the national character. When fully committed, Norton was able to ignore the depth and complexity of the issues that precipitated the War; victory would not merely resolve those issues, but purge and regenerate the nation.

Norton was not altogether indifferent to the question of slavery, but he was not an abolitionist until after Emancipation. Before then, he opposed only the extension of slavery beyond the Old South. Curtis, by contrast, was a convinced abolitionist more than five years before the War. In "The Duty of the American Scholar" (1856), Curtis wrote that "Against nature, against reason, against the human instinct, against the divine law, the institution of slavery is the most dreadful that philosophy contemplates or the imagination conceives." Moreover, Curtis denied the racial inferiority of the Negro; he found no grounds for excluding him from the egalitarianism of the Declaration of Independence. By 1865 Norton had come around to Curtis's views, but the move was not easy for him.[34]

Norton's political theory during the 1850's was unmistakably conservative. *Considerations on Some Recent Social Theories* (1853), his first work on the subject, was an attack on the errors of liberalism. It might have been written by almost any of Norton's Puritan predecessors. The distinction drawn by John Winthrop between natural and civil liberty in his "Little Speech on Liberty" in 1645 provided the basis for Norton's polemic two centuries later. Liberty defined as the absence of all restraint or complete freedom to do as one wished was seen by both men as ignoble, even barbaric. They insisted on a positive definition of liberty, a liberty that Winthrop called civil and Norton called moral. Both men believed that true liberty meant freedom to do one's moral duty. The proper nature of the relationship between this true liberty and the political liberty called for by nineteenth-century liberalism was the subject of Norton's book.

Norton began his discussion of political liberty by rejecting abstract, *a priori* notions about man's right to political liberty. The extent of a nation's political liberty, which meant for Norton the degree to which that nation was a democracy, depended on one factor alone, the influence exerted by Christianity on the national morals. As a nation raised its moral level, as it became truly invigorated with the spirit of Christianity, then, and only then, was Norton prepared to see a broadening of political liberty. And Norton was not sanguine in his expectations. He anticipated the advance of liberty to be an almost geologically slow process, but he was certain that progress would come, within the limits set by human nature. If false and insulting notions about the voice of the people as the voice of God were disregarded, strong leaders could come forward to direct and raise up the people. A certain minimal level of national prosperity was essential for any progress at all, Norton believed. Lacking it, Europe, including England, was about as likely to experience a social revolution as a peaceful advance in political liberty.

The conservatism of *Recent Social Theories* is rarely interrupted. In offering a definition of society, Norton advances the orthodox liberal view that society is nothing more than the collection of its individual members. He insists that sovereignty can derive ultimately only from the individual; "the fancied advantage of...what is called society" was no justification for sacrificing the individual. He also agrees with the liberals that there can be no opposition between the individual and the social good. "The progress of society is simply the progress of the individuals who compose it," he declared. Yet Norton's constant probing for the national spirit suggests that he did not consider society merely a collection of atoms. It is likely that Norton got his Benthamite notions about society from the first edition of Mill's *Political Economy*.[35] But how could Norton have accepted this Mill, the liberal Mill of the 1840's and 1850's, at the very time that he was most under the spell of Ruskin? Mill and Ruskin barely comprehended one another.

Norton's ambiguity is also Mill's. The difference between Mill's conservative and liberal writings seems hardly bridgeable at times.[36] Mill both affirms and denies an identity of interest between society and the individual; he is similarly ambiguous on the question of whether democracy, or whatever form of government best suits the conditions of the age, is the best form of government. It seems that Mill vacillated on these questions because neither traditional liberalism nor conservatism was adequate for his purposes. On one occasion, he wrote that the two categories could very properly coalesce. In the common task of raising the intellectual and moral level of the people, Mill thought logic urged cooperation between the Radicals and the Tories. Across the Atlantic where political ideologies were comparatively loose, a man like Norton could appreciate Mill's position.

But Norton was influenced, too, by Ruskin. The organic societies that Norton and Ruskin found in the Middle Ages were quite unlike any societies described by Mill, much less by the Radicals. Mill did occasionally use the increasingly popular concept of the national character. But his thought was so unswervingly directed toward securing social diversity that he could accept only the loosest interpretations of the concept. Whereas Norton and Ruskin were temperamentally inclined to seek unity, Mill aimed in the opposite direction. This is not to suggest that Mill encouraged social *dis*organization. His essay, "The Spirit of the Age," postulated the superiority of natural societies with common ideals and recognized leadership to ideologically confused and leaderless transitional societies. He even agreed with Ruskin that medieval society typified the former and Victorian England the latter. But Mill's rationalistic elitism forced him to view the great men of any age as members of society's standing opposition. Society included its multitude and its few, but even in superior societies there was no natural identity of ideals between them.

The key to reconciling Norton's political individualism and his artistic organicism lies not in John Stuart Mill, but in Christianity. It enabled Norton to hold to an almost atomistic view of society, and, simultaneously, to an organic view. Norton believed both that individuals were self-determining agents and that they were determined by the society they belonged to.[37] Morals and ethics arose from self-determination, and politics and culture from social determination. Norton often appeared to be a relativist about politics and culture, but he was an absolutist about morals and ethics. Christianity was indeed a positive advance over previous religions; its moral law was absolute. Furthermore, each man by virtue of his humanity was equipped with a conscience that enabled him, if he chose, to affirm the absolute moral law. Insofar as men were truly free, to return to Norton's definition of liberty, they were most impelled toward a common goal. Norton could insist, therefore, that a society of truly self-determining individuals would be the most perfectly homogeneous society. Self-interest would not threaten society because it would be identical with the Christian principle of self-denial. Christianity was the perfect cement for a liberal society.

Christianity reached far beyond ethics, too. If it was true, for example, that political principles derived from moral principles —a belief that gained increasing significance for Norton as the Civil War progressed—any clear-cut distinction between morality and other aspects of human conduct began to disappear. Norton's theory of art history had already obliterated the difference between morals and art; the Civil War integrated morals and politics for him. When the genteel group was most optimistic— and most systematic—its liberalism was anchored so securely in Christianity that it bore little similarity to the liberalism that Bentham had fathered. Insulated by theory against the particularizing tendencies in English liberalism, genteel thought was centripetal rather than centrifugal in its direction. The structure of genteel thought, irrespective of its immediate subject, was in constant danger of collapsing back onto its moral center. Between basic moral principles and the frequent, even trivial, circumstances to which the genteel authors applied them, there was a conspicuous absence of intermediate thinking. If the principle at issue was clear, its relevance to the case in point was seldom so. Moralism, in effect, functioned as a substitute for thinking.

When the Civil War broke out in 1861, Norton did not judge slavery by any abstract conception of human rights or by the actual situation of the Negro. "The slaves do not go about look-

ing unhappy, and are with difficulty, I fancy, persuaded to feel
so," he wrote while on a visit to a South Carolina cotton plantation in 1855. "Whips and chains, oaths and brutality, are as common, for all that one sees, in the free as the slave states." Slavery's indirect influence on the whites was another matter. "The
hardest trials and the bitterest results of slavery" fell on the
whites, not the blacks. Norton was never specific about the
mechanism of slavery's evil influence on the Southern whites.
He spoke of the dulling of white morals and white intellects,
but said nothing about how or why it happened.[38]

In the first years of the War Norton did not understand how
deeply slavery was at the heart of the conflict. To keep the North
free was his only initial concern. For this reason, he himself
would not have opposed secession.[39] Regarding the racial superiority of the whites as self-evident, Norton wrote in 1861 that the
whites would always govern the Negroes and would never amal-
gamate with them. The same "higher laws" that he would later
invoke for opposite ends he now used to justify the persistence
of "some form of subjection" for the Negro far into the future.[40]
But even before Norton reversed himself on the subject of slavery, before he accepted the abstract truth of the principles of
liberty and social equality that Curtis had accepted in 1856, he
began to champion the War as a moral crusade. Soon after its
outbreak the War had become for him a "religious war," a war
to uproot sin, although Norton expressed no political aim beyond preventing the expansion of slavery. Committed morally,
he now began to elaborate a political theory in support of the
War. The conflict could be posed as a series of antitheses: North-
liberty-democracy-America *vs.* South-feudalism-oligarchy-Eu-
rope.[41] In the last years of the War Norton was convinced that
both the flow of history and the recognition of true principles,
the former requiring the latter, inhered in the Northern cause.
He was willing to view the War as a war to save the Union and
not merely to save the North. Endowed as it was with the duty
of advancing civilization, acting as agent for both history and
the deity, the North was obliged both to conquer and to civilize
the South.[42]

The righteousness of Norton's political writing in the last two years of the War is astonishing when compared with the skeptical conservatism of *Recent Social Theories*. From the pragmatic attitude toward political and social institutions expressed in that volume, Norton had moved to the view that slavery was not only evil in its effects but basically opposed to the American doctrine of equality.

The development of Norton's ideas about slavery—from a concrete and pragmatic if biased concern with facts to a general and abstract concern with rights—was mirrored in his response to European criticism of the North during the Civil War. Conservative English intellectuals, Ruskin among them, were unsympathetic toward the North. In 1864, upset with the "horrible" American War and with Norton's view of it, Ruskin told Norton, "It is just as if I saw you washing your hands in blood, and whistling—and sentimentalizing to me."[43] Almost immediately thereafter, he broke off their correspondence. When the War ended, Ruskin explained: "I could no otherwise than by silence express the intensity of my adverse feeling to the things you were countenancing—and causing; for of course the good men in America were the real cause and strength of the war."[44]

While Ruskin was frustrating him by refusing to comprehend the morality of the Northern cause, Norton was busily enunciating a political theory that would exempt America from the follies of European opinion. He pressed his America/Europe dichotomy to the point of radical dissociation. The contrast between government in the Old and New Worlds was "almost complete," he observed; between America and Europe there was "irrepressible conflict."[45] In "American Political Ideals" (1864) Norton exulted that America had no past, that it was "unprecedented in history" and "the fruit of revolution." Forgetful now of what he had written in 1853, Norton did not fear the course of history because Europe would be forced irresistibly to emulate America. Now, he did not balk at asserting the right of revolution, and, although he had found the idea insulting in 1853, now he flatly asserted the superiority of men to their government. Exuding newfound confidence in the spirit of liberty, he now found it necessary to state that progress would never fully eliminate all government. A tentative opti-

mism arising from a hard look at social facts was no longer
Norton's mode. Not the facts of America, but her promise; not
her performance, but her rights and her mission, were the new
objects of Norton's attention. The gap between 1853 and 1865
was immense.[46]

In crossing it Norton invoked the name of Christianity. What
had transformed his skepticism into confidence, he said at the
end of the War, was a recognition that Christianity had become operative in America to a degree that made progress certain.[47] Estimates of the popular morality had always commanded
Norton's interest and called forth his judgment. Because his
estimates were low in the 1850's, he was pragmatically conservative at that time; when the War raised his opinions about the
American people (he pointed, for example, to the fine character
of the army) he became an unqualified liberal.[48] But however
drastic were the shifts in his thought, Norton consistently referred to the level of popular morals as an index of the state of
the nation and his own confidence in it.

But America was not the whole world; art had enforced that
lesson on Norton well before the Civil War. Why should a political advance in one country, and a backward country at that,
precipitate so much unrestrained rejoicing? In the course of history, nations had risen and fallen, though human nature had
changed little. If Christianity had become "operative" in America, as Norton believed, why there and why just then? What
was different about America, after all?

The answers to these questions offered by Norton and also
by Curtis did not require deep or original thinking. The traditional belief in America's uniqueness, shared to different degrees since the time of the Puritans by both liberals and conservatives, had always been suited to crisis. Now, in the blood-
iest crisis of all, it served its purpose. In the most unimpeachable
terms it justified the War and its consequences.

America *was* different from the rest of the world, the traditional belief ran, and Norton and Curtis agreed. Neither geography nor culture nor religion nor history had shaped America.
She was out of historical time. Providence had selected her to
establish a new dispensation in the world; it had directed the

flow of history toward her so that henceforth she would be at the cutting edge of history, the example toward which all nations were tending.

America would establish a new regime in the world, the reign of the principle of liberty. From the first, she had recognized her task in the impulse of religious liberty that sent her first settlers to her. She had seen immediately the necessary dependence of moral liberty on political and other forms of liberty. With these fundamentals undisputed from the start and embodied in a Constitution inspired by Providence, New England as "mother" for the continent instructed the newcomers. Fortunately, the abundance of America guaranteed a sufficient base for the nourishment of liberty. The eternal struggle between the rich and the poor, which had wrecked many a nation and worried them all, found no place in America.

America *was* different, different enough so that the place would counter the universal frailties of human nature. Looking to its wealth and its freedom, to the intellectual and moral superiority of its people, one could trust human nature. One could see the existence of a "moral community," the first truly united people in history. One could believe that this nation, defining itself only by a commitment to liberty, had a future of unending brightness. History could move geography, as many nations had discovered in their decline. But the human spirit was superior to historical conditions; a nation that defined itself by its devotion to principle need not fear the future. The Sinai of nations, as Curtis described America, could be expected to "subdue and harmonize" the world with liberty.[49]

But first the American North had to subdue and harmonize the American South. In 1865, neither Norton nor Curtis underestimated the extent of the problem. When no signs of true repentance were visible in the South, Norton demanded that its whole social order be regenerated. Anything that helped to accomplish this needed no defense. Both Norton and Curtis vigorously supported the program of Congressional Reconstruction as a step in the right direction. Curtis supported the Radicals during Johnson's impeachment trial, and not until 1871 did he begin to lose faith in Reconstruction. Even when his commit-

ment to Reconstruction was warmest, however, neither Curtis
nor Norton was concerned to do more for the former slave than
to secure him the vote and, perhaps, to educate him. When these
objectives were formally attained, or when, as in the case of
education, at least the first steps toward attaining them had been
taken, Curtis and Norton felt no compunction about handing
the problem of the welfare of the Negro back to his former
masters.[50] In this they shared in the broad consensus of Northern opinion.[51]

What distinguished the genteel political writers from other
Northerners was the extent to which they had viewed slavery
as a symbolic rather than a practical problem. The purity of
Northern principles, not the condition of the Negro, provided
both the beginning and the end of their political thought during
the decade of the 1860's. The abstract moralism of genteel
thought never touched the facts of the Negro's condition.

The few practical conclusions emerging from this symbolic
view of the conflict were not immediately applicable in the
South, but they would eventually be applicable not only there
but in all America. If one could now "trust" the American
people, as Norton and Curtis both believed the Civil War had
shown, if the spirit of Christianity was truly operative in the
country, America would now offer a finer example to the world
than ever before. Democratic institutions would be purged of
inefficiency and corruption. Materialism would be tempered
with a recognition of the truth of the laws of moral health. Culture, hitherto the most limited of American endeavors, would
flower in all the arts.[52]

The Civil War had freed America to advance into its promised future. The terms of that promise were clear. Equipped
with a comprehensive optimism and with a means for testing
that optimism, the genteel authors turned their attention to the
new "moral community" that America was building.

Scholars in Politics

FROM the end of the Civil War to the twentieth century, genteel political theory declined steadily into pessimism. By 1900 Gilder confessed in the *Century* that his early faith in the American public had been unwarranted, but he still felt that his hopes for the future were not altogether irrational.[1] The same year, Norton justified his early overconfidence in American politics to E. L. Godkin by pointing to the tremendous opportunities America had enjoyed. Of all the disappointments of his life, the failure of his hopes for America was the bitterest. In a late unpublished letter he described the collapse of those hopes as "the worst blow that modern civilization has had, perhaps a mortal blow. Indeed it seems to me that never before have thoughtful men been confronted with more difficult questions,—first of all, 'Is our civilization worth saving?' "[2]

Norton's alienation from America was more severe than that of his friends. His early-twentieth-century critics interpreted his revulsion from contemporary reality as a weak and sterile irresponsibility. This indictment of Norton, which was extended to cover the rest of the genteel group, was not wholly inaccurate. His critics oversimplified and misunderstood, but their complaint against the politics of the Gilded Age had some justification. Santayana exaggerated in suggesting that the philosophy of genteel America was idealism, but his instinct was correct. Genteel political thought, as developed by Norton and Curtis during the Civil War and elaborated in the following decades, rested on a fundamentally idealistic interpretation of human conduct. Only Norton ever questioned the starting point of that idealism, the fundamental moral law. His friends, despite their deepening dissatisfaction with American life after the Civil War, did not relinquish that anchor.

Neither, however, did most Americans in the Gilded Age. The intellectual revolution initiated by the theories of Charles Darwin around the turn of the century was anticipated in the academic disciplines in the 1870's and 1880's. But in the general intellectual life of the country during those decades, Darwin stimulated little more than religious controversy. The notion that human life and history were not directed by any ultimate principle was scarcely discussed. And when the religious controversy was settled, as it was settled for some by the philosopher John Fiske, it was settled in such a way as to preserve the sanctity of the moral law. Evolution was admitted, but its sting was removed. Evolution was just a new name for God's plan. In clinging to its presuppositions, therefore, genteel culture reacted to the intellectual advances of the age much as did the nation at large.

But the genteel reformers did have their particular style. A description of Gilder in the *New York Tribune* for 1895 conveys it perfectly. Gilder had been appointed by the Governor of New York to a commission to investigate tenement housing conditions. He took his job so seriously that he told the New York City fire chief to call him whenever a major blaze occurred in the tenement sections. Even in the middle of the night, he donned firemen's garb and inspected the scene. During his investigations for the commission, he discovered that the Trinity Church Corporation, which owned tenements, had succeeded in having a law requiring a water supply on every tenement floor declared unconstitutional. Gilder's commission secured a reversal, but the affair brought down "a veritable storm of public indignation" upon the Trinity Church and focused public attention on the commission's legislative proposals. After the bills were passed by the state legislature in 1895, the *New York Tribune* praised Gilder for his role in the affair. It singled out his "perfect rectitude, his unselfish zeal, his tact and his urbanity" when he appeared at the legislature's public hearings:

Mr. Gilder is a reformer, but he is also a gentleman. He did not appear at public hearings on his bills with a chip on his shoulder. There was no exasperating assumption of superiority on his part. Wherever tenement house reform needed a champion he was sure to be present, but there was no rancor or stubbornness in his contention. He made frank acknowledgement of his opponents' courtesy, and of the instruction which he had derived from their arguments. He was always ready to concede a point which did not sacrifice a principle.[3]

Gilder doubtless was flattered by the *Tribune* account, although today it might be read to suggest that for Gilder, no injustice was profound enough to provoke him to indecorous conduct. Yet if gentility meant an exaggerated emphasis on propriety, it was an exaggeration that was barely evident in its time. The style that seemed natural for Norton or Curtis seemed no less normal for American intellectuals generally until late in the nineteenth century. It may be true that American society has been uniquely pragmatic and experimental, but until the twentieth century this cannot be said of American intellectual life. There, not American uniqueness but American dependency on Europe, especially England, was all too obvious.

American ideas and forms of expression were clearly patterned after those of England. While provincial political status prevailed, provincial intellectual status was normal. After the American Revolution, American intellectuals continued to emulate English modes of thought. With no native standards for culture, they established their status by the only recognized standards of the day, English standards, and did what they could to secure English praise on English terms. But they became extremely touchy about doing so, and resented the patronizing attitudes of the English aristocracy. There were regular revolutions against the domination of foreign standards, as, for example, among nationalists after the War of 1812, and, again with the Transcendentalists, but the model of Europe was never shaken off in the nineteenth century. Almost generation by generation, American intellectual life assumed the pattern first of servile imitation and then of radical rejection of foreign influence. Genteel culture after the Civil War represents the imitative phase of this cycle. Its obeisance to English models made it appear at times almost foreign to America. Its insistence upon right principles and proper conduct seemed almost an attempt to outdo the English on their own terms. It found no greater satisfaction than on those occasions, usually celebrated in private, when evidence was discovered of English laxity or vulgarity.

Because the relationship of America to England remained a basic preoccupation for American intellectuals, one author in his lifetime could oscillate between imitation and rejection. The genteel writers if observed in three periods—before the Civil War, during and immediately after the War, and near the end of the century—nicely demonstrate the full cycle. What they were never able to do was to get beyond their problem. Nor was the pattern immediately broken in the twentieth century. Despising gentility as they did, its first critics only confirmed the American pattern by rushing to its other pole. The exiles came home again.

Fluctuating attitudes toward foreign aristocracies reflected a deep ambivalence felt by the genteel authors toward American middle-class society. Norton and Curtis were aware of America's continued movement toward a classless society. They might have been more sensitive to the subject than they were, but their generation saw a slackening in the trend. They were born early enough to see the traditional American political aristocracy disappear. They lived long enough to see a new American economic aristocracy emerge, an aristocracy whose investments were neither in shipping nor in railroads, the traditional New England bases of prosperity. Poised as they were between two aristocracies, the genteel authors found themselves in the most bourgeois age in American history.

As middle-class men, they displayed the moralistic style that has marked the bourgeois since his emergence in the seventeenth century.[4] Whether bourgeois vocations and the structural changes they initiated in society (as in the home, the family, the school) "explain" these middle-class thought patterns is unimportant here. What is significant for genteel America is the absence of either a peasantry or an aristocracy with values and modes of expression different from those of the middle classes. The genteel writers did not lament the absence of the former; pressure from below carried no social benefits for them. And although they never recommended the creation of an American aristocracy, their thought naturally gravitated back to the days of John Quincy Adams, to the days when American politics looked much more like English politics than it did half a century later. Curtis even complained that the mediocrity of American politics could be indirectly explained by the absence of a hereditary aristocracy. Without such a class to bring standards and prestige to the profession of politics, the "Best People" in America would not be attracted to political life.

It often seems as if the genteel circle, notwithstanding its democratic protestations, secretly saw itself as an aristocracy *manqué*. Its grumbling about America all too frequently reproduced the biases of the English upper classes. It elaborated general social and cultural critiques, but through them ran an undertone of resentment at the way Americans refused to defer to and reward the better people who, in any European country, would have constituted the aristocracy. Nevertheless, genteel culture remained essentially bourgeois.

Americans always exaggerated the distance between American politics and European politics in the nineteenth century. The seesaw of European politics between revolution and reaction afforded a spectacle that, from the American side of the ocean, seemed quite irrelevant. Yet, the Best People in America shared a kinship in fear with the European bourgeoisie. Both ultimately feared an alliance of the upper and lower classes against them. In nineteenth-century America that possibility appeared only twice, and both times the genteel writers resisted it with vigor.

The first of these threats grew out of the slavery controversy. For two full decades after the Civil War, the genteel reformers bitterly attacked the Democratic Party for its subservience to Southern interests during the conflict. They did not find any accident of geography in the harmony of interests between the

Southern aristocracy and the Democratic Party. The Southern alliance of aristocracy with democracy developed naturally, Curtis thought, from the principles of Thomas Jefferson. The ignorant barbarism that called itself democracy was all too prone to unite with aristocracy. Both parties to the alliance were foreign to the true spirit of America; only the interposition of classless America had prevented the country from duplicating the European experience.[5]

Curtis's bitter hostility toward the Democratic Party was mainly responsible for keeping him within Republican ranks until the Mugwump bolt of 1884.[6] Then, the conservative Cleveland allayed his fears about the Democratic Party. But in the political columns he wrote for *Harper's Weekly*, especially in the 1880's, Curtis concentrated more and more of his attention on the development of a new alliance between aristocracy and democracy. Created by industrialization, a new aristocracy of wealth alone had appeared. Created by the same process of industrialization, a new American proletariat had also appeared, composed almost entirely of the worst-educated immigrants ever to come to America, except for the Negroes. Curtis saw two equally horrifying possible results of this development: either the two new groups might combine to rule America, or they might fight each other in a bloody class war. By the time Curtis died in 1892, he had offered many suggestions in *Harper's* for controlling the growth of big capital and big labor. These suggestions, which will be discussed in Chapter 5, were palatable to neither. Always, Curtis maintained the bourgeois stance—small capital against big capital, skilled labor against unskilled labor. His economic program foreshadowed in many important respects the economic program of the Progressive movement. Since the Progressives were themselves middle-class men, it is not surprising that their concerns should have echoed Curtis's.

But to return to style. Of all the characteristics that foreign travelers considered to be conspicuously American, none received more frequent comment than the extent to which American life in the mid-nineteenth century had become permeated by evangelical religion. Since the time of the Revolution, American religion had been, by European standards, extremely decentralized and unstructured. The absence of a hierarchy in the Protestant churches had prevented the imposition from above of any single religious pattern; it also precluded opposition to religious change from below. The relatively unstructured Protestant churches of nineteenth-century America were the ideal setting for the popular religious movements, like the revivals, that regularly swept the country. And on the Western frontier, where it received the heartiest response, the revival bcame a more clearly defined social institution than most of the churches. Even in the cities—and the great upsurge of political and social reform in the pre–Civil War decades was an urban, not a rural, movement—it was impossible to escape the influence of evangelical religion. True, the revivals focused on the salvation of the individual soul and not the amelioration of society, but they repeatedly brought to Americans that quickened sense of the immediacy of God which fostered the habits of moralism and molded generations.[7] To give the tangible world a moral framework, which the genteel writers did as by second nature, was to do what Americans did. Later, this activity would be reserved for patriotic occasions, but in the mid-nineteenth century, and especially among the middle classes, the rhetoric of moralism was the national language.

Thus the style of genteel culture was not greatly different from the prevailing nineteenth-century national style, but it was unmistakably an exaggerated form of it. The extremism was at least partly a consequence of ignorance. In politics, for example, the moralism of the genteel reformers was not tested by the actual experience of officeholding. Genteel culture was always cut off from political power. Curtis, the most active of the group, was an unsuccessful candidate for three New York political positions—United States Representative in 1864, United States Senator in 1866, and governor in 1870. Though he had been active in Staten Island and New York State politics since the 1860's, and though he would be politically active through most of his later life, he always remained an amateur among the professionals. In 1870, as chairman of the New York Republican Convention, Curtis was approached by Senator Roscoe Conkling's men to see whether he would become a candidate for the governorship. Though he coveted the office and confirmed that he would not decline the nomination if it were offered by the Convention, he insisted that his name should be fairly presented. Conkling arranged for him to be nominated by an unsavory Tammany Republican and then directed his own forces to vote for another man. In effect, Curtis was used to defeat Horace Greeley, the third candidate. The experience left him resolutely distrustful of politicians.[8]

Prior to Progressivism, the reformers were sober about what could be accomplished in politics. The Liberal Republican movement of 1872 was a fiasco; disclosures of graft in the Grant administration underlined the futility of these early attempts at reform. Only in 1884 with the election of Grover Cleveland did the reformers find cause for optimism. Cleveland seemed an ideal President; he was opposed to high tariffs, firm in his commitment to the gold standard, friendly toward civil service reform, and, at least during his first administration, opposed to imperialism.

Gilder's support for Cleveland's principles provided the basis for the beginning in 1887 of a close friendship between the two men, sketched in Gilder's book, *Grover Cleveland: A Record of Friendship*. Gilder admired Cleveland's "rustic simplicity of thought" and his "moral fury."[9] He attended the Democratic National Convention of 1892 and Cleveland's second inauguration, and he was a frequent guest at the White House in the next four years. He reveled in his intimacy with the President. On one occasion, returning from a ball at one in the morning, he wrote to his wife that the President was "still working on decisions that may turn the course of modern history. I am going now to interrupt him and try to get him to bed."[10]

Gilder never swerved in his devotion to Cleveland. When the President alienated many of his independent supporters by forcing arbitration on Britain during the Venezuelan boundary dispute of 1895, Gilder stood by him. He approved Cleveland's action as "the introduction of ethics into international relations." Although in 1880 Gilder had argued against annexationist sentiment, contending that America should not subjugate foreigners who were "uncongenial" to democratic institutions, when the Spanish-American War actually broke out, he defended it. He thought the American people had gone into it "with a disinterested spirit, and with a pure intention, feeling that the 'oppressor' must be smitten." He supposed that the War could have been avoided, but "when slavery and freedom clash, slavery is doomed, and this Spanish piece of Medievalism in the new world was doomed too." On annexation, the *Century* took no clear stand, except to note that if "honor, duty, and humanity compel the action," the United States should take it. It did oppose ultimate statehood for the conquered territories: America's racial and religious troubles were already "disturbing enough" without adding "ineradicable race tendencies" and the "permanent" depressing element of tropical climate. The revolt in the Philippines simply puzzled the *Century*. The affair was "depressing from every point of view" and fraught with moral questions that were hard to decide.[11]

The questions raised by imperialism were less baffling to Charles Eliot Norton. From the time of Grant's schemes to annex Santo Domingo until the end of the Spanish American War, Norton was fiercely and consistently anti-imperialist. In his view, Cleveland's message on the Venezuela affair "shattered" his reputation. When war broke out with Spain, Norton was defiant. His argument blended liberal and racist assumptions: not only did colonialism deny American political ideals; it attacked the conditions that had made those ideals possible by threatening to introduce mongrel strains into the American character. Norton's acidity was irritating even to a fellow anti-imperialist, Senator Hoar of Massachusetts, who castigated him for his "habit of bitter and sneering speech" and the "bad influence" he exerted at Harvard. But Norton did not repent. In the midst of all the eulogies that followed McKinley's assassination, Norton called the dead President a "smug, canting, self-righteous servant of the Devil."[12]

But if Norton's anti-imperialism was unflinching, his rationale for it stemmed from sentiments he shared with the imperialists. Norton and Gilder agreed perfectly on the superiority of America to other nations, and on the superiority of the Anglo-Saxon race generally. Norton, however, doubted that America could assimilate different racial strains without serious jeopardy to her own institutions; he was anti-imperialist because he was isolationist. The true imperialists, on the other hand, men like Henry Cabot Lodge, were optimistic enough to believe in the possibilities of a new Anglo-Saxon empire, to be staffed by Americans. Norton and Lodge were expressions of the same mentality: in a mood of confidence they were imperialists; in a mood of self-doubt, isolationists. Their ideology, in the hands of a political insider like Lodge, would blossom into expansionism. But for an outsider, for a man politically impotent, temperament turned ideology inward. To defend America from ruin was the best that could be visualized.

A good index of the obsessively defensive stance of genteel politics is its increasing preoccupation with immigration after the Civil War. Thomas Bailey Aldrich represents the extreme of genteel opinion on immigration, but he represents the trend, too. A Mugwump and an anti-imperialist, Aldrich simplistically blamed all the major social ills of his day on foreigners. Whether the trouble was vagrancy, "that bitter blossom of civilization," or striking labor unions, immigrants were the troublemakers. They brought "unknown rites" and "tiger passions" to America that made them easy prey for the Boss Crokers of the day. Worse, they brought "foreign grievances," and such low standards of living that American wages spoiled them. Typically in Aldrich's *The Stillwater Tragedy* a drunken Italian heads the labor union, squanders his wages at the local pub, and gives "windy" speeches. By 1894 Aldrich thought the influx of immigrants had transformed the country so drastically that American democracy could only be considered a sorry failure. Always prone to apocalyptic thinking, Aldrich found his view of society growing blacker as the century closed. The advent of a new one promised nothing for him except more ignorant and unruly immigrants.[13]

Neither Curtis nor Gilder was so violent about immigration as Aldrich. But when the "noxious weeds and brambles" continued to pour onto America's shores, Curtis advocated restricting immigration in *Harper's Weekly*, and Gilder did likewise in the *Century*.[14] Norton, who would not permit America to shirk the responsibility for her failure, did not agree with Aldrich that immigration was the sole cause of America's decline. But their differences were only differences of emphasis. After 1870 Norton found joy only in his excursions to Italy. As the nineteenth century ended, Norton wrote, "I feel myself a stranger here, an exile in my own country."[15] Like Aldrich and Curtis he looked back with nostalgia to the life of the isolated New England village. Both Norton and Curtis, in fact, as already mentioned, took homes in Ashfield, Massachusetts. Both men felt comfortable in Ashfield. It was the last resort of the America they knew and loved.[16] But the "hard shrewd sense and the simpler manner" of their forefathers had vanished.[17] Middle-class, agrarian, Anglo-Saxon America had not survived the onslaught of immigration. She was no longer a single culture. And because her homogeneity had vanished, that "condition of great national power," her decline was foreseeable.

By 1900, the genteel reformers had effectively withdrawn from modern America. Their complaints about the state of contemporary affairs were comprehensive enough so that, to their critics, they seemed nothing but a group of hand-wringing reactionaries. Repelled by the developments transforming America—industrialization, urbanization, and especially immigration—they seemed to cling all the more firmly to a vanishing age. In politics, their opinions assumed an increasingly antidemocratic cast. Their crusade for civil service reform, overblown as were the hopes attached to it, did not succeed in restructuring American politics in the way they intended.

The civil service reform movement commanded Curtis's attention after the Civil War. All of his genteel friends looked upon it with favor; Norton and Gilder joined him in publicly urging its support. Gilder believed that civil service reform was as important as the War for Independence and the Civil War. "We have had three national problems," he wrote in a public letter at the time of the Cleveland-Blaine campaign of 1884, "the making, the purging, and the complete purification of our political institutions."[18] It was Curtis, however, who became most clearly identified in the national press as the spokesman for reform.

He was not its first. Already before the Civil War there had been sporadic expressions of concern over the state of the civil service.[19] The War itself saw most experienced Democrats swept from office at a time when the functions of government, and consequently the number of workers needed, were expanding rapidly. Recognizing the need for better-qualified people, Massachusetts Senator Charles Sumner introduced in 1864 a bill that would have provided for competitive examinations administered by a civil service commission. Congress took no action. A similar bill, introduced the next year by Rhode Island Representative Thomas Jenckes, marked the real beginning of the civil service reform movement.

Curtis joined the cause soon thereafter. Defeated by Roscoe Conkling for United States Senator from New York in 1866, Curtis took his fight with the Conkling machine into the arena of national politics. From then until his death in 1892, he was the most conspicuous champion of civil service reform. Like most of the reformers, he came from an old New England family. Like them, he represented the professions and the older financial and mercantile class; he had no ties to the new industrial elite. He lacked the college education that many of the reformers had, but in placing his support behind the Jenckes bill, which proposed a test of general knowledge rather than special skills for government employees, Curtis indicated his agreement with the European practice of tying government service to a university education.

The first struggles for reform centered on the appointive powers of President Johnson. The reformers did not at first oppose the President, but eventually they joined the drive for impeachment, even though it eclipsed the reform movement for a time. They were optimistic about President Grant until they saw his appointments. Their efforts then increased sharply, and in 1871 Congress passed a rider to the civil service appropriation bill empowering the President to appoint a commission to establish rules for examining applicants for government work.

Curtis was named chairman of the commission and succeeded in getting it to back the principle of competitive examinations. Grant promulgated the rules proposed by the commission in early 1872. A few months later the commission completed its classification of jobs, which Grant also accepted. It appeared that reform was well launched.

Within a year, however, reaction set in. When an appointment was made to the New York Customs House without proper review, Curtis resigned as commission chairman with a parting blast of criticism. Grant appointed another reformer as his successor, but by 1875 Congress had completely eliminated competitive examinations and the President acquiesced. Thereafter Curtis served the cause of reform from outside the government, but his influence did not diminish. He constantly badgered President Hayes about reform, and Hayes as often tried to pacify him. His exasperation over the lack of progress led to his first open break with the Republican Party. He recommended in *Harper's Weekly* in 1879 that New York voters "scratch" the Party candidate for governor, Alonzo Cornell. Twenty thousand voters did, but Cornell was elected anyway.[20]

In 1880 the New York Civil Service Reform Association, founded three years before, was revitalized and Curtis was named president, a position he held until his death. The organization fathered other state associations and, modeling itself after the loyal publication societies formed during the War, it printed and widely circulated reform pamphlets. Its efforts, however, did not perceptibly move Congress toward reform until a disappointed office-seeker shot President Garfield. In the summer of 1881, while the President remained critically ill, the reformers organized the National Civil Service Reform League with Curtis as president. Congress resisted a bombardment of petitions from the reformers for another two years, and then reluctantly passed the Pendleton Act establishing competitive examinations for part of the federal civil service. The bill was written by a legislative committee of the New York Civil Service Reform Association.

Reform was not at first so widespread as the reformers wished. The Pendleton Act covered less than half of all federal employees and did not even apply to municipal and state workers. The reformers, however, soon extended their success to the state level in New York and Massachusetts. And although national reform was halted for a time, the merit system continued to be extended by executive order in the 1880's and 1890's. From a very inauspicious beginning, the reformers had made steady if slow progress. When their movement began, there was no uniformity in federal personnel policies. Tenure was short and uncertain. Examinations were meaningless, nepotism was common, there was no uniform promotion policy and no training or retirement program. The Pendleton Act professionalized the federal civil service. In taking the first steps toward the creation of a national bureaucracy, the Act paralleled trends in the party system itself. Party leaders had resisted the efforts of the reformers to remove the government bureaucracy from local control, but the parties themselves were beginning to recognize the need for organization on a national scale.[21] The genteel reformers assisted in this move away from political localism.

At the time, however, the debate was conducted in quite different terms. Often Curtis and the reformers seemed merely to be repeating platitudes about the necessity of having good men in office. Their opponents, the professional politicians, knew better. They knew that an end to corruption in office could be achieved only by a significant rearrangement of American politics. Thus, debates on the reforms were bitterly vituperative. Many of the professionals were no less bothered by political corruption than were the reformers, but they thought the reformers naive about the realities of political life. They called Curtis "Calico Curtis" and said he was too dainty, too impractical for the hurly-burly of politics. The adjectives fit the American image of a European aristocrat; the reformers were regularly charged with advocating aristocratic ideas.

Curtis dismissed this as an irrelevant smear. But the charge did not die easily, for the good reason that there was truth to it. The reformers themselves preferred to be characterized in public by their announced motives—Christian conscience and efficiency in government. In private, however, they expressed antidemocratic sentiments. Because they deplored the corruption and incompetence of men in public office, they had increasing doubts about the electorate and the way it registered its decisions. When they spoke positively about American politics, they were likely to be thinking nostalgically of the age of John Quincy Adams, their golden age of political virtue.

Since then, as the reformers decided about 1870, American politics had declined. Once postwar political corruption became the topic of the day—the exposure of the Tweed Ring in New York City profoundly shocked the country—the reformers groped for an explanation of what had happened. Depressed by the mediocrity of Grant's political appointees, they found conclusive evidence in both national and local politics of a trend that had set in with the administration of Andrew Jackson. His initiation of the spoils system, according to the reformers, had greatly weakened American politics by introducing the practice of viewing public office as a reward for services rendered rather than as an obligation undertaken by the most talented. As public office became an occupation no different from other occupations, its aspirants were motivated by their private gain, not the public good. Moreover, the spoils system, based as it was on Jackson's view that any man could fulfill the responsibilities of office, undercut the long tenure and high status that public servants had traditionally enjoyed. A government dominated by the mediocre could no longer attract the talented. Were an honest and capable man to run for office, the political machines, through manipulation of untutored immigrants—another heritage of Jacksonianism—would guarantee his defeat. Left in the hands of men who did not understand correct political principles, government was, not surprisingly, subject to the vagaries of a high tariff, soft money, and imperialist expansionism.[22]

The reformers' myth of the decline of American politics obscured deeper misgivings. The genteel reformers had never been truly at ease with democracy. Although they seldom criticized American institutions before the Civil War, even then their attitude toward democracy had been cautious. In 1844 Curtis, always the most liberal of the group, was working in

Concord, Massachusetts, and listening to Emerson, Thoreau, and other Transcendentalists. But he never shared their optimism about democracy:

The theory of democracy is noble. It asserts the majesty of human nature. It is the wise man governing himself. It implies moderation, abstinence, temperance, heroism and religion.... But when it is not so—when it becomes among wild and sensual people the popular creed, then the majority governs, whether it order the canonization or the martyrdom of the best men.... Now I do not find in this American people that virtue which alone can render democracy either politic or just.... It is plain enough that we are not a people actually capable of self-government, however fair may be our theory.[23]

Curtis does not explicitly limit the right of universal suffrage here (as Norton does in *Recent Social Theories*), although he does imply that the suffrage may be restricted if men are not morally qualified for it. When Curtis later and almost alone among his friends supported woman suffrage on the grounds of natural right, it was because he believed that women would provide an efficient moral force in politics. For him the moral test had to precede an extension of the franchise.

During the Civil War, when the genteel group was most convinced of the uniqueness of America, it was, paradoxically, most enthusiastic about the universal truth of natural rights. After the War, as its distaste for America grew, it abandoned both ideas. Instead it attempted to restructure American politics by civil service reform in the hope of insulating it from the growing ignorance and barbarism of the American electorate. In lecture after lecture Curtis affirmed that the intention of the reformers was only to reintroduce into the American political system the kind of talented leaders that had been absent since the days of Andrew Jackson. He did not mention what was implicit in his argument—that the American voter could no longer be counted on to elect good men to office. The implication was evident enough, however; his disavowals were never successful in eliminating the aristocratic aura that clung to the civil service reform movement. Curtis did not want to deny that the reformers were inspired by English precedent. He openly criticized Americans for the national habit of supposing that they could learn nothing from foreign experience.

Beneath their rhetoric of talent and efficiency, however, the civil service reformers were open to the charge of aristocratic leanings. The men they sought to install in office were not just any collection of talented leaders, but an elite group with definite professional overtones. Typically, Curtis and Norton described the ideal politician as a scholar. Rejecting the popular view of the scholar as "unpractical and impracticable," Curtis said that his function for the state was to act as a public conscience by which public measures might be tested. The scholarly class, Curtis said, "is the upper house in the politics of the world."[24]

Reduced to its essentials as Curtis defined them, civil service reform would have substituted a class of scholars for the existing class of professional politicians. At the heart of his objection to the spoils system was his belief that its principle, self-interest, had created in America a special political class. The principle was false and corrupting, and the system operated, as his own experience testified, to bar from the political realm any who challenged it.

Curtis thought a new political principle was necessary: government ought to function in the public interest, not the private interest. He offered no definitions of what he meant by the public interest, but he was flatly opposed to what had become in America the prevailing practice of arriving at the public interest through the conflict of various private interests. He recognized that politics almost by definition was concerned with the reconciliation of opposing interests. But he thought that the principles of justice that ought to resolve such conflicts were no mere matter of majority opinion.

The true principles of the science of politics were not available to all men. Curtis virtually divided the body politic into the educated classes and the majority. The former were the only "true conservative force of the Republic." Only educated America could effectively oppose the tyranny of the majority and could assert the worth of self-reliance and the power of the individual. Only it could show that "progress springs from the minority, and that if it will but stand fast time will give it a victory." "Take from the country at this moment," Curtis wrote in 1882, "the educated power, which is contemned as romantic and sentimental, and you would take from the army its general, from the ship its compass, from national action its moral mainspring. It is not the demagogue and the shouting rabble; it is the people heeding the word of the thinker and the lesson of experience which secures the welfare of the American republic and enlarges human liberty."[25]

Curtis never suggested any more precise requirement for his new class of officeholders than that they be educated. His lectures do not mention wealth or family as desirable qualifications for office. He touched upon a model for his scholarly class only once, and on that occasion he had no feudal aristocracy in mind. Rather, he identified the scholarly class with the clergy "as of old."[26] Curtis was doubtless appealing here to the medieval practice of placing clergy and scholars in a single special, privileged class. By the nineteenth century, the medieval curriculum that derived all branches of knowledge from theology had long been discarded. But if the scholar of politics no longer had to go to the theologian for his concepts, the ultimately theological framework of knowledge had not disappeared. Despite the revolutionary changes that had secularized the world since the Middle Ages, Curtis continued to deal in a mode of thinking that, a generation after his death, would disappear into obscurity.

The political independence manifested in Curtis's notion of the scholar-politician is understandable in the context of his own political experience. His sympathies with the Liberal Republican movement in 1872, his bolt from Republican ranks in 1884 and his regular practice of "scratching" machine candidates form a pattern of politically independent behavior. But Curtis's independence arose not only from his dissatisfaction with the Republican Party, but also from his hostility to the party system in general. He believed that "the constant, watchful, deadly enemy of republican government from the beginning has been party spirit. ..."[27] He stated the theme many times in 1876 and 1877 as a result of his concern over the disputed presidential election. When that contest was settled, he was gratified that party spirit had yielded to patriotic instinct. Nevertheless, he always viewed the party system with suspicion. In the tendency to form parties that was as "useful in the State as the fire upon the household hearth," he wrote in 1877, "lurks, as in that fire, the deadliest peril.... The most plausible suspicion of the permanence of the American government is founded in the belief that party spirit cannot be restrained. It is indeed a master passion...."[28]

At the end of the Civil War Curtis and Norton both hoped that the party system would disappear.[29] When the Democratic Party revived much sooner than they had expected, they complained that there was no meaningful difference between the two parties.[30] The enormous amounts of time, effort, and money wasted on the party system seemed to them to profit no one except a class of professional politicians motivated by self-interest. Political conflict was but a meaningless scramble.

Party spirit carried all the negative connotations for Curtis and Norton that *faction* had carried in the eighteenth century; both terms suggested selfishness and unscrupulous behavior; both were intended to describe a primary threat to political stability. But although Hamilton, in *The Federalist Papers*, was able to outline a model for political stability by using faction to check faction, that idea repelled Curtis. Hamilton flatly dismissed the usefulness of religious or moral motives for restraining party spirit; Curtis, at least during the disputed election of 1876, thought that patriotism had been able to do it.[31] Skeptical as he was about human nature, Hamilton had no alternative to pragmatism in constructing his political system. Curtis, more optimistic and righteous about men, could not tolerate the possibility that an evil motive could be used to achieve good results.

The Federalist Papers offer the classical definition of American politics as interest politics, but the genteel reformers never accepted that definition. If Curtis had offered his own definition of a political party, it would have been reminiscent of the one offered by Edmund Burke in *Thoughts on the Cause of the Present Discontents*: "Party is a body of men united for promoting by their joint endeavors the national interest upon some particular principle in which they are all agreed." The genteel reformers, however, did not foresee the possibility of any ideological differentiation of parties in America, and sought instead to destroy the party system itself. And in attacking the patronage system, they were attacking its lifeblood. To have foreclosed the rewarding of political work by political appointments, on the scale that the genteel reformers wished, would have crippled the party system. That was what the quarrel between the reformers and the professional politicians was really all about. Perhaps if the genteel reformers had visualized a substitution of ideological politics for interest politics, their political theory would not have been as archaic as it was. Their attempts at restructuring American politics were designed, not to create a new politics, but to restore an old politics. It was false to assume as they did that pre-Jacksonian politics had not been interest-group politics, but even if that had been true, their effort to replace the professional politicians with a body of scholars would have been a hopeless one.

Genteel politics was most anachronistic in its concept of a class of men who have true views about politics because their education enables them to see how the fundamental moral law can order social relationships. The genteel reformers never recognized that education could carry with it a class interest of its own, an interest no more in harmony with the fundamental law than any other. Their partiality for men of their own class and background was appallingly narrow.

Had the genteel reformers had better intellectual resources at their disposal and had the theological framework of their views been less crippling, they might have been able to construct a more relevant if still conservative political theory. Burke's distinctions between the functions of the electorate and the functions of office might have provided a congenial starting point. His trenchant criticism of direct electoral control over the exercise of political office would have given the genteel reformers much to ponder. By distinguishing the functions of government from the functions of the governed, they might have adapted Burke to their own purposes. But although genteel politics was antidemocratic, it never ceased to be middle-class. Whether its failure to break out of the confines of the middle class is evidence of its own intellectual failure or of the narrowness of American politics is difficult to assess. It is true that genteel politics was not conservative enough to make Burke accessible to it. Yet at the same time it was too conservative to share the flexibility of another noted Englishman, a contemporary, James Bryce, whose *American Commonwealth* is virtually a catalogue of genteel prejudices.

Whereas the later editions of Bryce's highly respected volume show a continuing adjustment to American political change, the genteel reformers became more and more inflexible. Already in the 1870's Curtis was willing to consider a proposal that would have given men in all branches of the government lifetime tenure subject to popular approval. Norton, more skeptical, saw no hope for institutional reform at all.[32] In 1890 he thought that the older theories of republicanism had demonstrated their failure and had to be replaced. He feared that only "individual worth, and unorganized, extrapolitical action of its better classes" might save America.[33] At the end, the genteel reformers looked to the scholars still, but they resigned themselves to what they had once protested.

Economics for an Organic Society

THE decline in American political life was linked, in the minds of the genteel reformers, to a decline in the health of the economy. Except for Stedman they had few ties to the world of business, and they never engaged in organized attempts at reform in economics as they did in politics. However, they thought that business "bought" government all too often. Moreover, neither business nor government seemed able to cope with disorder in industrial America. Recurrent depressions and violent strikes appeared to be moving America toward a social revolution.

Their mounting anxiety after the Civil War over the close relationship of business and government did not lead the genteel group to call for a clear separation of the two. Though their intellectual antecedents were liberal, they were not the staunch defenders of laissez-faire that their critics have thought them. As they liked less and less the kind of men who entered government and the politics they pursued, they might logically have called for a general cutback in the functions of government. They did dampen their fervent support for the government after the War, but they stayed in the Whig wing of the Republican Party. They were always attracted to the idea that government had a positive obligation to promote the general welfare. They were not opposed to big government on principle, as laissez-faire liberals were.

The genteel critique of laissez-faire is amply documented in the writing of Norton and Curtis, although both men also described themselves as liberals. When Norton wrote in 1852 that government interference in private affairs should be resisted, he expressed their common view.[1] Yet, only a year later, in *Recent Social Theories*, he severely criticized liberalism. His positions are not contradictory, as I shall argue later. But they do show that Norton cannot be consistently classified as either a liberal or a conservative if the former of those categories derives from Bentham and the latter from Burke. What is true of Norton is also true of his friends, especially Curtis, who refused to be bound by any contemporary political labels.[2] In his editorials for *Harper's Weekly* he wrote favorably of Malthus, Sumner, and Spencer on the one hand, and Louis Blanc on the other.[3] When he spoke generally of progress and reform, Curtis considered himself to be of that camp.[4] Yet he called himself a conservative, too. He defined conservatism as "the rudder which holds the moving ship to its course" and reform as "the wind that forever fills the sails and moves the ship."[5] A judicious combination of the two was the only true road to progress.

Curtis would have preferred to let the matter rest there; like his friends, he was averse to anything he considered needless speculation. After the War, however, as he moved to support some forms of government regulation of the economy, he found his arguments blocked by doctrinaire liberals who continued to stand by the principles of laissez-faire. He sidestepped the argument whenever he could by calling for a pragmatic approach to economic problems. Norton, who understood the ideological issues better than Curtis, had his troubles, too. Neither of them ever produced a clear statement of economic principles.

They were hindered in doing so at least partly because they lived in a country where almost all discussion of political and economic principles was conducted in the language of liberalism.[6] After the Whigs decided in 1840 to woo the common man as avidly as their Democratic opponents, no political party outside the South openly advocated conservative ideas. The range of political and economic debate was considerably narrowed, and remained so until late in the century, when the Social Gospel movement and Populism offered a fresh look at basic principles.

The liberal framework was generally assumed; issues arose from the clash of special interests. The interests were real enough, but the conflicts between them neither demanded nor provided a broad perspective. Lacking that perspective and an audience as well, a conservative was unlikely to be able to criticize liberalism or even to understand that he himself was a conservative.

The difficulty was compounded for the genteel group because they had broken with the European world of kings and hereditary class structures that Burke defended. The genteel group had lost contact, too, with Burke's belief that the state embodied the divine will. During the Civil War they came back to that belief, but their religious roots were not deep enough to sustain it. What they needed but could not find was an *American* conservatism appropriate for a secular republic.

Despite their difficulties in locating themselves on the political spectrum, the genteel group can be recognized as conservatives. They were seldom optimistic about human nature or the human condition. They feared democracy and resisted its extension. They valued order, discipline, scholarship, tradition. They had a sense of the past, but little sense of the future. The world they cherished, a pre-industrial and pre-urban world, was the world of their fathers. They offered a conservative critique of capitalism, a critique founded upon their recollection and reconstruction of how pre-industrial capitalism had worked. The restoration of the harmony of those days—between government and business and among the social classes—was their object. They wanted society to work as an organism again, not as a cluster of competing groups. They frankly admitted that they looked backward for their golden age; so also did more than a few of the reformers of the Progressive movement after 1900. But the genteel group remained too conservative to see much hope in the future or any basis for a renewed trust in democracy.

Because the genteel writers never tried to accommodate themselves to industrial America, they remained indifferent to Spencer's attempt to adapt Social Darwinism to the period; in any case the notion of a social struggle for existence did not appeal to them at all. The whole late-nineteenth-century quarrel between Spencer and his opponents left Curtis, as it did Norton, largely untouched.

It is rather to the tradition of Whiggery, the tradition of a strong, paternalistic, central government, that Curtis's conservatism can be traced. Curtis realized that the powers of the central government had been hotly debated as far back as Hamilton and Jefferson. Although he glossed over the usual distinctions between Federalist and Anti-Federalist, he indicated his own preference for the former by giving a decidedly Whiggish flavor to his account of the eighteenth-century debates. Hamilton, the primary proponent of a strong national government, was for Curtis "the greatest of our great men" and Jefferson, the leading advocate of limited government, the least of them.

As the Civil War was ending, Curtis argued that it had vindicated Hamilton's contention that states' rights would prove stronger than nationalism in the course of American politics.[7] He felt it necessary in 1879 to declare that *Harper's Weekly* was not opposed to local self-government; it merely felt that American political difficulties resulted more often from the "exaggeration" of states' rights than from encroachments on them by the national government.[8] He delighted in pointing out that Jefferson himself had not been a rigid believer in laissez-faire. If he had been, Curtis argued, he would have opposed the public school and the post office, "the twin columns of public intelligence upon which the fabric of popular government rests." As it was, "Jefferson was a practical statesman just to the degree that he disregarded the absolutism of his own maxim." Curtis suggested that Jefferson's letter to Breckenridge justifying the Louisiana Purchase in terms of national advantage might have been written by the "Whiggest of Presidents."[9] Curtis's flexibility on economic issues and his sympathetic view of the national government as an agency for expressing and guiding the national will were evident.

They were evident, too, for Norton. In *Recent Social Theories*, Norton took a skeptical view of contemporary European liberalism. His objections to the European revolts of 1848 echoed Burke on the French Revolution: a cautious eye to human experience instead of hasty *a priori* generalizing was the best avenue to progress.[10] He always lamented the lack of "serious studies of social conditions."[11] His lifelong distaste for most reformers was reflected in his account of the International Congress of Peace and Liberty at Lausanne. The forms and institutions of government were not so important as the moral dispositions of men, he asserted at that time. Change would come only through "slow, historic processes," and from a close attention to the means at hand.[12] Norton advised caution and patience because the individual human being was "but a link...in a chain reaching back indefinitely into the past, reaching forward indefinitely into the future."[13]

But if Norton's hostility to reformers would have satisfied any laissez-faire capitalist, his attitude toward the state would not. In *Recent Social Theories* he defined liberty as freedom "from all restraints which may prevent the doing of what is right," and he did not worry about government action to compel the doing of what was right. Where men were in a degraded condition, such compulsion was reasonable. Thus he defended dictatorship as superior to democracy in certain cases. His qualitative definition of liberty allowed him to approve of any political system that would strongly encourage moral action. Yet only during the Civil War, and then only for a time, did Norton look to the government as a machine for social regeneration. He dismissed typical liberal objections to the authoritarian state as irrelevant to America. If the people were the state, there could be no antagonism between them. The constitutional phrase, "We the people," guaranteed the equation.[14] With the failure of Reconstruction, Norton no longer looked so hopefully to the state for direction. Well before this, he had betrayed a marked uneasiness with the Benthamite axiom that the economic interests of the individual and society were identical. In 1852 he published an article in the *North American Review* on various schemes of housing for the poor. Both a sense of charity and a fear of the lower classes motivated his plea that something had to be done to meet this "almost pre-eminently important" problem. He pointed out that the poor could do nothing for themselves; both public and private means must be employed to aid them. He advocated a system of inspection and regulation of housing by municipal authorities. That this was a step away from laissez-faire, he recognized. Governmental interference in private affairs "is to be deprecated, when the interests of the individual and society coincide," he said, "but when those interests differ, the government becomes unjust and partial, unless it interferes to bring them again to mutual harmony." Furthermore, Norton went on, there was much "foolish talk about the danger of a government invading the rights of property." That danger was small, he argued, compared with the danger of guarding "the assumed and fancied rights of property too zealously." The rights of property should "weigh nothing" compared with the rights of humanity. Laissez-faire economic doctrine to the contrary, individual interest and social interest often diverged. Indeed, laissez-faire economics in practice often led to a conflict between them. And Norton would not permit the individual to be set against the community.[15]

Neither would Norton permit the social classes to be ranged against each other, a position that underlay his increasing dissatisfaction with the course of post-War industrialism. Instead, Norton urged more social generosity and sympathy, more recognition of the "common ties of humanity" and the "duties of all classes toward each other."[16] That the social classes owed nothing to each other, as William Graham Sumner was to insist later, was inconceivable to Norton. In his early life he would have considered Sumner's stand a denial of the principles of Christianity. Even when he became an agnostic, he continued to test social ideas by a moral standard.

Except for his early articles showing concern for the poor, Norton wrote little about American social problems until after the Civil War. He concentrated instead on England, which he visited twice before 1860. English social conditions greatly upset him from the first. In London in 1856 he went to hear the Chartist orator Ernest Jones denounce the aristocracy. Norton thought the speech could have been stronger than it was, but the depressing working-class audience was "a bitterer denunciation of the social system" than anything the speaker said.[17] A decade later Norton wrote that the English poor were rightfully the enemies of society. "The solid crust of English society rests on a great dull mass of lava which sooner or later will be heated to a red heat and overflow and burn up whatever lies in its course."[18] In 1868 he wrote to Mill that the vast number of Englishmen had nothing to lose by violent revolution.[19]

In 1869 in "The Poverty of England," he described the condition of the poor as "a disgrace and a danger." As always, he maintained that the wealthy ought to assume more social responsibility, but he reserved the brunt of his attack for classical political economics, which he criticized as a repository for "current sophistry." "The laws of political economy," he wrote, "are not sufficient by themselves to regulate the relations of men one to another." Economic laws ought to correspond to morality, he thought, but the variety of dispositions and interests among men was so great that those laws "can hardly be absolutely applied even when fully understood."

To illustrate his ideas, Norton discussed some misconceptions attending classical wage theory. The notion that supply and demand were the sole economic consideration in setting wages he saw as a mask for selfishness. Only if all men were equally intelligent and independent could competition satisfactorily determine wages. The whole idea, he thought, tended to degrade and enslave labor. Moreover, no amount of theorizing could make labor and management equals in the bargaining process. The system by its very nature encouraged the hiring of workers at the lowest possible rate of pay. Emigration was no solution to the problem, and continence, under the circumstances, was highly unlikely. Norton, however, did not feel that capitalism should be replaced; only that certain functions of government should be expanded, the rich should assume more social duties, and the poor should be educated.[20]

The modesty of Norton's proposals is typical. However strong were their theoretical objections to the doctrine of laissez-faire, the genteel group were exceedingly cautious in recommending any actual retreat from capitalism. They were suspicious of economic liberalism, but their suspicions were conservative.

Their opinions on the labor question underline the point. In his first writing on the problems of labor, Curtis granted the right of labor to unionize and to strike. Both unions and strikes bothered him, however, because they forced him to consider the existence of economic classes with rival interests. Emphasizing that all men in America were laborers and that success came faithfully to "superior industry and sagacity," Curtis criticized the union movement for creating a special class of laborers. Labor and capital in America were "real friends," Curtis thought. Their problems could be solved through mutual understanding if each would plainly and calmly state its grievances. Strikes were useless because they hurt labor more than capital and seldom achieved their ends.[21]

Curtis did not deny that labor had legitimate complaints. He always protested the natural tendency of the employer to buy labor, like everything else, at the lowest possible price. Labor, for Curtis, was "merchandise plus a soul" and he expected employers to mix morals with economics when they set wages.[22] He approved a bill submitted in 1871 by Senator Hoar calling for an investigation of wages and hours, the division of profits between capital and labor, the general condition of the laboring class, and the effect upon it of existing laws. He said the bill asked the investigating senators to reject "phrases about supply and demand and the laws of political economy, knowing that there must be something wrong in laws which leave the mass of men poor, ignorant, and dissatisfied."[23]

The violent railway strikes of 1877 shocked Curtis and forced him to revise his thinking. Thereafter for a time the primary concern expressed in his articles on labor difficulties was the preservation of social order. However "hard in their dealings" employers might be, riot was no remedy. Realizing that his early hopes for harmony between labor and capital had been ill founded, he urged an expansion of both the state militias and the United States Army. He described all hostility between labor and capital and between strikers and nonstrikers as anarchy.[24] After Curtis had calmed down, he returned to exhorting labor not to separate itself from the rest of America. He referred to the "suggestive book" of Edward Atkinson, *Labor and Capital Allies, Not Enemies*.[25] He tried to forestall a new danger, that labor would form its own political party. He admitted that injustice could be remedied by legislation, but he wanted no government by special interests. The existing political parties provided adequate machinery for reform.[26]

In the telegraph strike of 1883, Curtis considered the public interest overriding. Cutting through disputes about the limits of government in his usual pragmatic fashion, Curtis declared, "Whatever is essential to the safety of the state, the state may rightfully do." Curtis observed that "the organized aggregation of capital will necessarily produce a similar organization in labor, and the conflicting interests of the two will perpetually menace the peace and welfare of the state, which it is agreed may properly provide for its own safety." The choices facing government were to ignore monopolies, to regulate them, or to prohibit them.[27] When the Southwestern Railway strike of 1886 broke out, Curtis recommended passage of a bill before the House establishing the machinery of voluntary arbitration for strikes involving the public interest.[28]

In May of 1886 just before the Chicago Haymarket riot, Curtis summarized what the American people had learned from the strikes. First, the "American view" of labor questions and the "American way" of dealing with them were being ignored because foreigners dominated the American labor movement. Second, politics and not strikes was the proper avenue for the appeals of labor. "The American government is not the enemy of the people," he argued; "it is their agent, and therefore it is simply stupid to be 'agin the government,' unless the majority is plainly oppressive, and even then the remedy is at the polls."[29]

The anarchist bombings in Chicago a week later stunned Curtis, though he derived a grim satisfaction from the outcome of the episode. The summary action of the police and the courts cheered him and renewed his confidence that the law could deal with social disorders. Noting the prominence of foreigners among the anarchists, he denied that anarchism was a logical result of the American labor movement and insisted that native Americans showed "no general disposition to resort to force as a solution of the situation." He traced much of the responsibility for the outbreak of violence in the labor movement to the domination of unions by foreign members and leaders "who have no knowledge of American institutions, no sympathy for American ideas, and who are profoundly ignorant of economic principles and of history."[30] But Curtis admitted that foreign immigration alone did not explain American strikes; to say that it did would be "grossly unjust." The labor problem was actually the "question which will test the essential character of our civilization," he argued. Labor might be dangerous, but when capital "is able and disposed first to buy legislation, and then to buy the interpretation of law by the courts, it becomes the enemy of society, disturbing the very foundation of all harmonious social understanding, and threatening violent revolution."[31]

While Curtis was struggling in the pages of *Harper's Weekly* to persuade labor and capital that they were true allies, the *Century*, in Gilder's hands, chose its side with no difficulty. Gilder himself, born in 1844, was the youngest of the genteel group. Raised in New Jersey and New York and educated in the various girls' schools at which his father taught, Gilder prepared for the law for a brief time, but enlisted in 1863 in the Union Army. His father died the next year and Gilder took a job as a railroad paymaster to support the family. In the late 1860's he reported for a Newark, New Jersey, newspaper and later owned another. He went to New York in 1870 to become editor of the new *Scribner's Monthly* and remained as editor when *Scribner's* became *The Century* in 1880. Before the Cleveland campaign of 1884, he had little interest in politics. Like Curtis, he became involved in civil service reform, but he was much more drawn to New York City politics—tenement house reform, kindergarten associations, and the unsuccessful mayoralty campaign of Seth Low in 1897. His ties to the world of culture were always stronger than Curtis's; he published five volumes of poetry after the Civil War and made his house a gathering place for actors and artists like his wife. His politics, purely a product of the Gilded Age, was marked by little generosity.

From the first, the *Century* was skeptical of labor; it was convinced that labor had misdirected its efforts by concentrating too hard on wages. Higher wages were desirable, naturally, but workers needed "to learn better how to use the income they now receive. . . ." Many laborers earned more than their subsistence required, but "hurtful and pernicious" pleasures like liquor and tobacco wasted their money. The poor should buy larger amounts to cut costs, buy for cash whenever possible, and eschew inferior goods and cheap ornaments.[32]

In these early editorials, Gilder underestimated the seriousness of labor difficulties, as he soon realized. As he became increasingly sensitive to labor violence, he accepted John Hay's *The Breadwinners* for serial publication in the *Century* and reacted severely against union threats to the public order. If the police could not handle these "banditti," he said, the militia ought to be called out with grape-shot and bayonets."[33] Gilder was especially bothered by references to dynamite.[34] In 1885 he censored part of an article that merely quoted an endorsement of dynamiting in England. "It would doubtless have been copied by dynamite journals as an endorsement of their methods," he wrote to William Dean Howells. He urged Howells to remove the word *dynamite* from an article of his own, lest some crank misinterpret it.[35]

The violence of 1886 called forth typical recommendations for repressive measures from Gilder.[36] From 1887 on, the *Century* gave prominent attention to restricting immigration as a solution to labor problems. It never specified what qualifications immigrants ought to have, but hinted that labor agitators ought to be excluded. By 1893 the magazine took the position that all American unions were controlled by foreigners, who restricted apprenticeships and excluded qualified Americans from them. This "effective conspiracy" had revolutionized American labor; the very term "American labor" was a "complete misnomer."[37] Until America got a genuine American laboring class, the *Century* maintained in 1894, "we shall continue to have labor troubles which will require the exercise of national power for their suppression."[38]

To deal with immigrants already in America, Gilder advised private societies and churches to train immigrants in true American principles.[39] He championed the free kindergarten movement and assumed the presidency of the Kindergarten Association, which he hoped would teach the proper principles of Americanism. His claims of success sometimes sounded extravagant, but perhaps it was true that a parent "stopped pawning her boy's clothes for drink when he entered the kindergarten." The ignorance of the immigrants who inhabited the tenement districts discouraged him, but he thought that "Dante's, Michelangelo's countrymen ought to be worth working over into Americans, no matter how troublesome the fresh material offered."[40] But the *Century* gave far more attention to keeping immigrants out than to training them.

The magazine did recognize that capitalism had its own tendencies toward disorder. As the depression of the 1870's turned into the recession of the 1880's, Gilder was troubled for an explanation. At first he pointed to overproduction, low wages, and "ruinous competition" at home. He said that all prominent men, whether they supported laissez-faire or Whiggery, agreed on the desirability of expanding foreign trade to solve domestic economic problems. If foreign demand was insufficient, it would have to be "worked up."[41] Gilder remained unsatisfied with this analysis, however, and expressed his puzzlement that the country should not be continuously prosperous. There was definitely something unnatural and morbid about the whole business, he wrote. He blamed labor for calling strikes in bad times and corporations for holding wages down to a point where trade was affected. It was in the employer's interest to have as "large a class of consumers as possible." The principles of political economy that dictated a niggardly wage policy were self-defeating, he thought. "It begins to look as though there may be a screw loose in this logic."[42]

Curtis was more willing than Gilder to think there was. Although in 1889 he complained that the extension of government functions sought by Sidney Webb would "threaten individual initiative and energy," usually he remained moderate on the subject of Socialism. On one occasion he dispassionately described it as a doctrine "of high expediency rather than abstract right."[43] Gilder, by contrast, placed the *Century* on the defensive whenever the topic of Socialism came up. He felt that its obvious intent and certain result would be to penalize the man of superior talent.[44] The leveling implications of the income tax, too, the *Century* opposed. It admitted that there were merits in the tax (some rich men devoid of ability lived on the interest of inherited fortunes), but thought that the maker of legitimate wealth had contributed to society "by leaving the general mass of wealth just so much larger than he found it, by furnishing long years of useful and profitable work to others less well equipped than he for the race of life, and by performing for years some specific service, in addition, to the public at large." Limiting wealth, therefore, would mean a net loss to the world.[45]

The trusts, however, were another matter. *Harper's Weekly* cartooned the coal, oil, sugar, and steel trusts in 1887 as hydra-headed cattle and octopi. In an obvious reference to his own strictures against anarchism, Curtis argued that Uncle Sam "should attend to dangerous domestic cattle as well as to noxious foreign vermin." Whatever the evils of labor, the "much greater and more menacing peril is that colossal organization of corporate wealth. . . ."[46] Gilder could not quite make up his mind. In 1888 the *Century* said that nothing since the Knights of Labor had so "startled" America as the appearance of trusts. It acknowledged that spokesmen for the trusts believed that they were a natural growth toward greater efficiency, but thought it difficult to see how the consumer could possibly gain as much from them as from competition. The *Century* was struck, too, with the parallel between capitalistic and socialistic collectivism. If the reduction of competition by private means could aid the consumer, as the trusts maintained, why should the government not carry the process further?[47]

In typical genteel fashion, the *Century* refused to judge the trusts solely on economic grounds. When Andrew Carnegie defended their economic benefits in the pages of the magazine in 1900, it replied that there was a moral question involved, too. The American social order was based on the attempt "to give every man a fair chance." The concentration of capital, however, "puts into the hands of a few men a power over the in-dustrial life of the country such as they never possessed before." The truth was that older moral and legal ideas based upon free competition had not survived. Carnegie's argument that competition would check the growth of trusts was, in this sense, a relic. Instead, the *Century* contended, the nation must have a "wider conception of the responsibilities of property and the duties of trusteeship."[48] It referred to Carnegie's notable "Gospel of Wealth" as a good standard for businessmen.[49] Gilder's own attitude toward Carnegie verged on the worshipful; he was highly gratified when Carnegie followed his philanthropic suggestions.[50]

The *Century* never took a firm editorial position on the question whether "public sentiment," like Carnegie's, or legislation would better meet the problems of a corporate economy. Obviously the former was preferred. The insufficiency of the private approach was implicitly conceded by the magazine, however, when it chose to devote a whole issue in 1902–1903 to a series of articles on the trusts. One of them by Albert Shaw on Roosevelt and the trusts vigorously defended the President's notions. The *Century's* last attention to the subject under Gilder came in 1904 when John Bates Clark advocated regulation instead of trust-busting in its columns.[51]

The relationship of government to the economy received much more detailed attention in *Harper's Weekly* than in the *Century*. Curtis was most confident in urging intervention whenever he could clearly appeal to the public safety. Railroad or steamship accidents, hotel or tenement fires, inevitably called forth his demands for government investigation and for laws requiring inspection and regulation of public facilities. Curtis was interested, too, in public welfare legislation. He urged prison, mental-hospital, and poor-house reform. Slum conditions led him to endorse progressive legislation regulating tenement houses. Citing the work of Charles Loring Brace, he urged child-labor laws.[52]

Curtis favored federal regulation of the national educational system.[53] In the 1880's when the Blair Bill to allot federal funds for state education was before Congress, Curtis at first justified it by the high illiteracy rate in the South.[54] By 1888, however, his increasing conservatism led him to worry more about the principle involved in the bill than about its possible good effects. He agreed with the *New York Evening Post* that the effect of the bill would be to encourage the states to rely too heavily on the federal government. Then, too, national expenditures for education would justify keeping a high budget surplus in the national treasury.[55] And Curtis felt that few things were more poisonous to public virtue than such a surplus.

Unlike Gilder, Curtis did not always oppose government aid to industry.[56] In 1868 he did support a change in the New York Constitution that would have prohibited all grants of money to any individual, corporation, or association except for educational and charitable purposes.[57] But he did not use the principle of laissez-faire as an abstract right as many American Spencerians did. He said it was impossible to say that there were not certain enterprises that the government should support.[58] When government subsidies for shipping came before Congress in the 1870's and 1880's, Curtis halfheartedly supported them as a means of strengthening America.[59]

Furthermore, Curtis was cautious about the free-trade movement. He favored a moderate tariff, but continually found new objections to lowering it beyond a certain level. In 1865 he feared that a low tariff would encourage the flow of gold out of America. In 1866 he subordinated the whole issue to Reconstruction. In 1871 he contended that tariff cuts would depress production and wages. A decade later he thought the tariff encouraged the diversification of labor, and observed that the "whole force" of the Whig tariff tradition was preserved in the philosophy of the Republican Party. Not until 1888 did Curtis admit that the Party had become protectionist for the sake of protectionism. By doing so, he thought, it reversed its historic acceptance of the principles of Henry Clay and Hugh McCulloch that the tariff was not intended to prevent foreign competition. His disillusionment with this transformation was reflected in his support for President Cleveland.[60]

In addition to a brief flirtation in 1873 with the suggestion that the government ought to run the railroads, Curtis from time to time advanced other proposals for government ownership of economic enterprise. Before the end of 1873, he argued that it was high time for the government to take over the telegraph. He pointed to reasons of economy, military efficiency, antimonopolism, and the natural relationship of the telegraph to the post office.[61] In 1881 he wrote that monopolies "disturbed the simple and natural industrial relations" that balanced supply and demand, and again called for the government to own and operate the telegraph. (That issue of *Harper's Weekly* featured a cover cartoon by Thomas Nast in which both government and competition attacked the monster, Monopoly.)[62]

Within two years, however, he reversed himself. In opposition to the anti-Jeffersonian ideas of Henry George he said that government ownership of the railroads and telegraph would introduce paternal government into America and destroy liberty.[63] But Curtis was still hostile toward the telegraph monopoly. Sidestepping the issue of whether the telegraph strike of 1883 was wise, he wrote that capital held such advantages over labor that no strike was without reason. But because the telegraph was a public employment, he sought government regulation so that service would not be suspended. "The general welfare and the public peace cannot be promoted by chopping logic and quoting what are called economical laws."[64]

When Curtis confronted the American railway system, his hostility was more evident. From his Reconstruction days, he had disapproved of the consolidation of competing lines; the public lost, not gained, from it.[65] He had also opposed further land grants to the railroads. In 1873 he placed himself on the side of government regulation of the railroads. "We must proceed upon the supposition that railroads are inevitable monopolies," he said, "and must regulate them as such."[66]

But Curtis's fondness for the farmer led him, for a time, beyond mere regulation. Noting the grievances of the Grangers, he declared that the government ought to build a cheap railroad for them if private capital would not. Perhaps the unusual intelligence and education in "the purest form of industry" explained Curtis's sympathy for Populism just before he died in 1892.[67] Curtis had previously advocated various plans to provide satisfactory railways for the farmer. For a time he thought that if the government would guarantee the interest on railway stocks, private capital could build a direct line from the Midwest to the East Coast.[68] All through the summer and early fall of the depression year of 1873, Curtis urged the government to build a railroad to the Midwest to aid the farmers. (During the same period, he also urged a government route connecting the coal fields of western Pennsylvania with the Coast.) In answer to the railroads' contention that they could not lower their rates, Curtis held that they had lost their usefulness in that case and could "no longer be permitted to exercise their exclusive monopoly." He regretted that the railway system had been built as it had; it would have been more trustworthy and rational if the government had done the job. Nothing beyond the comfort of the community and the wants of trade would have been required to justify the undertaking.[69]

After 1873 Curtis completely dropped his schemes for basic changes in the American economy. He objected to any "colossal" system of public works because it "leads straight to a concentration of almost resistless force in the hands of the government, fosters vast corruption, and directly threatens public liberty."[70] When he returned to the subject of railways, he now argued for regulation. In 1882 he pointed to the lack of ill results from regulation by the states.[71] A year before the Interstate Commerce Act (1887) was passed, he favored legislation along its lines.[72] He thought the act itself vague, but he approved Cleveland's appointments to the commission it established. A year later he agreed with Charles Francis Adams that the act had several weaknesses, but he hoped they could be remedied.[73] Apparently he was well enough satisfied with it, for he dropped the subject in that year and did not return to it. His death in 1892 removed him from the American scene before the economic convulsions of the 1890's. They might or might not have moved him further toward government regulation of the economy than his stand on the railroads.

Gilder's *Century*, in many ways more conservative than *Harper's Weekly*, did seem to be accommodating itself to the views of reformers as the century closed. Perhaps Gilder recognized that the stranglehold of big business on government could not be broken without legislative regulation. He looked hopefully to Theodore Roosevelt, an occasional contributor to the *Century*, as one who might initiate the needed reforms.[74] He secured articles arguing for the regulation of the economy from members of the Social Gospel movement, men like Theodore Munger, Lyman Abbott, Washington Gladden, and Richard Ely.[75] When the American Economic Association was formed in 1885 to combat the principles of orthodox political economy, the *Century* sympathized with its argument that men were not simply selfish, wealth-collecting creatures. It endorsed the Association's recommendation for an expansion of the functions of government, provided that civil service reform lessened the problems of patronage.[76]

In none of these areas did the *Century* advocate a fundamental revision of the American government. It recognized that economic nationalism had grown immensely since the Civil War, but it did not approve of radical departures from the traditional policy of private enterprise. Despite criticisms of laissez-faire economics, genteel reservations about capitalism remained conservative, not radical, reservations. The nostalgic wishes of the group to revert to a golden age suggest this conservatism, as does the persistent gap between its complaints and its proposals. Yet its theories foreshadow those of Progressivism. Genteel and Progressive thinkers alike were middle-class men alarmed when they saw big capital and big labor revising the rules that had rewarded moral effort with economic success. They argued that the traditionally peaceful American variety of economic competition was under assault by a fierce new order under which success would go to the powerful, and European-type class struggles and revolutions would threaten America. Their preoccupation—and for the genteel circle one might say their obsession—was to safeguard social harmony and order. When the sway of middle-class attitudes in government was challenged by the rise of corporate capital and by the influx of immigrants from Southern and Eastern Europe, the genteel writers rapidly backed away from viewing the federal government as an ally. Government was good so long as it was staffed by middle-class Anglo-Saxon Protestants with whom the genteel journalists could identify. When even the civil service reform crusade could not maintain this group in power, the withdrawal of genteel politics from contemporary America became nearly inevitable.

Viewed in a larger perspective, the genteel circle was fundamentally unsympathetic to the deepest forces of social change in American society—industrialization, urbanization, bureaucratization. It had no particular faith in technology and deplored the decline of agriculture and the rise of cities. Even if it had been able to muster a more democratic faith in the electorate and a more sympathetic concern for the poor—something that Progressivism itself did not uniformly manage—it could never discover a means for reform that seemed likely to be able to put its criticisms into effect. Alien to the world of big business and to the world of science, it was never persuaded that new methods were available to provide efficient government. Its economic thinking was hampered by the same anti-institutional bias that marked its political thinking. Rather than suggest ways in which the political or economic realm could be restructured, it persisted to the end in viewing institutional problems as problems of national character. It recognized that new institutions were in fact altering the national character, but as those alterations became more evident, it became less willing to propose significant reforms. In the end the genteel group seemed almost to revert to the individualism it had so long attacked. Unsuccessful in influencing the course of current politics and economics, the genteel writers turned to culture. There, for a time, they proved to be more potent.

In Defense of Beauty

ETWEEN the Civil War and World War I, the writing and the criticism of poetry in America increasingly became gentility's preferred province. More original poets like Emily Dickinson and Stephen Crane went unheard; there were no other critics of consequence. When Edmund Stedman died in 1908 the *New York Times* declared firmly that the "deanery" of American letters had been vacated.[1] Stedman himself would have demurred; he had protested the title for years because it made him sound like "an odious prig."[2] Yet he was so often called on to grace the meetings of colleges or clubs or associations[3] with his occasional verse that there could be no doubt of the high esteem in which he was held in American cultural circles. As the *Springfield Republican* wrote, he was perhaps the most representative man of letters in America and, for a generation, America's official poet.[4] He was, also, as the *Times* asserted, America's single most authoritative literary critic.[5]

Like many of the other genteel authors, Stedman came to his career by the journalistic route. Reared by an uncle in the town of Norwich, Connecticut, Stedman spent two years at Yale, studied law for a few months, and in 1853 bought a partnership in the *Norwich Tribune*. The paper failed in six months. After another partnership, this time in the *Mountain County Herald*, Stedman decided that the twelve-hour days his job demanded were too long and not profitable enough, and bought into Ingraham clockmakers in New York. That venture proved no more successful and, short on money, he moved into a Fourierist cooperative sponsored by Stephen Pearl Andrews.

He lived there from 1858 to 1860. He won his first notice as a poet for "The Diamond Wedding," which appeared in the *New York Tribune* in 1859. The ballad was a satire on the New York nuptials of a rich Cuban, Marquis Don Esteban de Santa Cruz de Oviedo and his much younger New York bride, Frances Amelia Bartlett. Stedman implied that the wedding was a mercenary sale because the groom was fabulously rich, whereas the bride's father was a mere ex-lieutenant in the United States Navy. Bartlett demanded that Stedman issue a retraction of the poem. Stedman refused. He offered Bartlett a duel, but Bartlett declined, saying Stedman was not his social equal. Threats of prosecution for libel were eventually withdrawn, probably because the family grew tired of publicity.[6]

The affair opened the *Tribune* to Stedman. It brought him a job on the paper and contacts that enabled him to publish his first volume of poems. Soon afterward he entered banking and finally in 1865 opened the brokerage firm he ran for most of his life. His colleagues on the Stock Exchange promptly dubbed him the "broker-poet," a tag he detested. It was not, however, entirely inapt. He continued to write poetry, and his brokerage office used a telegraphic code in which *Keats* meant "cancel order to buy" and *Shelley*, "select and sell at discretion."[7] Stedman's literary and critical interests remained primary in his life. He always described his business as merely support for his art. He saw little nobility in business. "All the princely merchants of my acquaintance are princely snobs," he wrote. "If they do a decent act—if they build a temple 'to Science and Art,' like ——, or give royal international dinners, like ——, it is in the one case in order that 'Science and Art' may groan under the weight of being *obliged* to speak well of a rich old nincompoop after he is rotten, and, in the other, that all the *little* English and American snobs may vie in fulsome laudation of the *great snob*—whose wine they drink!"[8]

In competition with the princely snobs, Stedman avidly sought to assert his own claims. When in 1871 he thought his literary reputation was beyond question, he wrote to Yale asking to be granted the bachelor's and master's degrees that had been denied him because he was expelled for an adolescent prank. He received the degrees, but for years afterward he dreamed that his request had been denied.[9] When he wrote and delivered a poem for Yale's bicentennial celebration in 1901, he said he felt he was at last "getting through Yale."[10] If any one member of the genteel group typified the need for status that genteel culture answered, it was Stedman.

His style of life was always precisely calculated for elegant effect. Like Aldrich, Stedman was inclined to dandyism. Howells, impressed with Stedman's collection of several hundred neckties, proclaimed him a "worldly splendor in dress."[11] Stedman shared Aldrich's fastidiousness, too. At his dinner parties, he planned the minutest details—the menu, the table setting, even the flower arrangements, and suffered intense chagrin at the slightest disruption of his scheme. "The accidental or haphazard was not permitted, the logical, artistic, systematic, was demanded."[12]

In criticism, as in life, Stedman insisted upon observing the right rules of beauty.[13] His attachment to them, like Norton's, was unmistakably didactic in tone, but he was careful, at least at first, to dissociate his didacticism from the didacticism of the Brahmins. Stedman and his friends were perfectly willing that poetry should teach, so long as it taught beauty for its own sake and not for the sake of politics or religion or morals. What this principle meant in practice was that the genteel poet looked for themes outside his own time and place. A poem from Stoddard's *Songs of Summer*, which Stedman credited with first achieving the ideal of beauty for its own sake, illustrates the point.

> We parted in the streets of Ispahan.
> I stopped my camel at the city gate;
> Why did I stop? I left my heart behind.
>
> I heard the sighing of the garden palms,
> I saw the roses burning up with love;
> I saw thee not: thou wert no longer there.
>
> We parted in the streets of Ispahan.
> A moon has passed since that unhappy day;
> It seems an age: the days are long as years!

I send thee gifts by every caravan;
I send thee flasks of attar, spices, pearls;
I write thee songs on golden-powdered scrolls.

I meet the caravans when they return.
"What news?" I ask: the drivers shake their heads:
We parted in the streets of Ispahan.[14]

In his many volumes of literary criticism, Stedman consistently defended art against the didacticism of his predecessors. *Victorian Poets* gave unfavorable notice to the line of English didactic poetry that stemmed from Wordsworth.[15] He thought even Keats had been tainted by the didactic; the final lines of "Ode on a Grecian Urn" were too preachy for Stedman's taste and marred an otherwise excellent poem.[16] Stedman did recognize that Keats was the fountainhead of a very different school from Wordsworth's, the school of art for art's sake.[17] But although Keats exemplified genteel ideals, the Victorian art school did not win the approval of the genteel writers. In virtually every piece of criticism that Stedman wrote, he objected as strenuously to art for art's sake as he did to didacticism.

When Stedman referred to the art school, he meant Rossetti, Gautier, Morris, and Swinburne, and the early Tennyson. He called their work the poetry of the fin de siècle.[18] If these poets were as careful to avoid themes of contemporary social concern as the genteel poets were, they were still too deficient in passion for his taste. By passion he did not mean sensualism, as found in Swinburne.[19] Their emotions were too obviously contrived; Swinburne's "excessive richness of epithet and sound" was too cloying, its odor "too intoxicating to endure."[20] Stedman preferred the more sincere, spontaneous emotion of Shelley.[21] In America he found no genuine emotion in the great poets of the older generation. To a man he thought them "too thin-blooded."[22] He called Whittier "almost virginal," and of Longfellow he said that he dealt with the piteous "as tranquilly as the nuns who broider on tapestry the torments of the doomed in hell."[23]

Despite his call for passion in poetry, Stedman wanted no subjectivism. In *The Nature and Elements of Poetry* he distinguished the objective poetry of the pagans from the subjective poetry of the Christians.[24] The former represented willing self-effacement and the simple zest of artistic creation; the latter spoke for the distinction of individuality and the luxury of human feeling. It was undeniable, Stedman thought, that Christianity's intensification of self-expression had subjected the poet to dangers he had been free of in pagan times—egotism, conceit, the disturbed vision of over-introspection, and delirious extremes of feeling. The ancients took life as they found it and accepted death as nature's law.

Stedman recognized that life could no longer be lived as the ancients had lived it, and he was bound by his romanticism to believe that the moderns were superior to the ancients. If the opposite were true, he noted, it would contradict the law of evolution. But he was not optimistic and conceded a "loss" with the movement of time.[25] His *Victorian Poets* was replete with judgments on the relative objectivity or subjectivity of the poets considered. Ironically, Stedman considered Matthew Arnold, the Victorian poet who was most objective in his intention, among the least objective of the Victorian poets. Arnold's best poetry was his saddest.[26] In the 1875 edition of *Victorian Poets,* Stedman attacked Arnold's sadness "as an unconscious confession of his own special restrictions."[27] Yet he admitted that Arnold's very unrest and bewilderment gave him a representative position.[28] Although he later thought better of Arnold, he remained hostile to subjectivism.[29] When his own *Poems* appeared in 1873, he wrote, "You won't find any morbid egotism in my volume."[30]

Stedman was always careful to insist that poetic passion was an objective quality, bearing no relationship to the private experience of the poet. None of the particular ingredients of poetic composition—imagination, emotion, intellection—in great poetry at least, sprang from the poet's private self. But Stedman's use of the words *passion* and *subjective* was ambivalent. His aesthetics was torn by conflicting impulses to assert romanticism and to restrain it.

In his survey of American poetry, if one discounts nonaesthetic apologies, it is clear that Stedman lamented the thinbloodedness of the American tradition. In turning to English poetry, he found the opposite extreme: the Victorians were plagued with an excess of what the Americans lacked. English poetry was marred by sensuality and despair; the Victorians erred in permitting their private and personal experience to inform their poetry. Much as Henry James had done for his novels, Stedman found the theme of his criticism in the contrast between American and European experience, although he did not self-consciously exploit it. And just as James remained undecided whether life in America or in Europe held the greater attraction, so did Stedman. His criticism is eclectic to the point of formlessness, but his critical location falls somewhere between the poles of American and English poetry.

In the introduction to *Poets of America* Stedman explained why American poetry had lagged behind European poetry in its development. He pointed first to "all the drags" of the word *colonial*. In America the contest with nature absorbed the epic passion. Because it lacked stimulation, poetry remained latent and born poets silent. Republicanism also acted to retard culture. Although it lifted "our people quite above the dullness and stolidity of the middle classes elsewhere, it did not speedily raise them to the pitch of high emotion." Republicanism was "a leveller, and in its early stages raises a multitude to the level of the commonplace. . . ." American independence and material comfort, too, were antithetical to poetry. America had "so many happy little households" that all the darker contrasts of life were missing. All of these factors conspired to place politics above art in America and led to the despotic requirement that the American must be "a good citizen first of all." He had to rear and maintain a family and serve the interests of his community and nation. Privation for the sake of an artistic ideal was frowned upon. Even if he tried poetry, the newness of his country robbed him of themes. Although, on the one hand, Americans were not superstitious, on the other hand, they lacked legends and a sense of the past. The customs they did have were as heterogeneous as the people themselves. American poets were caught between imitating European standards and expressing the dominant American ethos that worshipped the good citizen and ignored the poet.[31]

The genteel authors sought with some success to avoid doing either, but many critics argued that they never broke free of European models and ideals. Even in its day genteel poetry was commonly criticized for lack of originality. The genteel poets themselves privately agreed that they were sometimes imitative, although they insisted that their later poetry was original.[32] They felt that their chosen path was especially difficult because American culture lagged behind European culture. To attempt a romantic revolution in America after similar European movements had subsided could not be so clear an undertaking as it had been for the Schlegels and Schiller or Wordsworth and Coleridge. For they knew well that European romanticism had bred a reaction. The obvious qualities of Victorian poetry—restraint, scholarship, analysis, artistic perfection—were antiromantic. The Victorian period was a critical period, Stedman said, suspicious of cant and melodramatic affectation. The inspiration and eccentricity of the early romantics had given way to mediocrity.[33]

Although the genteel poets protested this turn of events, they were part of it. In considering a successor to Tennyson as poet laureate, Stedman thought poets and critics would accord the honor to Swinburne, his first choice, but philistines would block it. He thought conservatives would object to William Morris, his second choice, so he suggested that Austin Dobson, whom he placed in the Victorian art school, be given the title.[34]

Stedman's distaste for developments in Victorian poetry led him to turn back to part of the first generation of English romantics for his ideal. What he wanted was a kind of poetry that would eschew the didacticism of New England as well as the emotionalism of Byron. It would not succumb to the almost neoclassical emphasis on form of the Victorian art school, but would continue to express the sincere and sensuous, but not sensual, emotion of Shelley.

Because of their attitude toward American culture, the genteel poets suffered from a crippling sense of inferiority. At no time in their lives were they able to feel the literary patriotism that inspired so many of America's first-rate artists in the nineteenth century. Had the debate over national self-expression that engrossed romantic America been less puerile than it was, perhaps the genteel artists might have begun their careers with a more clearly articulated critical position than they did. But American literary criticism before the Civil War was an ill-defined activity. It imitated European standards and rejected them by turns. It lacked knowledge and confidence. It was be-mired in an incredible bog of petty personalities. With the par-tial exception of Poe, no American literary critic before the Civil War had a critical system.

The genteel poets' original dissent from the Brahmins re-flected the romantic drift of the time. Although they dramatized their struggle for independence, it was far less painful than their accounts imply. If genteel poetry did strike some new notes in its formative period, its rebellion was nevertheless fashionable. From the beginning the genteel authors had a shrewd eye for the marketable; Bayard Taylor is the best example, but they were all infected with the commercialism they despised in Amer-ican business. The genteel authors used their positions on the pre-eminent Eastern literary magazines—*Harper's, The Atlantic Monthly, Scribner's,* and *The Century*—to dominate the literary audience that had developed in the decades before the Civil War. At the same time, they catered to this audience, composed mainly of middle-class women.

The genteel romanticism of the 1840's and 1850's concentrated on destructive criticism of the old order, the Puritan way of life. But after the Civil War, when industrialism transformed America from a nation of zealots into a nation of philistines, genteel literature found less to approve in the new order than in the old. Inevitably a note of wistfulness for vanished days crept into it, and a change of tactics. Destructive criticism gave way to defensive exhortation; romantic rebels became apostles of culture. With the loss of its youthful optimism, genteel litera-ture ossified. Its energy was channeled solely into the mainte-nance of traditional taste. Not a single major development in American society was reflected in the literature of the genteel tradition; it remained in 1900 what it had been in 1850.

Moreover, well before 1900 the genteel literary critics had taken over the Brahmins' role of policing the purity of literature. Stedman complained about having to enforce what he called the *virginibus* maxim (print nothing to offend a virgin), but his grumbling was mild enough.[35] He would never have openly praised Longfellow as a "good, *safe, family* poet," as William Winter did, but his *Poets of America* was laced with similar implications.[36]

The *virginibus* maxim was often carried to ridiculous lengths. In 1896 Gilder bought a story for the *Century* and then balked at a passage in it: "the bullet had left a little blue mark over the brown nipple." The author argued that since the nipple was male the wording was not lascivious, and pointed to a recent issue of the *Century* that had unblushingly exposed the male nipple in an illustration of the Olympic Games. Gilder would not be moved.[37] Josiah Holland, Gilder's superior on the old *Scribner's Monthly*, possessed a sensitivity on matters of moral taste that could only be described as exquisite. When it was proposed to illustrate a poem in which a young woman in the privacy of her room reflects upon her evening out, Holland objected, saying, "How is it possible for the readers of this magazine to imagine Mr. Church [the artist], who, I understand, is a bachelor, in the young lady's room at such an hour as he would have to sketch her?" It occurred to him to suggest that the poet make the girl the artist's wife. At this, the poet asked, "How is it possible to suppose *me* in *Mrs. Church's bedroom?*"[38] The impasse could not be resolved.

Without being led to such tortuous extremes, the genteel critics acquiesced in the kind of censorship that was common before the Civil War. While on the editorial board of *Putnam's Monthly* in 1853, Curtis cut the sentence, "I am not sure but this Catholic religion would be an admirable one if the priests were omitted," from Thoreau's *A Yankee in Canada*. Three parts of the manuscript had already been published, but Thoreau demanded its return. Curtis cut the manuscript of *Cape Cod* as well and Thoreau withdrew it also.[39] Gilder freely admitted that he had edited *Huckleberry Finn* for what he called a miscellaneous audience before it appeared in the *Century* in 1882.[40] He could not accommodate himself at all to Stephen Crane's *Maggie*; it was too honest. When Crane asked Gilder why he had published Arthur Morrison's slum story, "A Child of the

Jago," Gilder replied, "But Mr. Morrison is an Englishman."[41] Crane had to find another outlet for his naturalistic novel. Later, Gilder rejected *The Red Badge of Courage*, too.[42]

Just as his friends did, Stedman deferred to prevailing standards of taste. When James Fields, the prospective publisher for his early poem "Pan in Wall Street," suggested that he substitute *trousers* for *pants* in a line of the poem—*"pants* being a word below the mark of so excellent a piece"—Stedman rewrote the entire stanza to suit the substitution.[43] The roles were reversed twenty years later when Stedman, looking over the manuscript of Twain's *A Connecticut Yankee in King Arthur's Court*, detected the offensive word *sewer* three times. A poor and commonplace term, unworthy of the writer, he wrote Twain.[44]

Examples of this kind of censorship are manifold and easily found. What is difficult to discover is any general statement of the grounds for it. Clearly, religious and moral issues were more sensitive than political or economic ones throughout the Gilded Age. Publishers did not routinely suppress heretical views on the latter questions even when they were personally disturbed by them.[45] A definition of a model magazine article by Robert Underwood Johnson, Gilder's assistant editor, gives some indication why this may have been the case. The ideal article, Johnson argued, would interest both the reader who knew all about its subject and the reader who knew nothing about it.[46] The inclusiveness of his formulation expresses the typical aim of the genteel magazines, to encompass the entire reading audience. And for some reason it was assumed that religious and moral heresies were less acceptable to that audience than political or economic ones. No indication exists that publishers either examined or questioned that assumption. Gilder came the closest to spelling out the rules that were not to be transgressed: no vulgar slang; no explicit references to sex, or, in more genteel phraseology, to the generative processes; no disrespectful treatment of Christianity; no unhappy endings for any work of fiction.[47]

With the major magazines straitjacketed in this way, the personal journalism of the revolutionary little magazines that began to appear in the 1890's found a ready following. The Chicago *Chap-Book* (1894), first of these avant-garde American magazines to appear, was modeled after the notorious *Yellow Book* of fin de siècle England.[48] Its literary editor, Henry Harland, interestingly enough, was a devoted friend of Stedman's. "I owe you everything," he confessed on one occasion.[49] Judged from a distance, the *Yellow Book* looks tame enough and Stedman's ties to its editor not shocking. Judged likewise, Stedman's mild defense of Swinburne in *Victorian Poets* also seems unexceptionable, yet he was obliged to assure the reader of his own moral credentials before even touching upon the poet.[50] Although the genteel critics became enforcers in the cause of moral literature, it was not a cause they themselves initiated. They became identified with it in the end only because they fell prey to the same fears that plagued their audience.

The genteel turn to tradition was a reflex reaction to intellectual as well as social change. In his introduction to *Victorian Poets* Stedman characterized the world of the nineteenth century as a time of transition.[51] In both England and America the development of what Stedman called the new learning had sapped the strength of traditional beliefs.[52] Science, for that is what Stedman meant by the new learning, had weakened religious certainty and replaced the old purposeful cosmology with a chance-governed one in which man was accorded a precarious position. It had cast its spell so firmly on the age that fact had robbed fancy of all virtue and the poet of a job.[53] As much in self-justification, therefore, as from any desire to confront the problems of the modern world, Stedman undertook to incorporate science into his aesthetics. He worried so much about the threat of science to poetry that he felt obliged to render his aesthetics impervious to criticism by assimilating the very method that science called its own. Admitting a great deal, he said that if there was anything novel in his *Nature and Elements of Poetry*, it resulted from his attempt "to confront the scientific nature and methods of the thing discussed."[54]

In a time of transition, Stedman felt that the only sensible thing to do was to be as modest and moderate as possible. By this he meant in part that his aesthetics would be universalist and eclectic; unfortunately it was often merely ambiguous. Not only did Stedman's definitions enlist all men and all places, but they dissolved the distinctions other critics had made. He waved away, for example, the debate between romanticism and classicism with the weak objection that quarrels between schools of poetry seemed to be most labored when the creative faculties were inactive.[55] He blunted the definitions formerly accepted for the two terms, making romanticism represent the eternally innovative spirit and classicism the fixed and academic. And as he did in virtually every discussion of opposites, he combined the two and found both in the greatest art.[56]

Despite his attention to the interrelationship of literature and culture, Stedman's treatment of the problems confronting late-nineteenth-century poetry is not persuasive because Stedman himself could not view them as real problems. For all his talk of such contemporary issues as the threat of science, for example, Stedman was not sufficiently unsettled to see any need for altering his traditional definitions of the nature and purpose of poetry. His aesthetics was basically a defense of poetic idealism: poetry is "the most ideal and comprehensive of those arts which intensify life and suggest life's highest possibilities."[57] Stedman's idealism was not classical, although he was well read in the classics and often cited them. Nor was it neoclassical; he had little sympathy for that period in literature. But the idealism that Stedman saw in Keats and Shelley seemed as worthy to him in 1900 as it had fifty years earlier. Never in his criticism of late-nineteenth-century poetry did he so much as hint at a desire for innovation; the standard to which he repaired was always the standard of the past. Deferring to the doctrine of evolution, he said that poetry would change and improve. Nevertheless, he was not only averse to relativism but firmly judicial in measuring the present by the past.[58]

Stedman tried in *The Nature and Elements of Poetry* to make poetry compatible with science. He opened the book with a comparison of the force of poetry to force as science viewed it.[59] He defined the spirit of poetry as "a force, an energy, both subtle and compulsive; a primal force, like that energy the discovery of whose unities is the grand physical achievement of this century." Just as physical force manifested itself in substance, as light in coal, so poetic force expressed itself in written poetry.[60] He admitted that poetry was not a science, "yet a scientific comprehension of any art is possible and essential."[61]

His definition of poetry as "rhythmical, imaginative language, expressing the invention, taste, thought, passion, and insight, of the human soul" distinguished poetry from the other arts because of its language, which at best takes wings.[62] He drew on science to justify the rhythmic nature of poetry, relating it to the discovery that the movement of all matter is vibratory. Naturally, therefore, rhythm will most thrill the body and soul, and will invest words with a mysterious and potent influence beyond their normal meanings.[63]

Stedman gave credit to the Lake School for raising the problem of the general relationship of science to poetry.[64] He paraphrased Wordsworth when he said that the poet must treat nature and life "as they *seem*, rather than as they are...."[65] Like Wordsworth and Coleridge, he limited the subjectivist implications of impressionism by giving the poet the function of piercing deeper than the scientist into objective reality. But he went beyond them to add that the poet must exercise an "insight that pierces to spiritual actualities, to the meaning of phenomena, and to the relations of all this scientific knowledge." Beyond "the phantasmal look of things and full scientific attainment there is a universal coherence—there are infinite meanings...."[66]

Stedman's idealistic romanticism stems from Shelley, who was influenced by Platonism, rather than from Wordsworth and Coleridge, whose approach to poetry was more empirical.[67] But his foggy handling of scientific concepts and the illogical analogies he drew between science and poetry obscure what might have been a reasonable statement of classical idealism. He praised, for example, the new learning of the nineteenth century as "the passage from a childlike and phenomenal way of regarding things to the absolute, scientific penetration of their true entities and relations."[68] As he describes it, Stedman's science seems to be of Newtonian vintage. Of course, his purpose was not to understand science, but to defend poetry from its challenge. So he insisted that the poet saw deeper into the universe than the scientist. And in the course of human progress, the fantasy of the poet preceded scientific invention and discovery.[69]

Stedman's idealism is difficult to identify more clearly than this. His repugnance toward philosophical thinking often led him to the verge of a general anti-intellectualism. He often criticized authors for reasoning "too curiously" or "too closely."[70] Metaphysics especially drew his fire; he wrote James McCosh that the Scottish philosophy "seems to me little better than admirable mental gymnastics." And there is no reason to suppose that any other philosophical system would have pleased him any more. As he put it—although his aesthetics suggests the opposite —his temperament was "averse to abstractions" and dwelt only on the concrete, either as seen and experienced, or as poetically imagined.[71]

Stedman rejected Berkeleyan idealism, which assumed the existence of nothing but the individual soul or ego.[72] He abhorred absolute idealism because he thought it necessitated a relativism that would deny beauty, something no one who loved art could do.[73] But in answer to the question whether there was an ultimate reality, transcending sense experience and knowable only by the mind, Stedman's statement about the "phantasmal look of things" suggests that he believed there was. His idealism is also apparent in his view that the artist was "a congener, even a part, of the universal soul—that divinity whose eternal function it is to create."[74] High-level artistic creation was in a sense revelation, too. Although the artist must be obedient to his own "inner light," he could not invent "forms and methods and symbols out of keeping with what we term the nature of things."[75] In fact, the Deity "has taken us into his workshop. We see that he creates, as we construct, slowly and patiently, through and by evolution, one step leading to the next. I reassert, then, that as far as the poet, the artist, is creative, he becomes a sharer of the divine imagination and power, and even of the divine responsibility."[76]

Stedman here invoked a traditional view of poetic genius originating in the Renaissance and revitalized by romanticism. He always vigorously defended the doctrine of genius; when William Dean Howells denied it, Stedman pointed out that Howells himself fell back on "natural aptitude" to explain great and original things. Aptitude was not enough for Stedman, however, unless it suggested something so unique and compelling as to be almost supernatural. Stedman's own Platonism inclined him to see the source of artistic greatness in supernatural guidance. But he followed Shelley in naturalizing the quality of genius; it was an inborn thing that operated by intuition and not by any supernatural faculty. He tried to rid the concept of the metaphysical trappings it carried both in Plato and in Emerson without limiting its power. Genius was a quality essentially different from talent; it was creative and original, unlike taste. If all men had a spark of the genius in them, only the true genius saw into the real world, the world of Ideality.[77]

In its Emersonian form, the doctrine of genius provides a useful standard for comparison with Stedman's aesthetics. In Emerson, as in Stedman, the beautiful, the true, and the good were aspects of the same reality. Emerson's theory of genius used the terms poet and thinker, or even man, interchangeably, but although Stedman used them less flexibly, he agreed with Emerson that the genius who saw through to the true unity of things was simply man writ large. The difference between Emerson and Stedman is mainly a matter of sensibility. Emerson's Transcendentalism was vigorously open-minded. It looked to all experience, including the simplest, as a potential source of truth. It respected the private visions of all men in the hope that true vision would be there. If its tone was didactic, that was because it had something to say: if only a man would be himself, he would discover his own divinity.

The genteel poets, while clinging to the Transcendental standard of an ideal realm where the true and the good and the beautiful coalesced, were like mystics gone flat. They continued to believe in something beyond themselves, which, however, they could not see. They clung to the received structure of ideas not as men who fear the deluge—they had no doubts of their ability to endure—but as men who fear its discomforts and unpleasantness. In self-defense they preserved and repaired the traditional aesthetics. Viewed from the outside, that structure, though loose in places and rather too accommodating, did not reveal its own hollowness.

The traditional aesthetics defined the truth of poetry as idealism. After the Civil War, genteel idealism was threatened by the rise of realism and the critical debate initiated by it. Henry James and especially William Dean Howells, whose own relationship to the genteel group is ambiguous, openly attacked the notion that literature should offer an idealized version of life for its readers to imitate. Stedman responded to these arguments in two very typical ways: first, by appealing to tradition and, second, by minimizing the difference between himself and his opponents in an attempt to blunt their attack and to salvage some authority for his own position.

Against the realists' plea for a literature of precision, Stedman invoked the romantic preference for suggestiveness, a preference he attempted to attribute to Nature herself. Stedman was one of the first major American critics to give Whitman a favorable review, but, not surprisingly, he objected to Whitman's realism. Whitman violated nature, Stedman contended, when he "draws away the final veil. It is not squeamishness that leaves something to the imagination, that hints at guerdons still unknown. Suggestion, or half-concealment, produces the choicest effects, and is the surest road to truth."[78] Adding a notion that was typical of the genteel mind, Stedman said that Whitman overlooked nature's own law. "For, if there is nothing in her which is mean or base, there is much that is ugly and disagreeable.... Even Mother Earth takes note of this and resolves, or disguises and beautifies, what is repulsive upon her surface...." The delight of art was not to make nature "ranker than she is" but to "heighten her beguilement" and "to portray what she might be in ideal combinations."[79]

In *The Nature and Elements of Poetry* Stedman again attacked Whitman for dwelling on "the underside of things." "Realism, in the sense of naturalism, is the firm ground of all the arts, but the poet, then, is not a realist merely as concerns the things that are seen. He draws these not as they are, but as they

are or may be at their best."[80] In poetry, as in all art, deviation
from fact is not only justified, but required; nothing is more life-
less than "servilely accurate imitation" of nature.[81] But if the
poet must idealize nature, he must also know it. Stedman's *Poets
of America* abounds with praise for the true American feeling
for nature. Yet Stedman criticized Bryant, whom he called the
foremost poet of nature, as "careless of scientific realities."[82] Trying as he did so often to conflate opposed categories, Stedman
said, "Every workman must be a realist in knowledge, an idealist
for interpretation, and the antagonism between realists and ro-
mancers is a forced one...."[83]

But Stedman's compromise settled nothing. His discussion of
the debate over realism entirely ignored the fact that not only a
method of treatment but a motive was involved. In the novels of
Howells, for example, realism sprang from a strong faith in democracy and a drive to reform it. Stedman's distaste for the common man limited his sympathy for Howells's efforts. He did not
like to be confronted with the commonplace in literature; it was
not real but "superficial." His irritation was summed up in one
definition of realism: "the persistent contemplation of boorish
and motiveless weaklings, although they swarm around us, and
add to the daily weariness of humdrum life."[84]

In his criticism, Stedman made some concessions, usually
grudging, to the realists. He apparently thought well of both
Turgenev and Ibsen.[85] Henry James's involved style displeased
him. For realism to be successful, he argued, its method must be
unconscious, not as scrutinizing as biology.[86] His relations with
Mark Twain were friendly enough for Twain to send him *A
Connecticut Yankee* for comment. His criticisms were trivial
and overshadowed by his praise for Twain's "magnificently riot-
ous and rollicking imagination and humor" and for the "good
taste" of the entire book.[87] After reading Howells's *The Lady of
the Arostook* he wrote that he found it "absolutely *realistic*," but
he warned Howells not to "banish idealism entirely from our
tastes" and chided him for giving up poetry.[88] In Kipling's realism he found proof for his own position that "ideality and experience are not antagonistic." Again avoiding the unpleasantness

of having to resolve antagonistic schools, he praised the realistic novels of his friend Stoddard's wife. "The method is nothing—nothing—compared with the quality of the practitioner."[89]

To the realists and especially the naturalists it often seemed as if the genteel poets were simply prudish in their distaste for the franker literature of the day. But from the beginning the genteel group had been devoted to expressing the beautiful, not the real. Stedman always held that the one indispensable ingredient of poetry was beauty.[90] Beauty would enforce on human intelligence "a perception of its fitness," Stedman believed; he was confident that one man's perceptions of beauty were approximately the same as another's. At bottom, beauty was traceable to the "truths of nature, to the perfection of the universe, to that sense of the fitness of things which is common to us all in our respective degrees...."[91]

Founded in nature, beauty was of universal validity. Stedman was no more attracted than the realists were (Howells said his aim was to describe the typical man in typical circumstances) to a literature that celebrated the particular or the personal. He followed the English romantics, not the German, in his emphasis on the universal as seen through the particular.[92] True beauty partook of the infinite, not the temporal, he said.[93] It was expressed in an "absolute simplicity of kind, but limitless variety of guise and adaptation."[94] Any poem that produced a serious and lasting impression—and like Wordsworth and Coleridge Stedman believed that endurance was the ultimate test of poetic worth—would in the end "be found to have a beauty, not merely of its own, but allied to universal types."[95]

In *The Nature and Elements of Poetry* Stedman conceded that every race or nation had its own ideal of beauty. Earlier in his life Stedman had written poetry with antique themes, but when Lowell objected that such themes were inappropriate to a new land, he agreed. In late life he urged the artist's use of home models but insisted that the poet of America "must avoid expression of its transient passions and characteristics. Seize upon the essential, lasting traits, and let the others be accessory."[96] That poetry is truest which is "universal in its passion and thought, but national in motive and in all the properties of the craft."[97]

Genteel criticism was almost always able to accommodate itself to New England's more insistent demands. In its formative days, it sharply distinguished between its own and New England's ideals, between beauty for its own sake and beauty for the sake of morals. Lowell, for one, balked at the new direction in poetry; he did not hesitate to discourage the genteel poets from venturing too far from the paths of his own generation. Because they were prudent and discreet, the genteel poets were always able to maintain friendly relations with the New England school. Had their rejection of moralism in poetry been as dramatic as they thought it was, this could not have been so. But the genteel poets agreed with the view of the English romantics that although poetry had intrinsic value, it was also a means to moral and social effects. Keats came closest to the art-for-art's-sake ideal, but even his objections to moralism were only technical.[98] Tennyson, whom Stedman ranked as the foremost Victorian poet, used moral effects to the point of preachment in the *Idylls of the King*, yet Stedman thought that "through all of his writings, of every style, there runs, overtly or covertly, the truest, noblest, broadest philosophy of the age."[99]

What genteel criticism actually rejected, then, was only the direct or too explicit teaching of morals. And in America, despite Lowell's fretting, there were important precedents for the genteel view. Edgar Allen Poe's identification of didacticism in art with heresy was so influential that it was followed by American critics almost as a matter of course throughout the nineteenth century.[100] For Stedman, Poe's subordination of ethical truth to beauty was not so much wrong as irrelevant. Like Emerson, who also abhorred the "heresy of the didactic," Stedman insisted that the true, the good, and the beautiful were facets of the same higher reality. The kind of didacticism Stedman criticized was the "gospel of half-truths," the prosaic morals that were actually injurious to morality by making it repulsive. When true ethics or philosophic truth was expressed in a poem, the result was a "higher didacticism" to which Poe's criticism did not apply. Stedman credited Pope, the "chief of English moralist-poets," with this achievement.[101] Despite its initial protests, genteel criticism did not succeed in establishing its independence; it pre-

served and scarcely modified the traditional view of the nature
and purposes of poetry.

When Stedman turned his attention from the nature of poetry
to the poetic process itself, he was no more innovative. On the
exact nature of artistic creation he was vague. Although he credited the Lake School with introducing modern conceptions of
poetic imagination, Stedman seems wholly to have missed Coleridge's distinction between the primary and the secondary imagination. He defined poetic imagination as the ability of the artist
to conceive both forcefully and clearly, as if by an inner eye or
inner ear, the "actualities and possibilities" of things.[102] Imagination was the crucial poetic faculty: "artistic ability is coordinate
with the clearness and staying power of the imagination."[103]

In the processes of artistic creation, the imagination and the
passions were closely related. Stedman was not sure which came
first, and so called them twins.[104] He believed that the stimulus
of passion was more essential to the poetic powers than anything
except the imagination. He defined poetic passion as "intensity
of emotion" and gave Wordsworth and Mill particular credit for
stressing the need for it. He deplored the Victorian tendency to
cover sentiment with an aristocratic reserve for art's sake.[105] His
criticism, especially in *Victorian Poets,* but also in *Poets of
America,* reiterated a plea for intensity, sincerity, passion. He
thought an over-decorative aestheticism was the bane of the age.
At times his emphasis on intensity almost echoes Walter Pater's
dictum that the purpose of life was "to burn with a hard, gem-
like flame." "For what can be of more value than intense and
memorable sensations? What else make up that history which
alone is worth the name of life?" Stedman asked. "We know
by instinct that they are right who declare all passion good *per
se . . . ,*" he said.[106]

His romantic reliance upon instinct also served him as a means
of avoiding any discussion whatever of the techniques of poetic
composition. Unlike neoclassical treatises on aesthetics, *The Nature and Elements of Poetry* for all its talk of laws and rules simply "assumed the need for artistic perfection."[107] Stedman worried that if the poet were too highly cultured, too thoroughly
acquainted with past models, his work would lack spontane-

ity.[108] The "instinctive" or "natural" poet was better off: he never worried about technical questions in advance, but composed "by ear" and touched the result up later.[109] Against all the restrictions so often imposed on poetry by tradition, Stedman maintained that the most novel form was permissible, if it was artistic.[110] He would countenance no interference with the "absolute liberty of art."[111] Romanticism had reinstated poetry as an art, and Stedman had no wish to return to the neoclassical insistence on rules for composition.[112]

But if Stedman almost unthinkingly accepted the notion that each poem was an organic creation exemplifying its own rules, that idea was scarcely as emancipating for him as it had been for Coleridge. He could, while accepting the organic premise, nevertheless maintain that the poet had no need for a new style.[113] His technical modes, although suggested by intuition, were shaped by environment, and came originally from reading and experience. The poet had to study the past to learn "what can be done and what cannot be done acceptably."[114] Moreover, the intellect was of great importance in writing poetry. The poet's conceptions were spontaneous, certainly, but working them out was an act of intellect.[115] No regard for careless verse led him to esteem Tennyson above all Victorian poets.[116] And if at one place he praised Poe's statement that poetry had been his passion, not his purpose, at another he conjectured that more purpose would have helped.[117] He dismissed Poe's aesthetics with the patronizing observation that it was "not bad for a neophyte."[118]

Were the phrase not so anomalous, Stedman's aesthetics might best be described as an antiromantic romanticism. Stedman's own intellectual tradition was basically the English romantic tradition, but the issue that concerned him—as distinguished from the issues that concerned the first generation of English romantics to whom he remained loyal—was an issue raised by his attempt to affirm romanticism and at the same time to restrain it. The terms in which he cast his problem, subjectivism and objectivism, were not his own, but were derived through Coleridge from the German romantics. Because they never ceased to trouble him, they provide the best insight into his aesthetics.

Stedman associated objectivism with what he described as the pagan virtues of self-effacement and zest for life, and subjectivism with the Christian virtues of individuality and human feeling. Fearing the dangers of self-expression, Stedman pointedly insisted that the sufferings of modern man arose, not from his objective situation, but from his hypersensitivity. There was little recognition in his aesthetics of the relevance of sociological change for literary theory. He was unaware that the German definitions of *subjective* and *objective* were full of nostalgia for a vanishing social order under which life was simpler and freer. In Stedman's hands the terminology was no less nostalgic, but the nostalgia was disguised, perhaps even from himself. His social and political thinking actually looked back to the vanished age of pre-Jacksonian America; but no more than Bayard Taylor was willing to give up civilization for nature was Stedman willing to question the superiority of the moderns to the ancients. His weak appeal to evolution did not resolve the conflict thus created, or conceal his unwilling doubts of that superiority. Stedman's criticisms of Matthew Arnold in the face of his own assertion that Arnold was both subjective and representative only underlined his reluctance to confront the depth of his isolation from contemporary civilization. Refusing even to cultivate his detachment and self-consciousness at certain times to support his imaginative life as Tennyson did, Stedman was left with but one appropriate ideal both for art and for life, the ideal of Stoicism.

Because Stedman tried to believe that the modern world, if seen objectively, provided no excuse for a sad and troubled poetry, he explained away the poets who thought otherwise. Some were simply wrong, others too young. He thought Byron represented the "limbo of life" between youth and maturity: "There is a space of life between, in which the soul is in a ferment, the character undecided, the way of life uncertain, the ambition thick-sighted: thence proceed mawkishness, and all the thousand bitters...."[119] And some poets, the ones who lacked "health" as Stedman defined it, never grew up to see things as they truly were. Bryant was not such a man; he "never whined nor found fault with condition or nature."[120]

Stedman especially admired such an attitude. He resorted to it himself in the face of repeated financial reverses and recurrent illness, but particularly when he realized that he had failed to become a first-rate poet. He seldom indulged his feeling that the pure dreams and ideals of his youth had been sorely tried. He did not mean to reassert the Calvinist ethic of self-denial. His own concern for the life of beauty maintained the value of human existence for its own sake. It seems more likely that what he had in mind was not self-denial, but a stoical faith based on the conviction that life was far from a pleasant affair, but that to live it at all, one had to swallow one's doubts and act. Action was good in itself if intensity was the purpose of existence as Stedman maintained in *The Nature and Elements*. The good poet, then, "warbled cheering and trustful music," and poetry served as an incentive to life, not as an escape from it.[121]

The Poet's World

As a spokesman for official doctrine, Stedman articulated the genteel ideal of poetry as an incentive to life. Yet the genteel poets themselves were never much cheered by that ideal and often discussed their calling in the dreariest of accents. They shared with the genteel reformers a basic revulsion from the America that emerged from the Civil War. But their special position as poets marked them with a deeper pessimism.

Unlike the genteel reformers, Thomas Bailey Aldrich, Richard Henry Stoddard, and George Henry Boker were primarily literary figures. Of the three, only Aldrich secured an audience, but that audience—even for his prose—was never so wide nor his work so well known as Bayard Taylor's, because literature could not compete with travel accounts. Taylor remained the closest of friends with Boker and Stoddard until his death in 1878, but he was less exclusively committed to poetry than they were and will figure only in the last part of this chapter.

The poet's world as seen by Stoddard, Boker, and Aldrich was a dark and tentative world. In recoil from contemporary life, the poet nevertheless inhabited a region that was not a private world of the imagination. For different reasons for each of the poets, reality intruded too forcefully to permit poetry ever to become the refuge they hoped it might.

With Richard Henry Stoddard life was never gentle. His early years were not only poverty-stricken, but completely devoid of intellectual and cultural stimulus. He received almost no formal education. He worked at odd jobs from an early age, and in 1848 just before he met Taylor, his first intellectual and literary companion, he had been an apprentice iron-molder for three years. With Taylor's encouragement he began writing poetry. His literary acquaintances secured for him a position as Inspector of Customs at the Port of New York, which he held until 1870. From 1860 until his death he held various editorial positions on the *New York World*, the *Aldine*, and the *Mail and Express*. His financial circumstances were never comfortable, and throughout his adult life he was plagued with ill health. His poetry never sold well.[1]

Aldrich's career, like Stoddard's, was partly a career in journalism. But Aldrich climbed as high as it was possible to climb in that field, becoming editor of the prestigious *Atlantic Monthly* in 1881, and holding that position for ten years. Moreover, his poetry pleased established literary figures so well that Ticknor and Fields admitted him at the age of twenty-nine to the company of Lowell, Holmes, Whittier, and Longfellow by publishing his poems in its select Blue and Gold Series. The popularity of his many short stories and several novels brought him an income appropriate to his status, and confirmed him in the comfortable, respectable, New England ways he had been born to.[2]

The life and career of George Boker seem at first glance to provide even less of a source for pessimism than Aldrich's do. Boker was a millionaire and a scion of Philadelphia society. He was one of America's most eminent playwrights. He was also a successful diplomat, serving as minister to Turkey from 1871 to 1875 and then as minister to Russia for the next three years. Yet Boker did not win his wealth easily; long years of bitter litigation were necessary before his inheritance was cleared. And his success as a playwright never contented him; he always felt his audience too indifferent. He was bitter over the fact that his best play *Francesca da Rimini* had to wait thirty years for a successful staging. As for his diplomatic service, he was more impressed by the political motives that led to his recall from Russia in 1878 than he was by his successes in office before that time.[3]

Different as were the lives of Stoddard, Aldrich, and Boker, there was nonetheless common to them a deeper pessimism about the direction of change in America than was felt by others in the genteel group. Had they been genteel politicians instead of genteel poets, or had their profession been almost any but what it was, they might not have expected so much from themselves and valued so little what they did. But when society showed what scant interest it had in the genteel ideal of the poet, the genteel poet could scarcely avoid feeling betrayed. He could disguise his doubts about his talent by chastising the American audience that read poetry and insulting the audience that did not. But he could not hide his fears that the whole world of poetry had been undermined by the forces of social change. He might try to transform his poet's world into a private world, as Boker and Stoddard did for a time, or he might from the beginning, as Aldrich did, hold that to be both impossible and undesirable. Either way, as a thing to be escaped from or simply avoided, reality weighed heavily on the mind of the genteel poet. An account of the poet's world must begin with that outer world so apparently inhospitable to poetry.

In the 1850's when the genteel poets first gained recognition, they wanted nothing to do with politics. When Boker advised Stoddard to "get out of your age as far as you can," he was speaking about more than literary matters.[4] The Civil War later directed genteel political thinking into an optimistic affirmation of America; it exerted the same effect on genteel poetry. In neither case, however, was the effect a lasting one. When it became clear that the war to heal the American character had failed, the War itself, and especially the exuberant genteel response to it, became an embarrassing episode. Only four years after the War, Boker gave up contemporary themes and returned to his former view that the poet should be free to range through the ages:

> No, nor to any time, howe'er
> Remote or strange, can be confined
> These human hearts whose boundless sphere
> But broadens with the general mind.

He with art's mystery poorly deals
Who cramps within a narrow band
That whose ethereal nature feels
The strength of God's sustaining hand.

Not for myself, but for my art
I claim all ages, every clime;
And I shall scorn the lines that part
Country from country, time from time.[5]

Boker's plea for cosmopolitan poetry reflected a distaste for America and for her themes. How can art manage in the world of the "panting engine?" he asked. How can it compete for attention with a "wire that tells the price of corn and rags?" For Boker there was nothing good in a world of material progress and moral apathy. He was unsympathetic to a science that advanced "without knowing where or why," a science that tugged at the "pillars of the sky." The beautiful props of heaven —faith, love, imagination, law—were "crumbling at the base, and veined throughout with many a ghastly flaw." America had become an ugly place; there was no beauty in a "smoking gorge" or a "thousand buzzing wheels." He was sickened by prophets of progress who did not see that "all the holiest things of earth are stealthy Mammon's lawful prey.[6]

It was not strange that a millionaire should lament the "weary, endless clink of gold."[7] Boker hated materialism even more than his impecunious friend Stoddard did. Stoddard's shortage of "cursed, cursed gold" troubled him constantly, but Boker's surplus of it gave him little peace.[8] Boker had inherited his wealth from his father, who had been president of the Girard Bank in Philadelphia. When he died in 1858, he was charged with fraud, and a long legal struggle ensued that tied up the estate. Boker became so irritated with the slanderous tactics of his father's enemies that he wrote *The Book of the Dead* as an act of vengeance. It was not published until 1882, but even then it caused a local sensation. Boker's suit was finally settled in 1873, when over a million dollars came into his hands.[9] Even before then, Boker had developed a hearty detestation for the life of business. "If there is anything that I loathe with my whole soul it is trade,"

he said. "The low, dirty, lying, swindling rascality that is prac-
ticed under the flag of trade not only affects me morally, but it
makes me sick at the stomach."[10]

Boker's and Stoddard's abhorrence of the world of commerce
contrasted sharply with the attitudes of Thomas Bailey Aldrich.
Aldrich had grown up in Portsmouth, New Hampshire, where
he had been captivated by the gentle charm of that declining
seaport town. Capitalism, for Aldrich, was always part of the
respected past. His views on politics and economics were no
more sophisticated than Boker's, but whereas Boker had personal reasons for hating the world of wealth, Aldrich habitually
invested that world with the nostalgia of the past. The index
of Boker's disaffection from America was his hatred of the
wealthy; Aldrich, who never much quarreled with Mammon,
reserved his animus for the poor.[11]

"Whoever disparages money," Aldrich said, "disparages every
step in the progress of the human race." He believed that too
much gold had seldom ruined men, but too little had often done
so. "What noble enterprises have been checked and fine souls . . .
blighted in the gloom of poverty the world will never know."[12]
Socialism was anathema to Aldrich. He did not bother to point
out its faults; that it was rooted in envy was enough for him.
He scornfully described Socialists as "the walking delegates of
a higher civilization who have nothing to divide."[13]

Although not quite out of the mainstream of genteel thinking,
Aldrich's political theory can barely be called democratic. The
political corruption of the day so infuriated him that he rarely
expressed the few democratic sentiments he had. He confessed
in 1899 that he had "never been very deeply impressed by the
administrative abilities of what we call the lower classes. The
reign of terror in France is a fine illustration of the kind of government which the masses give us when they have the opportunity."[14]

Aldrich did have some commitment to the idea of freedom
and self-determination. Like most of Boston, he thought, he was
not happy about the Spanish-American War.[15] His anti-imperialism, however, was not much more than a warning against the
mongrelization of America. Here Aldrich spoke the concern

of genteel culture, but his characteristically shrill note suggested that his fears were deeper than those of his politically active friends like Curtis. Genteel culture as a whole cannot be described as moderate, but measured against it, the genteel poets often verge on the hysterical and the paranoid.

The traditional nature of Aldrich's values is apparent. They were bourgeois values and they were what Aldrich assumed to be native American values. The ideal life for him was always the life of the isolated New England village. The "hard shrewd sense and the simpler manner" of his forefathers were the ways of virtue.[16] The democracy that he praised had vanished along with the older and simpler New England. As he suggested in 1894, democracy might be called "The Light that Failed."[17] The lower orders had risen; the "canaille" had taken possession of the new world.[18] Aldrich could see no good in it, and in his pessimistic moments, like Henry Adams, he expected a holocaust to end it all.[19]

Aloof from the contemporary world of social problems, Aldrich, Boker, and Stoddard devoted their energies to art. "We must both cling the closer to that worship which is the consecration of our lives," Taylor wrote Stoddard, to "the unselfish homage of that spirit of art and beauty which men call Poetry." "Let us work our way, whatever the toil and sorrow," he continued, "from vestibule to chancel, from chancel to shrine, from the lowest footstool of the temple to the high priest's place beside the altar."[20] Stoddard agreed, and so did the third member of their "trinity," Boker. "What a wonderful, what a holy gift is this Poetry," he wrote Stoddard. "How should it not be prized, how should it not be cultivated!"[21]

For all three men, poetry ranked above the other arts, and the poet above other men. Non-poets were of a "lower organization."[22] They lacked the "mental nerves" to pick up the sharp sensations of the imagination.[23] If nature were to "spoil" millions of men in making a genius or two, Aldrich thought the gain would be great.[24] The psychology of genius demanded that the poet suffer before attaining true creativity. Not for the genius was the placid content of ordinary men; the insensitive lacked the highs and lows of deep emotional experience.[25] The genius could never be sleek and happy. The lovers of art "must hunger and waste and burn, ere the beautiful heathen heart will stir."[26]

If poetry was a high and arduous calling, it was also intended as a refuge. Only seldom was it used to confront the contemporary; instead it allowed the poet to escape his day. No one else in the period wrote so many poems with antique and medieval settings as Aldrich, Stoddard, and Boker. Of all Boker's plays only two had modern settings. One of these, *The World A Mask*, was a satire on the tendency of society to elevate respectability above virtue. The other, *The Bankrupt*, dealt with the return of a wealthy master criminal to a city in the northern United States. It was a thin and unconvincing attempt at realism. Boker's biographer Edward S. Bradley concludes that he was just not suited to the genre.[27] Boker himself when working on *The World A Mask* wrote to Stoddard, "I have felt what it is to debase a gift of God. I have degraded myself to write a play for the rabble....I was a fool, a poet no longer."[28] During the production of *The Bankrupt*, Boker was deeply depressed about his work and even doubted his own sanity.[29] Bradley's judgment that *The Bankrupt* was Boker's worst play seems fair.[30] Boker, like Stoddard and Aldrich, wrote his best poetry when he avoided contemporary life.[31]

No insignificant part of the genteel poets' alienation from the America of their day stemmed from what they thought to be hostile criticism. Stedman and Aldrich constantly complained of the patronizing tone in the literary columns of the New York *Nation*. Aldrich went so far as to suggest that the foreign birth of its editor E. L. Godkin and his literary critic John Richard Dennett was responsible for their antagonism. He felt that they "have no sympathy with us or our institutions, and it is an impertinence for them to sit in judgment on our politics or our literature."[32]

What Aldrich wanted was sympathetic criticism. Readers did poets a "grievous wrong," he said, if they did not bring as much beauty to poetry as poets did.[33] Boker was more cynical. He was prepared to provide sympathetic criticism, at least to his friends. "Never judge of my opinions by what I say of my friends in a newspaper," he wrote to a friend; "for I hold the bookselling part of literature to be a trade—*an everlasting effort to gull the public.*" "Criticisms are written for the purpose of promoting a book's success with the public," he said, "and not to ventilate our own critical ability, or to show how shrewd we can be at picking holes in literary merit."[34] Boker's friends were not so candid, but they generally agreed with him, as the bland affability and unctuousness of much genteel literary criticism shows.

The genteel poets realized that hostile critics were insignificant compared to an indifferent public. "The only critic whose verdict is worth a fig is the great Public," Aldrich wrote.[35] The problem was not to cater to the public taste, but to weather it.[36] If success never came, or came too late, the consequences could be dire. "I am an old man now," Boker wrote in 1882 when Lawrence Barrett's production of *Francesca da Rimini* brought him his first success, "a tremulus of ashes, from which the early fire has burned out.... God knows what I might have done when my mind was a furnace and my heart as glowing iron within the fire. If there has been any loss to the world, it has been the world's own fault; *for I was as much choked off and silenced, as though the act had been one of design.*"[37]

It galled Boker, too, that the poets of Longfellow's generation enjoyed an established fame, while he and his friends had to struggle for recognition. In fact, the genteel poets were in a delicate position. It would have been disastrous to risk openly offending the established American poets. Their influence was essential in securing journalistic positions and an occasional favorable review that counted. The cultural circles of Boston, New York, and Philadelphia, where the genteel poets congregated, were small and tightly knit. A good word here and there from the right people was sufficient to launch a man's career. Or with these people against him, he might almost vanish from the American scene, as Melville did after his early success. So virtually all public criticism by the genteel poets maintained a reverent posture toward the older generation. Direct letters were similarly deferential and admiring in tone.[38] Even when genteel editors supplanted the older men, they treated their work with the greatest delicacy.[39]

In short, one would never have guessed that the genteel poets actually had little regard for the skill of their predecessors. Stoddard, for example, chafed with impatience for the time when the "old duffers" of New England would be dead.[40] Boker thought that he and his friends "should not expect to be popular in an age when Longfellow is a great poet." He advised waiting until "Longfellow & Co." had passed away.[41] If one knew the real views of the genteel poets and crtics, one could read between the lines of their published criticism. Stoddard's *Recollections* revealed some of these views, but it did not appear until 1903, when Longfellow and Lowell were dead.[42] Stedman, who wrote earlier, had more need of tact, and no one could have handled the problem more deftly. Some actually thought he was too genial.[43] But even in Stedman's work, a close reading will reveal the disguised criticism. His *Poets of America* conceals a basic dissatisfaction with the poetry of New England's great generation beneath a defense of that poetry on nonaesthetic grounds. For one who knew, however, as presumably his friends did, that Stedman did not consider good character or representative qualities adequate justification for poor poetry, *Poets of America* must have had its amusing side.

But private jokes did not console the genteel poets for the length of New England's shadow. And just as they emerged from it, they saw a worse threat in the rise of literary realism. It was almost as if they never had a chance, caught as they were between moralists on the one hand and vulgarians on the other. Their romanticism flowered briefly in the 1850's, but before they could develop it they saw it sink into sentimental feminine fiction. That kind of romanticism was not at all to their liking.[44] Although sentimental himself in the lugubrious "Babie Bell," Aldrich generally criticized romanticism when he thought it verged on the sentimental.[45] In *The Story of a Bad Boy,* Aldrich satirized the sorrowful self-indulgence of the youthful Tom who, scorned in love, buried his natural effervescence in lonely walks and memorized the "more turgid poems" of Byron. He was a Blighted Being, and like all of his kind, had no purpose in life, "except to be as blighted as possible."[46]

But genteel realism was one thing, and Howells's variety quite another. Aldrich and his friends objected, not to the methods, but to the subject matter of literary realism.[47] Aldrich's critcism echoed Stedman's, but its disdainful air was Aldrich's own. It was sufficient for him that realism worshipped the tedious, the dull, and the commonplace. No one doubted that men were not always noble, but photographing them in their pajamas did not help matters.[48] Realism plainly had an obsession with the disagreeable corners of human experience. Aldrich did not like books like *A Mummer's Wife* that left a bad taste in the mouth. Zola and Flaubert were anathema to him; he thought them "malarious." "Art should create nothing but what is beautiful," Aldrich said, "and leave real life to do the rest."[49] As editor of the *Atlantic* he added realism to his "list of subjects not to be touched."[50] He was skeptical enough to believe that any discussion of the controversy would only encourage his enemies. "It is plain," he wrote in 1896, "that the poetry in demand today must be strong, and picturesque, and slangish, with a dash of obscenity. Henceforth the Muse shall wear a cabbage, and not a rose on her bosom."[51]

The kind of rose Aldrich and his friends offered to the Muse differed from man to man. Boker, as a playwright, naturally praised the dramatic in poetry above the lyric. His themes were best drawn, as in *Francesca da Rimini*, from tragic situations that he saw as universal. Boker felt, however, that because they lacked the contemporaneity demanded by realism, he never received his due. In his nondramatic verse, Boker looked back, like his friends, to Keats and Shelley and Tennyson.[52] Stoddard and Aldrich increasingly fell into the art school.[53] For almost all of his mature life, Aldrich loved the work of the Cavalier poet, Robert Herrick. He said he would be content if his lyrics, like Herrick's, could be brief "and polished as the bosom of a star."[54] Stoddard, in the 1880's, declared that the only two poets he cared about were Frederick Locker-Lampson and Austin Dobson.[55]

There was a distinct drift among the genteel poets away from the romanticism of their youth and toward the verse of the art school. Beginning as rebels of a sort, the genteel romantics sought to escape from their age through their poetry. The Civil War lured them back to it for a time, but post-War America undercut the possibilities for a renewed romantic vision. The reasons they themselves gave for this are not convincing. As middle-class men of letters they did indeed deplore the new rich and the new poor, but the truer source of their malaise lay in the fact that they were poets, and, by choice and by temperament, traditional poets. As poets their ultimate failure and Stedman's, too, lay in their inability to recognize that not only their poetry but the very art of poetry faced a crisis at least as grave as the one the romantics they worshipped had met and mastered.

By the beginning of the nineteenth century the appearance of a new, middle-class reading public had demanded from poetry a new purpose and a new language. The poets obliged and for fifty years enjoyed public approval. As the audience grew, however, it turned increasingly to a new form of literature that spoke to its concerns and in its idiom. Not even long-standing religious prejudice was sufficient to inhibit the widespread success of the novel once Dickens turned it to a realistic recording of the ways of men who never had appeared in novels before. Once its focus was shifted from the gentry to the middle classes, the realistic novel had a secure audience.

In America this development occurred later, in the post–Civil War realism of Twain and Howells and, after 1900, in literary naturalism. The audience for poetry did not diminish—in fact more poetry was published in 1890 than ever before—but the art of poetry declined.[56] The genteel poets themselves wasted energy they might have devoted to poetry in resisting the rise of realism. They hated realism for depicting a vulgar and boring world, and they had a substantial self-interest in defeating it. They were moved not so much by fear for their livelihood— Boker and Stoddard were not supported by their art—as by fear for their position in the world of American culture. And, committed as they were to the traditional literary culture for their prestige, they refused to see the need for new forms to invigorate their art. Had they been as isolated as they claimed they were, they might have used their isolation creatively, as Emily Dickinson did. But for Boker and Stoddard in 1890 as for Taylor in 1850, the ideal of art was no more profound than the ideal of boyish escape. Except perhaps for Thomas Bailey Aldrich, the genteel poet found no impulse for creativity.

Aldrich is a partial exception to some of these generalizations. He was, for one thing, a better poet than either Boker or Stoddard. He was also more respected and more popular than they; his prose fiction sold widely and was translated into several languages. More than Boker and Stoddard, he represented the continuation of the established literary culture. Boker and Stoddard never quite commanded the respect of that culture, though they never broke with it. Their attitude was a frustrating mixture of self-doubt and hatred of the culture that ignored them. Aldrich, by contrast, although he did see that American culture was losing its grip on American society, never feared for his own status within that culture. Unlike Boker and Stoddard he did not exhibit the reflex of romantic alienation to any great degree. His early poetry sounded much like theirs, but a humorously skeptical touch was evident in his Oriental poetry, a genre that in less disciplined and detached hands was the occasion for so much genteel swooning. He usually avoided the sentimental and the silly by scoffing at it; he avoided the serious by simply avoiding it. His poetry and his prose were devoted to the mid-range of human experience; his interest was neither in the great and compelling events of the world nor in the private nuances of the self. His style, appropriate for his subject, was the ironic style, mildly pitched and carefully executed. In a world from which both tragedy and joy were barred, he confined himself to the good-humored voice.

It is an irony he would not have appreciated that the limited world of his art was not so very dissimilar from the world of Howells, the one realist New England could stomach even though it deplored the waste of talent. Realism, for Howells, deliberately mirrored a world of the mid-range of human action because it championed democracy. Idealism, for Aldrich, limited its world to the mid-ground because it could no longer imagine a world that transcended the normal and it feared the world that ran beneath. If irony was potentially a complex attitude for confronting reality, as Henry James demonstrated, it was also, as Aldrich showed, a means of burying reality.

The particular quality of Aldrich's poetry was never better captured than by Paul Elmer More, who placed Aldrich in the long line of cultured society poets beginning in classical Rome. In that line More placed Martial, Catullus, Suckling, Herrick, Prior, Pope, Vincent Bourne, Cowper, Lamb, Dobson, and Lang. More found the essence of society verse in irony, not grim but self-deprecating, half a confession of weakness and half a veiling of strength. Reticence and suggestion were its manner and regret for an idealized past its tone. Although touched by the tragic brevity and insufficiency of life, it expressed no grief louder than a sigh and no amusement at human folly stronger than a smile. Spontaneity was overlaid with polish and urbanity with bashfulness.[57]

More could well have added that an age with a taste for realism could feel no warmth for such poetry. When Aldrich hinted that his workmanship was "more costly" than his subjects, he turned upside down the priority of the literary realists. Stedman's various histories of the poetry of the nineteenth century were undistinguished, but his perception was sure when he linked the art school to the fin de siècle. Aldrich believed, as Oscar Wilde did, that the subject of a work of art was trivial compared with the quality of its style.[58] Or, to put it differently, both men took style itself as the subject of their art. They reversed the realists' maxim that art should imitate life and insisted instead that life should imitate art.

For the genteel poets, however, the doctrine of imitation was scarcely more than an expression of their desire and need to instruct and elevate American society. They had embarked on their careers determined to free art from morals, but as established poets they continued the didactic tradition of New England. The lesson was somewhat altered—the new morality was kinder to aesthetics than the old—but its aim was essentially unchanged. Literature remained primarily educational and disciplinary in function.

For Wilde, although the doctrine of imitation had its conservative objectives, it looked forward to the literature of the twentieth century. The art of style for Wilde not only attacked dominant notions about the priority of life over art, but in rejecting the idea that experience had any inherent meaning, it opened the door to a radically subjective and personal literature.[59] Wilde himself moved only tentatively in the direction his theories indicated. Usually his radicalism was confined to scoffing at the bourgeois ingredients of Victorian culture, an attitude not at all unpalatable to the English aristocracy. On its assertive side, the style that Wilde opposed to the Victorian style of the conventional, the respectable, the prudent, and the hard-working was the style of spontaneous expression, of luxury, of laziness.[60]

His style was more than a revived romanticism. As a means for expressing the subjective self, Wilde opened the literature of romanticism to new qualities like insincerity and duplicity, which he saw as devices to multiply personality. In his own role as poseur, however, he rarely seemed interested in going beyond the boyish.[61] Despite all his sympathies for the frivolous and the irrelevant, they seem to be only that, sympathies. He was willing to accept the world he lived in and his own perspectives as firm instead of shaping a new literature of the self that might question both the world and the man. Perhaps in that sense, and in the same sense for Aldrich, his romanticism is appropriately described as decadent.

Of course it is in quite another sense that Wilde is customarily called decadent. But, from any viewpoint less intolerant than that of Victorian England, one might regret Wilde's homosexuality more because it failed to enrich his art than for any other reason. For this failure it would be fairer to blame England than Wilde. Yet for all the sexual inhibition of Victorian culture, England did have an aristocracy at least free enough from bourgeois influence so that a degree of sexual freedom—or, more modestly, the freedom to speculate about the possibilities of sexual freedom—could be defended. In America there was far less freedom of sexual expression; to find it, one had to be beneath society in the urban slums or outside it on the frontier.

Homosexual gatherings where men of different social classes mixed were possible in England, but almost inconceivable in America.[62] Perhaps for the same reason—the attitudes of at least some of the English aristocracy—the art of the English decadents did find a sufficient audience to enjoy some freedom of development.

It was neither Wilde's homosexuality nor his art that lost him his aristocratic support, but only his views on Socialism, which, had he understood the subject better, he might never have fallen into. Aldrich, as the best poet of the American art school and as a man whose sexual practices and artistic theories had no tincture of radicalism about them, never could find the sympathetic and sophisticated audience that England afforded to Wilde. The American audience for the works of the art school confirmed its respectability by its reading; the English audience, secure in its self-esteem, could tolerate a mocking of the respectable. The relaxed temper of the English fin de siècle could find no space to flourish in the more bourgeois society of America.

Prevented as they were by their own incapacities and by society's indifference and hostility from producing a meaningful and satisfying art, the genteel poets translated their attractions to a cult of art into a cult of love. Barred by both personal and social restraints from becoming aesthetes, they nourished instead a devotion to the doctrine of romantic love. They believed in an art of beauty, to be sure, but they were unanimously agreed that the greatest human experience was not the creation of poetry, but love. A few lines from "In an Atelier" by Aldrich voiced their common feeling: "Ah, Fanny, I am sick at heart, / It is so little one can do; / We talk our jargon—live for Art! / I'd much prefer to live for you."[63]

Stoddard saw love as the culmination of the poet's growth. Following Wordsworth, he emphasized the sympathy children felt for nature. But nature could not satisfy the poet, who felt a growing need for beauty. And even beauty created other wants that could be satisfied only by love, "the sum of human needs."[64] Besides its solace for the disheartened artist, love offered an escape from the perplexities of the day. Obsessed with the transience of life, Stoddard advised his readers to "seize the hours before they fly."[65] Only love was "mightier than Death."[66] Aldrich suggested that love made theories of evolution irrelevant:

> Graybeards, who seek to bridge the chasm
> 'Twixt man to-day and protoplasm,
> Who theorize and probe and gape,
> And finally evolve an ape—
> Yours is a harmless sort of cult,
> If you are pleased with the result.
> Some folks admit, with cynic grace,
> That you have rather proved your case.
> These dogmatists are so severe!
> Enough for me that Hilda's here,
> Enough, that having long survived
> Pre-Eveic forms, she has arrived—
> An illustration the completest
> Of the survival of the sweetest.[67]

Taylor, more frightened of science than Aldrich, affirmed the supremacy of love as Aldrich did, but with an undertone of worry. In "Cupido" love is the last salvation of man in a world made lonely by science.[68] Boker struck the same dark note by calling love "the sole surviving passion / That enlinks a dull existence / With the dull and ruthless present."[69]

There is a seemingly deliberate confusion of art and love in genteel poetry. As romantics the genteel poets inherited the notion of sensibility used by their predecessors to open art to a broader rendering of human experience and, simultaneously, to broaden that experience itself. In their attempt to emancipate both art and life from rigid conventions, the early romantics often blurred distinctions between different forms of self-expression. By doing the same, the genteel poets testified again to their lineage. But their reiteration of traditional romantic formulations is also understandable in light of their own situation. Because they could not respect the only audience their poetry commanded, they could not really respect their poetry. Had they been able to, they might have seen as Oscar Wilde did that the spheres of art and life were different. Art was not an inferior form of lovemaking, as the genteel poets, admitting their own inadequacy, believed. Art did involve self-expression, but the self projected in art was not the self expressed in love. Wilde saw what the American poets could not see, that art was an ordering of experience that was itself orderless. In choosing his mask, the artist did indeed choose a self, but one of many selves.

Against this psychology of art, the genteel poets held firm to their romantic preconceptions. The self, for them, could be only one self, the inner, private being that gave identity to a man, the same self that the early romantics also intuitively affirmed and sought to unshackle. All sincere expression—and the genteel poets demanded nothing so much as sincerity—sprang from the same source. Their insistence on this point, ironically, led to hypocrisy. Because they considered poetry self-revelatory, they rigorously barred any expression of private experience from poetry. Immodesty in art was as much a clue to an immodest self as was immodesty in society. Art, therefore, was confined to the sphere of the publicly acceptable. It is no wonder that the genteel poets found an art of that sort—even though they themselves could conceive of no alternative—less appealing than the art of love.

The facts of genteel love, however, did not come up to expectations. Aldrich's courtship, for example, was a dreary business. He fell in love for the first time in 1855 with a woman four years older than he, "beautiful as a Madonna and learned as Minerva—everything that a dweller in 'book-world' could have dared to dream of." He said that he could not marry at that time, offering no explanation except his friends' opposition.[70] He thought his Minerva was too "queenly" and a trifle too noble, anyway.[71]

It is not clear when he first met his wife-to-be, but he was engaged in the early 1860's. From the start, Aldrich's mother protested "as she never before protested against anything involving a wish of mine." Apparently, she did not believe in the strength of Lillian's love, and warned that she would never be happy married to a "poor literary man."[72] Aldrich's "overcare" for Lillian led him to break their engagement in April, 1863, but by fall they were back together again.[73] Plans for marriage then were wrecked by the intervention of Mrs. Aldrich. Interestingly enough, Aldrich did not seem to resent his mother's meddling. He was happy when she visited him, and wrote Lillian during the height of their difficulties that "a Mother's love, more unselfish than any other love, is rather difficult to be merited."[74]

Aldrich's reasons for being attracted to his fiancée reflect the subordinate position of women in the nineteenth century. In his personal letters to her, Aldrich referred to Lillian as "Toddlekins" and "my Dear Child"; he was pleased when she accepted his advice "like a good girl."[75] Revealingly, Aldrich confessed that he was most attracted to Lillian when she was ill. His happiest night one winter he spent tending her during convalescence.[76] And when she was capricious Aldrich wrote to her, "deliciously cruel to me, you become a sumptuous epicurean cannibal."[77] Aldrich's mother was finally reconciled to the marriage, and it took place in 1865. In one vital respect Lillian Aldrich subscribed to the Victorian sentiments of her husband: she firmly opposed all moves to extend the suffrage to women.

The private life of Edmund Stedman does not properly belong in this chapter, but because his experience with courtship and marriage parallels Aldrich's, it may be mentioned here. If it is not obvious in the case of Aldrich, it ought to be obvious in the case of Stedman that the genteel exaltation of love was very much a compensation for emotional deprivation.

Stedman was extraordinarily close to his mother. If some inherent emotional sensitivity inclined him to her, the fact of his early and long separation from her stimulated that sensitivity. His youthful avowals of affection for her occasionally assumed a pathetic quality, deepened by his inability to communicate well with his stepfather.[78] In characteristic nineteenth-century fashion he venerated his mother as an angel; his despair at separation from her evoked a comparison of the two of them to Evangeline and her love.[79] Very likely the emotional starvation of his childhood had something to do with the "morbid sensitiveness" his biographers found prominent in his personality.[80] Throughout his life, Stedman suffered from severe hypochondriasis. From childhood through mid-life he believed he had consumption and would die young; when doctors assured him this was false, he became convinced he had heart disease. With that disproved as well, he turned to neurasthenia.[81]

In his letters, Stedman did not blame his mother for her early separation from him. His father had died of illness at sea when he was two years old. His grandfather said he would not support the widow and her children, but he promised that if the children would go to be raised by his brother in Norwich, Connecticut, he would divide between them when they came of age the inheritance he had reserved for their father. Stedman's mother at first hoped to avoid this arrangement by supporting herself and her children by writing for magazines like the *Knickerbocker, Godey's Lady's Book*, and *Graham's Magazine*. Unable to earn enough money, however, she consented to the separation from her children. When six years later she married William Burnett Kinney, owner and editor of the *Newark Daily Advertiser*, both Stedman and his brother "begged piteously" to be taken to their new father's home, but Kinney refused. Knowing that the Stedman family was very wealthy, Kinney apparently thought it would be better for his stepchildren to remain in Norwich to win their inheritance. Stedman's mother assured him she was disappointed by Kinney's decision, but Stedman may nevertheless have blamed her subconsciously for the decision.[82] The cry for sympathy revealed in a pathetic college prank of his was almost certainly aimed at his mother and not at his friends, as he believed. Leaving a suicide note where it would be found by his college classmates, Stedman hid under his bed to see what effect his note would have. He was discovered before he could test for any reaction.[83]

Stedman's behavior in this episode illuminates his motives in marrying and his choice of a bride. Four years after the wedding, Stedman admitted to his mother that caprice, sympathy, rivalry, and most of all pride, had led to his marriage. At that time, his mother and his wife had not yet met, and Stedman, explaining the fact that his wife was too sensitive to write, described Laura to his mother. His sketch of her makes clear that she was a very different woman from his mother. He conceded that she lacked literary or scientific accomplishments, but referred to those as superficial adornments. He said he "always went on the theory that I had enough literary education for the family—that I needed in a wife a resting-place, where I could be *nursed, comforted* and *loved*. Laura has been all this—and, like the wife of Schiller, understands me, if she does not my books."[84] Laura fitted the qualifications of a Victorian wife, but she also satisfied the need for simple affection that Stedman's mother had not met. Stedman thought his mother exceptional because of her literary interests, but she may have been more typical than he imagined. As a middle-class woman, confined to the home by middle-class prejudice, she may have controlled her frustration behind the mask of coldness that so many Victorian sons complained of and let literature, produced and read in privacy, be her compensation. We know too little of Mrs. Kinney to do more than speculate about her. But there would be wry justice in a nineteenth-century wife and mother's denying her husband and her sons the affection they aimed to monopolize.

Distinctions between male and female nature were unimportant to Stedman as a boy. But, confirming the social pattern that had withheld from him what he needed then, Stedman grew up to the norms of his culture and drew those distinctions sharply. Against the embarrassingly honest explanation he had given his mother for his marriage, he later insisted that a male artist ideally should marry only when mutual comprehension was possible. An affectionate but inartistic and commonplace wife "vastly imperilled" an artist's growth and marital happiness. A man should "marry art, and be true to it alone" unless his marriage was ideal, Stedman wrote in *Victorian Poets*. A woman, by contrast, could develop her artistic nature only through marriage, even if it were not ideal. Her artistic and spiritual natures were "so closely interwrought" as to make marriage essential. The female poet, drawing upon marriage, fulfilled her "highest mission" in the expression of love poetry. The subjectivity of her utterances, as with Elizabeth Barrett Browning, was defensible because women were less conceited and more tactful than men. Men as a rule were safe only with objective poetry.[85]

Like most Victorians Stedman saw the family as the center of life, a bulwark against the outside world. Women were intended to "make men strong and fill the home with sunshine." They had a "sacred right" and duty to be wives and mothers.

Outside the home women were to be conventional. They should profess religion and care less about literary and intellectual matters than about their families. Men, of course, could do the rest.[86]

Aldrich's and Stedman's marriages, however typical they may have been for their day, were very much unlike those of Stoddard and Boker. Stoddard's wife, Elizabeth Drew Barstow Stoddard, never exemplified the ideals of propriety that were commonly associated with gentility. She fancied herself a Bohemian. She wrote her husband in 1865 that she wished she were "sitting in the gutter in Bleeker St., or at an apple stand."[87] When Lowell returned a story she had submitted to the *Atlantic* because parts of it were too frank and needed revising, she asked him, "Do I disturb your artistic sense by my want of refinement? I must own that I am coarse by nature. At times I have an overwhelming perception of the back side of truth."[88]

"The Pythoness," as Boker and Taylor frequently called Mrs. Stoddard, also had what must have appeared to them an overwhelming frankness. "I have no more respect for Lizzie's opinion than you have," Boker wrote Taylor, "but once in a while her poisoned shafts hit the white...." Describing an evening with the Stoddards, Boker quoted Mrs. Stoddard:

"George, you, Dick, Bayard, Stedman, Aldrich, Read, the whole lot of you youngsters, have all been dreary failures as poets. Not one of you has won even a third class position as a poet. There is not one of you who can justly lay claim to popularity, in any true sense of the term. You have not even attained to such a position as is held by that weakling Longfellow, for whom no one can challenge more than a third class place, as compared with the mass of English poets. Since you began to write, a half dozen English poets—Swinburne being an example—have arisen, and secured the fame to which you in vain aspired. It was not time that you lacked therefore to become known, but poetic ability. The world is not unappreciative of real genius, as you flatter yourselves is the case, only you are not up to the required standard. You are all failures, and the sooner you stop writing the things that no public will read, the better for your peace of mind. Is not this the truth," she said, turning to me very sadly. "God's truth," my lips and my conscience cried with one voice. "God's truth," echoed poor Dick, with his heart's sickness in his face.[89]

Mrs. Stoddard was a sensitive and temperamental woman, and getting along with her was no easy matter. She was partly responsible for a permanent breach between her husband and Aldrich. She disliked the wives of Taylor and Stedman, neither of whom was attracted to Bohemianism, and stirred up trouble with them over trivial matters. The intimate coherence that had marked the genteel circle in the 1850's did not long survive Stoddard's marriage. The comrades complained increasingly in their letters of "that damned Lizzie!" Tolerant as always, Stedman got along well enough with her in private and praised her novels in public, but Taylor privately thought she was "hopelessly diseased, mentally and morally." Exactly what bothered him about Mrs. Stoddard is not evident from his letters, but a reference in one of Aldrich's letters to Edwin Booth's mortification at his "folly" with Lizzie suggests, at the least, that she was too flirtatious for genteel taste. Invoking the universal curative, Aldrich wrote his wife that he would rather see Mrs. Stoddard "holding him [her child] to her bosom, than have her write the most superb American novel ever dreamed of. It will be better for her. She needed the softening influences which the cares of a fragil [sic] life will entail upon her."[90]

But the most radical departures from genteel behavior were Boker's. A Philadelphia socialite, Boker possessed from his college days onward a calmness and poise that gave him the appearance of almost patrician restraint.[91] Without ever breaking with his wife, Boker managed a series of love affairs spanning most of his adult life. His volume of *Sonnets*, published posthumously, celebrated three affairs beginning about 1852 and extending almost until his death. His first and longest (fifteen years) was with a prominent Philadelphia woman who was unhappily married. The lovers carried their discretion to great lengths and were never discovered. Boker's appointment as minister to Turkey terminated the affair in 1871. Boker's second affair was a brief dalliance in the summer of 1877 in Paris. His third began in 1881 and lasted almost until his death.[92]

The *Sonnets* themselves were appropriately subtitled "A Sequence on Profane Love." The concept of love articulated in them overturned traditional mores in one sense. Like Browning and Swinburne, Boker presented love as an irresistible force, beautiful in itself. He confessed to "no remorse" at loving "above the law."[93] As he declared to his lady:

> If thou art sinful, there are thousands then
> Who howl from pulpits, and make dreary night
> Of texts as barefaced as the morning light,
> Who more deserve the Angel's damning pen—
> That tribe of bitter and self-righteous men
> Who, in God's name, fill earth with wild affright,
> Afflict our very virtues with a blight,
> Till heaven's great dome becomes a murky den.[94]

Love was to be not a sin but a joy and a refuge. Boker described it as "God's deputy—alone sublime, / The last, sad, lingering angel." Threats of hell would not deter him. "When my lips upon her lips should feed," he wrote, "I would possess her though hell yawned in view, / Ablaze to punish the presumptuous deed."[95]

Yet Boker's conception of love preserves intact the traditional dualism of the sexes. For man, love is lust; for woman, it is sacrifice. In Sonnet LXX he declares that his lady is "pure and fine" and that she takes "small pleasure in the close embrace."

> Her tender pity shames this heat of mine,
> That bows her soul unto a lowly place,
> To meet the cravings of my abject race,
> With yielding smiles and patience all divine,
> So much she suffers for her dear love's sake,
> So much forgives, so calmly puts aside
> Her own distaste, her stately virgin pride;
> And all for me, who like a satyr slake
> My brutish thirst within a crystal tide,
> And stain it with the dusty stir I make.[96]

He confesses to shame that he could "day by day, / Deface her virgin temple, foully roll / In orgies that pollute the sacred bowl, / Merely because she will not say me nay." He wishes instead to share his lady's "Whiteness," to drop beneath the "earth that sullies me."[97]

In his letters, Boker's attitude toward his mistresses was not so worshipful. In 1856 he sent Stoddard a laconic account of his troubles. "She thought she could play with edged tools," he wrote, "and so she picked me up and began, but I finished the matter, as Mother Nature directs; and now the lady howls in my ears, night and day, about her ruin, and her remorse, and her poor husband, and Christ knows what. If she let me alone, she would not have suffered. However, I feel like a thief, and the Devil only knows where it will all end."[98]

Boker's love affairs set him apart from his friends and gave him a superiority that he used to tease his less experienced comrades. "My astonishment cannot be suppressed!" he wrote Stoddard in 1850.

So you have been feeling a "lady's thighs," have you? Have ladies thighs; and where are they situated? Is it a pleasant amusement this said feeling of "a lady's thighs"? What is the perception produced by the same? Does it open any new moral perception; or is it only a harmless, silly enjoyment of the beautiful through the sense of touch, like passing the finger ends over a highly polished substance of any kind—say ice for instance? To what does it conduct? How long can you continue the pastime without exhausting it? Really this is very strange! I intend asking the first "lady" I meet to allow me to feel her thighs. Would the request be altogether proper?[99]

Stoddard, of course, never doubted that Boker was a gentleman. He knew that gentility exercised its claims only upon a man's public behavior. Prudes might object, but the genteel circle never thought itself prudish. It was no lack of acquaintance with the facts of life that dictated the withholding of those facts from public view. A little more frankness in literature would not have dismayed the genteel poets, but they assumed that it would have antagonized the reading audience, especially in America. In 1868 when Swinburne was planning to publish a novel anonymously in America, Boker wrote Stoddard that he ought to tone down the sexual element.[100] His letter is a commentary on the reading public, but also on Boker's own sophistication. It reveals a man whose indelicacy was leagues beyond the realism of Howells and James. Boker advised that Swinburne's hero

should not copulate with the heroine in an unnatural manner. The con, rectum and the mouth may be permitted—and surely here are holes enough to serve the purpose of a great imagination—into any one of these he may introduce his nine inches stiff, limber or even double; but I would not have him burst open her delicate shell-like ear with his penis, and beget in her dreamy head another Pallas. The villain of the story should not bugger his mother in the first chapter; at least I should not open with this domestic incident, usual as it may be, and therefore perfectly defensible on natural grounds. I should not form too many "groups" after the manner of *de Sade*; for that great master has almost exhausted those situations. I do not say that in the last scene or climax, all the characters may not shag and bugger together in a ring, say in the form of a Round Robin; but a little of that goes a long way....[101]

Elizabeth Stoddard was not overstating the case when she wrote to Stedman that Boker "could weep with his victims, but he was the sort of man that would have taken the Virgin Mary from the Ass, before Joseph, and helped her kindly into an adjoining hedge."[102]

Boker's sexuality took its style from the complete separation of private and public spheres of conduct, the former freed because it was secret and the latter controlled because it was visible. A man could be himself at home, he believed, but in public, rules for work and manners for society imposed their masks. The genteel poets posited the same sort of relationship between public and private behavior as they did between the artist as artist and the artist as man. They tried to convince their readers that a man's poetry had nothing to do with his life, but their worrisome preoccupation with poetic subjectivity indicated that they could not believe themselves. Their very concern that their art not reflect personal experience betrayed the fundamental artificiality of the line they drew between public and private. The line was useful, however; the privatization of experience that it enforced aided both the timid and the bold. The sexually repressed could cloak their frustration in the refuge of home, and the sexually predatory could pursue their adventures out of public light. In bourgeois society Stedman and Boker complemented one another.

They were complementary not only in the possibilities that privacy offered them, but in the language of privacy itself. Most of the genteel poets spoke of sex in terms of Home and Mother; only Boker drew on the vocabulary of pornography, and even he, only in private. The difference of their language, however, did not arise because they were describing two different realities. Boker's letters, though not his poetry, admitted the sexuality of women that genteel culture publicly denied. But Boker's own sexuality did not really diverge from the genteel concept of womanhood and of relations between the sexes. The sexual aggressiveness expressed in his letters was elicited by the pure and queenly female that his poems adored, but aggression underlay genteel behavior toward women in general, whether they were to be seduced outside marriage or confined by it to home and motherhood. In at least one of his affairs, Boker became aware that one ingredient of his sexual pleasure was the knowledge that he had degraded a woman. No one can say whether his genteel friends felt this in their more conventional sexual relationships, but the fact that they were attracted to sick and helpless women suggests that they had fantasies not so different from Boker's reality. From neither perspective were women regarded as human beings. Genteel culture substituted a caste of sex for a caste of class.

The inferior position of women appears also in the suppressed homosexuality of both genteel America and Victorian England. Repression was firmer in America than in England, but genteel literature found socially acceptable ways to hint at homosexual inclinations. Bayard Taylor's work is filled with a frank admiration for male beauty, whether in Bedouin boys or in less voluptuous New England lads.[108] When the nature of attraction between males became problematical, as in "Twin Love" and *John Godfrey's Fortunes*, he was able to sanctify physical intimacy by confining it within the bonds of kinship. Brothers and cousins kiss each other, share the same beds, and refer without the least hint of impropriety to the "magnetism" that binds them together.

"Twin Love" is about the relationship between twins named David and Jonathan. It is not a modern version of the Biblical tale, but the use of Biblical names enables Taylor to treat a relationship that otherwise would have discomfited if not offended his readers. In Taylor's story David and Jonathan are inseparably joined by a bond suggestive of the supernatural. The first rift between them occurs when Jonathan decides to marry Ruth. He does not see this as dividing him from his brother, as David does. He tries to reassure David: " 'Ruth is ours, and I bring her kiss to you,' he said, pressing his lips to David's. But the arms flung around him trembled and David whispered, 'Now the change begins.' " Jonathan and Ruth marry, and David goes West. Later, with Ruth on her deathbed, Jonathan calls mentally to David and he returns. For a few weeks all three live happily although Ruth's illness worsens, and she notices "the mysterious need which united them, the fullness and joy wherewith each completed himself in the other." After Ruth's death, the brothers resume living as they had before Ruth's appearance, walking hand in hand, sleeping in the same bed, sharing the same wardrobe. Jonathan's children call David father. The twins talk of "our Ruth," and look forward to the time when "death will make them one when at the same moment he summons both."[104]

"Twin Love" can be viewed as a carefully drawn expression of and defense against homosexuality. There is no reason to believe that Taylor intended it—or was even capable of seeing it—as such. However, in a passage deleted from his published letters, Taylor quoted August Bufleb, a German friend who accompanied him on an Egyptian expedition, as saying that Taylor's face "expressed all that he sought in his youth and never found in women."[105] Some time after the expedition, Taylor married his friend's niece.[106]

Whether Taylor himself was consciously attracted to homosexuality is unimportant. Genteel literature is marked by a persistent homosexual strain that is scarcely surprising in view of the strictures against the portrayal of heterosexual experience. Of course the strain is disguised and almost unconscious. The genteel treatment of the homosexual theme confirms the pattern of sexuality that is to be found in the official or public views of genteel culture and in its private or pornographic views. In all cases, woman is fixed in a sexually passive, which is to say inferior, role.

Toward the end of the nineteenth century as the woman suffrage movement became an issue of national concern, genteel culture reacted with predictable fright. Had it been better acquainted with the motives of the suffragettes, it might well have sympathized with them as Curtis, alone in his circle, did.[107] As it was, Taylor's views were typical of the genteel position. In his novel *Hannah Thurston*, Taylor's thinly veiled spokesman Maxwell Woodbury says that "Woman is too finely organized for the hard, coarse business of the world, and it is for her own sake that man desires to save her from it. He stands between her and human nature in the rough." "Can woman refine human nature by gaining the vote?" asks Hannah, an advocate of women's rights. "On the contrary," replies Woodbury, "it would drag her down to unutterable depths. If woman had the right of suffrage there would be less swearing among the rowdies at the polls, the first time they voted, but at the end of five years both sexes would swear together. . . . She would soon either be driven from the field, or brought down to the same level. Nay, she would go below it, for the rudest woman would be injured by associations through which the most refined man might pass unharmed."

Taylor believed that the woman suffrage movement offered a threat to men as well as women. Explicitly defending the value of male aggressiveness against a feminizing culture, Taylor has Woodbury appeal to fixed laws for the sexes. Although the human race is improving, Woodbury argues, "between the natures of the sexes there is a gulf as wide as all time. The laws by which each is governed are not altogether arbitrary; they have grown, age after age, out of that difference in mental and moral development." Whatever is, is not always right, Woodbury continues, "but you may be sure there is no permanent and universal relation founded on error. You would banish profanity, excesses, brute force from among men, would you not? Have you ever reflected that these things are distorted forms of that energy which has conquered the world? Mountains are not torn down, rivers bridged, wildernesses subdued, cities built, states founded, and eternal dikes raised against barbarism by the eaters of vegetables and drinkers of water! Every man who is worth the name possesses something of the coarse, original fiber of the race."[108] Woodbury is not defending capitalism, of course, but civilization; yet Taylor gives him a nice understanding of the support for both.

Besides her refinement, woman suffered other disabilities as a political being. In "Mrs. Strongitharm's Report" Taylor pictured women legislators as uninformed, gullible prey to lobbyists. One woman says she "always skipped the dry, stupid stuff about the tariff, and finance, and stay laws and exemption laws, and railroad company squabbles; and for the life of me I can't see to this day, what connection there is between these things and Women's Rights." Also, Mrs. Strongitharm's colleagues do not really want to be in politics. Once they win the right of suffrage, they lose interest in exercising it, and refuse to go to the elections if they become delegates, pleading the excuses of canning, darning and other housework.[109]

Unfortunately for politics but fortunately for domesticity, woman's nature was susceptible to the influences of men. The "superior reason" of men gave them "a vast power which most women do not understand."[110] In politics, male superiority could be put to base ends, but in love all was resolved. No matter how strong-minded a woman, her instincts outran her ideas; her ideas ran wild only because her heart was unsatisfied. Love would make "short work" of theories about human rights.[111]

When Taylor spoke of love, he meant marriage, of course. For him the purest life was wedded life; "the best of Christians are fathers and mothers."[112] In marriage, woman found her career, wholly absorbing her energies in the manifold duties of domesticity. Women who did not like cooking or sewing received scant sympathy from Taylor. "We have already a sufficient crop of young women," he observed, "who turn their wholesome necessity of household duties into a piteous aesthetic *Weltschmerz* —to say nothing of the young men who feed their own vanity by calling labor degrading, and lamenting over the deterioration of their souls, whenever they must earn their bread."[113]

In her marriage, too, woman must accept a definitely subordinate position. To Woodbury in *Hannah Thurston* "the relation of protector was indispensable; the rudest blows of life must first fall upon his shield. The idea of independent strength, existing side by side with his, yet without requiring its support, was unnatural and repulsive."[114] Woodbury is a sufficiently sensitive and intelligent man to grant to Hannah her independence in their marriage. The novel ends, however, with Hannah begging her husband to take back her independence; she loves him and that is enough for her.

Taylor's arguments against woman suffrage are typical of those advanced by opponents of the movement both within the genteel group and outside it. The anti's were agreed, as Gilder told a meeting of the National League for the Civic Education of Women in 1908, that the home and the family were "the foundations of the best things that humanity has yet achieved." The suffragists represented "a new, insidious and possibly disastrous attack upon the fundamentals of civilization."[115] Yet George William Curtis, the respected editor of *Harper's Weekly*, did not share the fears of his genteel friends. Although Curtis was too individualistic before the Civil War to support the suffrage movement or any other political movement, he later reversed himself and gave numerous speeches championing the cause of woman suffrage.[116]

The Civil War brought to high tide Curtis's belief in natural rights, and thereafter he could see no reason why women should be grouped with idiots and criminals in being barred from the franchise.[117] Using phrases such as "traditional prejudice" and "mere sentimentality," Curtis dismissed objections to woman suffrage that were based on conventional conceptions of the nature of women. "There is no more reason that men should assume to decide participation in politics to be unwomanly," he observed, "than that women should decide for men that it is unmanly. It is not our prerogative to keep women feminine." He did not by any means deny that female nature was different from male. In fact, he hoped that women would provide a conscience in politics. "If we would purge politics," he said, "let us turn upon them the great stream of the purest human influence we know."[118] Curtis was scornful of panicky men who conjured up the vision of "a mighty exodus of the whole female world, in bloomers and spectacles, from the nursery and kitchen to the polls." Their fear seemed to be, he said, that the home would be left a "howling wilderness of cradles and a chaos of undarned stockings and buttonless shirts."[119] He frankly appealed to women to enter politics as a means of protecting the values of the home and family, not of altering them. Legislative issues he thought women competent to deal with were political issues that were also moral issues—fraud and corruption, hospitals, tenements, prisons, gambling, drunkenness, prostitution.

Curtis himself had good reasons for looking to women as political allies. The genteel reformers and the suffragettes made similar diagnoses of the ills of American politics; both were naive enough to hope for the restoration of political virtue by the reintroduction of conscience into government. As it turned out, the adoption of the merit system for political recruitment and the extension of the franchise to women were scarcely radical in effect. In their common concern for the preservation of what they thought were traditional American values, neither movement actually questioned the existing social and economic structure. Because the suffrage movement did not threaten the principle of the division of labor that had confined women to the home in the first place, it proposed nothing that would endanger middle-class family structure or measurably alter women's role within it.

In supporting the suffrage movement, Curtis understood what the genteel poets did not, that its aims were as conservative as theirs. The suffrage movement was not a step toward the sexual emancipation of women. Curtis's actions in its behalf confirmed and did not question the genteel pattern of sexuality. In sex, just as in politics and in art, genteel creativity arose from the one emotion it truly felt, fear. The poet's dark world was the inner world of genteel culture.

Exit Religion

FOR ALL their disillusionment with the real world, the genteel authors were never much interested in turning toward the supernatural for solace. They were sentimentally nostalgic about the religious certainty of past generations, but they cared only that much. Religion was always just an appurtenance of the comfortable and cultured world in which the genteel group moved. In youth they had had their brush with orthodoxy, but later they found it irrelevant. In maturity they forgot it and rested easy in the superiority of their own religious liberalism. They occasionally worried over religious issues, but their worries were mainly personal, not social. At best religion offered private reassurance and meaning.

For all of the group but Norton, the origins of genteel religion were synonymous with anti-Puritanism. In *The Story of a Bad Boy*, Aldrich gave a typical view of the dreary New England Sabbath.[1] Stoddard, always more antagonistic toward the Puritan spirit than Aldrich, recalled that in his early life at Hingham, Massachusetts, his relatives and their friends actually looked forward to dying. It seemed to be "the most laudable industry of the time," he remarked.[2] Stoddard carried his attitude over into literature; both he and Boker avoided religious themes in their poetry. Boker undoubtedly agreed when Stoddard said that from an early age he "could never endure religious verse...."[3] Aldrich felt the same way. He described George Washington

Cable as "speckled all over with the most offensive piety. He drools religion...."[4]

In his courting days in the early 1860's, Aldrich expressed a simple faith in the love of God and a piousness that was not shared by his friends.[5] But he, like they, had already moved beyond a belief in preachers, forms, or creeds.[6] They agreed that the way man lived was more important than what he believed.[7] Aldrich called his religion the "New Faith." Praising Stedman's book on the widely known liberal pastor O. B. Frothingham, he said Frothingham's church was the only one worth attending and declared he would join it if he lived in New York.[8]

Genteel religion had little theology. Stoddard confessed to Stedman's mother in 1867 that he had not been a "bit of a Christian" for years.[9] He and Boker called their beliefs "the new religion" and were smug about its superiority over the older "prejudices."[10] Boker had acquired a hearty contempt for orthodox religion when he attended Princeton from 1838 to 1842. The restrictiveness of the conservative Presbyterians who controlled the school pushed him in the opposite direction, and he became a convinced rationalist. Among his favorite writers were Condorcet, Voltaire, Juvenal, Boccaccio, and Rabelais.[11] Once his adolescent inquiry had exhausted itself, Boker was uninterested in religion. He praised the pantheism of Stoddard's poetry, but probably only for the irritation it caused the orthodox.[12] Theology figured in his long sonnet sequence only as an obstacle.[13]

Taylor's religion was less negative in intent, but he, too, had little theology. He always believed that nature showed evidence of some "informing and directing Will"; Darwin did not shake him from that.[14] He did not believe, at first, in the Unitarian doctrine that Christ was a man.[15] In time his Unitarianism became more evident, and in his last and major works it was marked. After the Civil War as Taylor searched for the middle way, he thought the question of religion transcended all others in importance. "Merely *negative* argument will not answer;" he wrote, "very few human souls can accept it, and then through their own inherent power, lift themselves upon *positive* ground." He even conceded the usefulness of orthodoxy; "nine-tenths of the morality we have (such as it is—but we cannot spare it) comes through that doctrine."[16]

Taylor's tolerance of orthodoxy was undoubtedly backtracking, but it never threatened his liberal religious principles. In *The Masque of the Gods*, the first of three religious plays he wrote in the last decade of his life, Taylor presented a naturalistic explanation for religion. Men have torn the mask from the face of the gods, he maintained, "to find the mock of the face of Man." But the gods were not just men's creations; they were also dim perceptions of some unknown and supreme God, whom Taylor called "A Voice From Space." Influenced by nineteenth-century evolutionary theories, Taylor saw a progressive development in religion through historical time. He believed that Christ was the highest manifestation of the religious spirit yet to appear, the only begotten son of the true God. But he added that Christ himself was not perfect and would be superseded in time. The play ended on the confident note "that in some riper time Thy perfect Truth shall come." The Christian religion would give way to the "*over*christian."[17]

In 1874 Taylor published a second religious drama, *The Prophet*.[18] Some controversy attended this play because of its obvious criticism of the Mormons, which Taylor minimized publicly but admitted privately.[19] The crisis of the play presents the institution of plural marriage as a tragedy. In an attempt to resist it, the Prophet's wife, a good and pure creature, searches her Bible in vain.[20] Mrs. Taylor's notes to the play reinforce a point that the play itself makes clear: Taylor's attack on religious literalism applied as well to orthodox Protestants as to Mormons.[21]

Prince Deukalion (1878) was Taylor's *magnum opus*. The play derives from classical mythology. Deukalion, the human representative of Prometheus, longs for the return of Prometheus's spirit to earth. In Act I, set in A.D. 300, man rejects nature. Christianity has replaced beauty, grace, and joy with "atoning pain and crowned repentance."[22] In Act II, set in the time of Dante, the slight cheer Deukalion finds in Dante's "scarcely self-confessed ambition" to be a poet is overshad-

owed by the apathy of his world.[23] Not until the romantic period
of the nineteenth century, the setting for Act III, does man again
exult in nature. He finds joy in the world, pride in the mind,
strength to forget the ill and to work for the good, freedom to
seek dreams, and patience to find truth and eternal beauty.

Yet the nineteenth century suffers from two inhibiting influences. One is dogmatic religion with its inherited passivity and
otherworldliness, and the other is science.[24] In his play Taylor
forces science to concede that the absence of proof is no deterrent
to a belief in the doctrine of immortality. The hope of eternal
life, he says in closing his play, is no "unproven solace" but

> Proven by its need!—
> By fates so large no fortune can fulfill;
> By wrong no earthly justice can atone;
> By promises of love that keep love pure;
> And all rich instincts, powerless of aim,
> Save chance, and time, and aspiration wed
> To freer forces, follow! By the trust
> Of the chilled Good that at life's very end
> Puts forth a root, and feels its blossom sure!
> Yea, by the law!—since every being holds
> Its final purpose in the primal cell,
> And here the radiant destiny o'erflows
> Its visible bounds, enlarges what it took
> From sources past discovery, and predicts
> No end, or, if an end, the end of all![25]

Taylor's *Prince Deukalion* closes on a very strong note of positive religion. We *must* have immortality, Taylor wrote in 1877,
a year before his death. "If there is no future for me, a Devil,
and not a God, governs the universe."[26]

Like Taylor, Aldrich was troubled about religion and especially about immortality. While editor of the *Atlantic* in the
1880's, he enforced a moratorium on religious questions. He rejected or asked authors to revise manuscripts that would have
offended readers with traditional religious views.[27] He discouraged religious speculation on insoluble questions. It was useless
to ponder whether God was good, he wrote to Horace Scudder
in 1882.[28] He agreed with Tennyson's statement that "there lies

more faith in honest doubt, believe me, than in half the creeds."
Tennyson had "summed up the whole matter" to his satisfaction, and it needed no repeating.[29] Always regretful that the conviction of New England had disappeared, Aldrich envied his
grandfather's "unquestioning faith." "He used to read a big
Bible covered with rough green baize," Aldrich wrote, "and believed every word he read, even the typographical errors."[30]
Even Stoddard, for all his hatred of the Puritans, thought old-
time religion had been a comfort to the people and wished that
"such hope, such certainty, such rest be ours."[31]

But Aldrich and Stoddard agreed that almost all religious
belief was conjectural. The frontier at which Taylor's religion
halted, the doctrine of the immortality of the soul, gave them
pause, but did not deter either man. Aldrich frankly admitted
that nothing could be known about "the other side of death,"[32]
and when his son became fatally ill in 1903, his doubts were
strengthened.[33] The death of a friend in 1899 depressed Stoddard
similarly. "God rest his soul, if he has a soul, and there be a
God," he wrote.[34] The disillusionment they felt when faced
with the possibility that there was no God and no immortality
was summed up by Aldrich:

> Valor, love, undoubting trust,
> Patience, and fidelity
> Lie beneath this carven stone.
> If the end of these be dust,
> And their doom oblivion,
> *Then is Life a mockery.*[35]

Almost every figure in the genteel group was willing at least
to toy with the idea that life was indeed a mockery—every one,
that is, except Gilder. Youngest of all the group, he exemplified
the final attempt of genteel culture to resuscitate traditional religious views. Gilder's poems, his editorials in the *Century*, and
his letters frequently lapsed into a vapid optimism that was as
much softheaded as softhearted. He himself admitted as much
and explained it as an inheritance from his "ancestral orthodox
religionist strain." He thought that the Methodist Episcopalian-
ism of his father and the Huguenot strain in his mother's reli-

gious background had given him a certain complacency. "Un-
toward events surely cut me, depress me," he wrote in 1909, "but
a spirit of fatalism—an appreciation or apparent discernment in
events of a benevolent fate—has done much to keep me from
despair, even from overanxiety."[36] Gilder's confidence was
founded in his belief in the existence of a fundamental law that
manifested the divine plan. Throughout his life he clung tena-
ciously to that belief although he considered himself a religious
liberal. In 1894 he wrote to Helen Keller that he was a Christian
only in the broad sense that did not depend upon the "obfusca-
tions of theology." Nevertheless, perhaps theology had "its uses,
like the equator and other respectables."[37]

Gilder believed that God himself did not change, but that
man's perceptions of Him did. He hoped that what men saw as
a "Mysterious Force" in ancient times had been replaced by a
"friendlier plan."[38] Interpreting the evolution of religion in
what he thought was a Darwinistic fashion, Gilder argued in the
Century that it was nobler to think of God as coherent and logical than as capricious.[39] Gilder recognized that Darwin could
be read differently. Even in the midst of joy, as Gilder declared
in one of his poems, reflections on the cosmos were depressing.

> The awful void of space wherein our earth,
> An atom in the unending whirl of stars,
> Circles, all helpless, to a nameless doom;
> The swift, indifferent marshalling of fate
> Whereby the world moves on, rewarding vice
> And punishing angelic innocence
> As't were the crime of crimes; the brute,
>   dull, slow
> Persistence in the stifled mind of man
> Of forces that drive all his being back
> Into the slime; the silent cruelty
> Of nature, that doth crush the unseen soul
> Hidden within its sensitive shell of flesh;
> The anguish and the sorrow of all time,
> These are forever with me. . . .[40]

But Gilder hastened to conclude his poem by recalling his
mother's face, which reassured him that the right must reign

somewhere. The sentimentality of his conclusion makes suspect the "unescapable anguish" which, in another of his poems, he declared was the lot of mankind.[41]

Gilder repeatedly blamed scholars for his momentary doubts. They wearied him, he complained in "The Doubter"; they "hurt and bruised" his soul and confused his brain.[42] He decided to salvage his soul and his sanity by stifling his doubts on one fundamental issue—the divinity of Christ.[43] The pragmatic habit of mind increasingly appealed to Gilder as his convictions about the fundamental moral law wavered. Without ever explicitly denying the existence of such a law, he turned to speaking of the uses of religion. He suppressed his skepticism about the divinity of Christ by contending that Christ gave to existence a "reason sane."[44] Like Taylor, he asserted that Christianity could never be discarded because it provided an "aid to moral effort which no mere system of ethics, however evolved, claims to supply."[45] To think of Christ as a mere human being was for Gilder "the blackest thought the human brain may harbor."[46]

Gilder tried especially hard to discover a justification for the doctrine of immortality. In looking to the life principle itself for some basis for this belief, he seemed to reach toward philosophical idealism. But his justifications, unlike Royce's, were not rational; he felt that the heart could see where the mind could not. Because the human heart cried out, "Naught is but life," Gilder concluded that the force of its declaration implied there was truth in the feeling. Where reason could offer nothing, the heart maintained that life was immortal.[47] From this suggestion of immortality, Gilder did not deduce the traditional Christian heaven. From the nature of life exemplified on earth, Gilder felt that pain and suffering were inherent in it. Wherever there was life, on earth or beyond it, there would be pain. "For in all worlds," he wrote, "there is no Life without a pang, and can be naught." Adhering to the transcendental naturalism that characterized his discussion of the life principle, he avoided traditional theological explanations of evil. Pain was a simple fact of the human condition. Men, being what they were, could not comprehend happiness without sadness. The latter was the "eternal cost" of the former.[48]

There was neither joy nor conviction in Gilder's affirmations. They did not console him or save him from drifting into a passive agnosticism like that of his friends. He resisted more earnestly than they, but in 1905 he confessed that, despite all he had written, "if put on the rack of categorical questioning I fear I would prove a sad enough 'agnostic.'" His particular dilemma was that the "old leaven" of his fathers lurked in his mind and his heart. The New England cosmology went deep, and Gilder admitted that he could not help thinking "in and with" its symbols.[49]

The other genteel poets discovered their symbols elsewhere. The natural life, not the supernatural, attracted them. Yet even nature, once an avenue to the divine, had lost its ability to comfort. Stoddard and Taylor, like Stedman, agreed that Wordsworth's vision of the brotherhood of man and nature aptly described only immature life. Stoddard was impressed with Wordsworth's "Ode on Intimations of Immortality." He sketched his own childhood delight in nature: "The gush of feelings, pure and undefiled,/ The deep and rapturous gladness./ The nameless sadness,/ The vision that overpowered the visionary child." In adulthood, too, his life was "blent" with nature's. "The soul of man detects and sympathizes/ With its old shapes of matter, long outworn;/ And matter, too, to new sensations born,/ Detects the soul of man with spiritual purposes."[50] But in 1870, disregarding the fact that he had written a good deal of it, Stoddard complained that he did not like nature verse. "God made the country—well, what of it?.... I am not a bird, or a fish, as far as I know, and I want to see men, houses, streets, and I want fresh newspapers and books, old and new. I want the feel of the pavement under my feet, and sight of the multitudinous life of cities before my eyes."[51]

Nevertheless, Stoddard did not stop praising nature and criticizing city life after 1870.[52] His early objections to Calvinist theology remained with him all his life in the form of a pantheistic identification of God and nature. Despite his strong religious skepticism, he never quite shook off the belief that nature was a source of truth and morals and an object of beauty.[53] But Stoddard knew, as Stedman had written in *The Nature and*

Elements of Poetry, that nature did not participate sympathetically in human sentiment and passion. The belief that it did was only a "pathetic fallacy," said Stedman, using Ruskin's term. The poet must see that "the chances of life seem much at haphazard.... Rain still falls upon the just and the unjust.... The natural law appears the wind of destiny. Man, in his conflicts with the elements, with tyranny, with superstition, with society, most of all with his own passions, is still frequently overthrown. It *seems* as if the good are not necessarily rewarded except by their own virtue, or, if self-respecting, except by their own pride, holding to the last; the evil are not cast down, unless by their own self-contempt, and the very evil flourish without conscience or remorse.... Thus Nature, in her drama, has no temporary pity, no regret."[54]

Toward the end of his life Stedman expressed this view in a rather striking image from the animal world. On one occasion he pictured nature as a lioness who batters man playfully at first, but "soon shows she means business" and smashes him. The lioness is as little concerned with her victim as the blacksmith at the anvil, or the potter at the wheel. Nature—"so resolute, so implacable, the unnatural Mother"—cared only for the species, not the individual.[55] But man did have some sort of a "true and spiritual rapport" with Nature, and therefore it was "just as well" that some should cling to the belief in a sympathetic universe. The force of emotion dictated it, and feeling was perhaps truer and deeper than thought.[56]

Stedman and his friends, though they occasionally voiced romantic complaints about life in the city, were city men at heart. Their experience had not prepared them to see rural and small-town America as places of emotional impoverishment, a conception that dominated American literature after 1910, but neither had it prepared them to write the traditional romantic praise for nature that is sometimes evident in their poetry. There, where metaphors suggesting peacefulness, unselfishness, and creativity are repeatedly invoked, nature figures as little more than a refuge from the city. Even when the genteel group elaborated its myth of a pure and homogeneous rural populace in pre-Jacksonian days, it confined the potency of nature to the past.

American religion did assimilate the Darwinian concept of evolution and survive, but for the genteel poets, at least, the romantic view of nature could not. The loss was crucial for them because in their own intellectual development nature had assumed many of the traditional functions of religion. Stoddard, for one, could no longer be reassured. Faced with the fact that man was a transient being, Stoddard came to believe that nature, far from being a repository for certitudes, was just as transient as man himself.[57] Obsessed with this belief, Stoddard devoted poem after poem to the prospect of death. "For what was Earth but the great tomb of men, / And suns and planets but sepulchral urns / Filled with the awful ashes of the Past?"[58]

If Stoddard's gloom was especially acute, he was not alone in it. All the genteel poets clung to romanticism without the support they once had had in nature. The eighteenth century had found comfort in the fact that nature, even if cold and mechanical, was unchanging by virtue of the eternal laws that controlled it. But the genteel poets followed the romantics of the early nineteenth century in seeking to humanize the mechanical universe by projecting human passions into it. From their success, Stoddard in particular reaped bitter fruit. He had made nature human, but as a consequence, he had made it mortal. Nature now, like men, suffered under the sentence of death; the cycle of the seasons lost its dignity. The order of nature was evidence of truth, yes, but of the truth that there was only one truth—death. The very unification of nature and man achieved by romanticism bred new alienation.

For as Stoddard's age enforced clarity of vision upon him he knew that the differences, not the similarities, between men and nature were what counted. Stoddard had preached the rich and full life; he had meant the individual life. From birth he had been temperamentally unable—although he tried repeatedly—to understand that a general law possessed dignity precisely because it was general and spared no individual. That Stoddard agonized over death, and nature did not, was all that mattered. For consolation he turned to Stoicism. He found in Marcus Aurelius an awareness that human life was "worthless" and the entire universe nothing more than "ebb and flow."[59] Ironically, the romantic rebel came to advise men to retire into themselves to find "the seat of all tranquility." Rest, not emotional intensity, was Stoddard's final goal in life. Deliberately, he put behind him the activity of his youth, and turned instead to "the good ordering of the mind."[60]

Although Aldrich and Boker were free of Stoddard's funereal tone, the transience of existence suggested to them also that whatever meaning tradition had brought to life had largely vanished. In a world of constant and undefined change, certainties were few. The gods were vague, they believed, and the purposes of existence entirely conjectural. Furthermore, if one believed that no new knowledge would show the way to truth— and certainly the new science had not done so—one necessarily became pessimistic. As man matured, it was his portion to suffer this disillusionment. As Aldrich wrote to a friend in 1904, "When one is young, one doesn't know any better than to be happy."[61] Forty years earlier, too, he had been convinced that knowing human nature meant knowing sorrowful things.[62] Stoddard summed the matter up in *The King's Bell* by permitting the bell of happiness to ring only at the hour of death. The King declares:

> Happy, alas, who's happy here on earth?
> Why man is wretched from his very birth.
> Frail as a flower's his hold on life, none know
> Whether the human bud will fade or flow;
> For hours on hours his lips are sealed in sleep,
> And when at last he wakes—it is to weep.[63]

Aldrich was well aware of the doubt and pessimism that marked the end of the nineteenth century.[64] But neither he nor his friends would have permitted any mere historical explanation for their pessimism. They would have insisted that it transcended time and place. Against the cosmic optimism that Royce attempted to revive in their day, they maintained that however good human life might be, there was profound sorrow in human existence. They were conservative enough to believe that the conditions that made for progress or retrogression did not touch that fact. Elizabeth Stoddard, who was more extreme in her sentiments that her husband's friends, was also more candid. Her analysis was simple. "Oh my God," she wrote to Stedman, "what an awful blunder life is, worse than a crime."[65]

Neither extreme of genteel religious thinking, the attempt of Taylor and Gilder to prop up the traditional idealism nor the decline of Stoddard and his circle into an emasculating pessimism upon finding nature indifferent to them, made any contribution to the theological controversies of the 1880's and 1890's. The genteel group had little contact with the Social Gospel movement to turn Protestantism from a religion of personal and private concern into a religion of moderate social action. Although reformers like Washington Gladden, Richard Ely, and Theodore T. Munger occasionally wrote for the *Century,* the religious liberalism of genteel culture remained within the economically and socially conservative Unitarian church.[66]

Charles Eliot Norton, always his own man, is an exception here, too. A rationalist by training and conviction, Norton was never tempted by emotional or intuitive appeals for the preservation of traditional religion. But neither did he permit his own doubts to interfere with what he regarded as the self-evident obligations of men toward one another. Uninterested in what interested the genteel poets, nature, and interested in what did not interest them, science, Norton was able to relinquish the one and base his hopes for the future on the other.

In the middle of the nineteenth century Norton's social and political ideas rested on a belief in a fundamental moral law. But Norton did not look to nature for evidence of the fundamental law. In fact, he pointedly distinguished the sphere of nature, where the laws of scientific determinism held, from the sphere of man, which was free and self-determined. Norton never explored the source and nature of the moral law and the manner in which men perceived it. The topic would have struck him as too metaphysical, and, like his friends, he had a prejudice against abstract philosophy. He preferred a philosophy like Santayana's that turned "speculative inquiry to moral ends—in other words to the uses of life."[67] Yet he rejected William James's pragmatism. Norton apparently misread James, for he thought pragmatism worth "just about as much as the systems of metaphysical speculation which have preceded it...."[68] He did not understand that for all James's efforts to legitimitize the will to believe, James was no more interested in theology for its own sake than he was. Both men searched for a morality that could be founded only in human experience.

Norton was reared as a Unitarian. His father was a famous minister of the pre-War period and a fierce opponent of Emerson. Charles was no lover of Transcendentalism either; he dismissed it as a lot of muddled thinking. But by 1867 he was willing to say of Unitarianism what Emerson had said thirty years before, that the Unitarian protest against dogma and creed had nearly done its work and was in danger itself of "hardening" into a church. "The deepest religious thought," Norton wrote, "the wisest religious life is outside of Unitarianism at present, is not to be found, indeed, within the limit of any churches." Any conformity of doctrine whatsoever, he thought, must be abandoned. "We must have a free Church, to which all who are seeking the highest and best they know, and are trying to express their highest convictions in life, may come and be welcomed on equal terms, whether they call themselves Unitarians or Trinitarians, Christians or unbelievers."[69]

What Norton had in mind was a kind of moral society. If men were to have "utter freedom of individual opinion," common ideas could not be the basis for organization because no creed was broad enough for any two men. He admitted that his ideas were open to the charge that they failed to distinguish between religion and morality. And he admitted that religious and moral duties were "often indistinguishable." But he thought that religion was a "matter of absolute requirements; morals is a science and practice of the higher expediency."[70]

Norton's notion of moral expediency was not meant to conflict with the idea of a fundamental moral law. It simply restated his conviction that morality must devote itself to social concerns. Norton's free church would be a loose fellowship of all men for developing the religious character of the community and for "inspiring and regulating active efforts for the improvement of man." It would apply the spirit of religion to the difficulties of society. Its work would be "practical humanity."[71]

In another sense, Norton meant something revolutionary by moral expediency. Until the end of the nineteenth century Norton was unable to free himself from the typical Victorian and genteel belief that morality depended on organized religion. His arguments for a free church questioned it, certainly, but in 1875 he thought that the liberality of his own ideas would be a danger to America if widespread. Unlike England, where the aristocracy afforded "a fixed standard in the midst of the fluctuations of personal convictions or popular emotions," America had to rely upon extragovernmental organizations like the church for social order.[72] Yet in 1869 Norton had written to Ruskin that if a man in America were persecuted for atheism, he should "feel bound to declare myself on his side." The question of the existence of God had to be regarded as an open one, he felt, "and as one *which had no intrinsic relation with moral character*. I believe an Atheist may be as good, as enlightened, as unselfish, and may conduct his whole life from motives as pure, and under sanctions as strong as a Theist."[73] In 1897 Norton finally made himself clear. Casting aside all nostalgia for the past, he declared that "the loss of religious faith among the most civilized portion of the race is a step from childishness toward maturity." He had no fear for the morality of the race. "Our morals seem to me the result and expression of the *secular experience of mankind*. As such they have a solid foundation."[74]

When Norton spoke of morals as the "higher expediency" he meant that they ought to be calculated by means of liberal rationalism. He defended Bentham's utilitarian system against the attacks of Sir Henry Maine. He believed that Bentham's utility principle had to be weighed against customs ideas, and motives, but, granted that, he would apply it not only to laws but to morals as well. He admitted that there were difficulties in determining the objective happiness of a people, but insisted that utilitarianism was the best way. There was no such thing as "*absolute*" morality, he wrote in 1875.

What had happened to the fundamental moral law? During the Civil War, Norton had been certain that man was subject to "the purposes of God in the creation of the world." He had denied the Positivistic assumption that social laws could be discovered that would explain man's actions. Man was a "higher power" than the nature that surrounded him. Free men's actions were the stuff of history; although men were subject to "moral connections," they were not bound by scientific causation.[75] But as Norton lost all interest in religion and grew increasingly worried about the state of civilization in America, he turned to science as his only hope for the future. By 1878 he wrote that "the thought of any who have any capacity for thought" was moving toward Positivism.[76] When he had rejected guesses about the beginning and end of existence as "altogether futile," he was ready (in 1902) to assert that human thought and action were explainable. "If we could collect enough knowledge," he wrote, "our faculties, as they at present exist, would be sufficient to enable us to account, I believe, for what is now inexplicable to us in human conduct."[77]

In the 1880's Norton had been depressed because "the whole view of human existence which the world has held up to this time seems to be changing, and the new view is not yet clearly outlined...." But he felt that although man would have fewer "glowing illusions" about himself, he would be more independent because of it.[78] He granted that the substitution of natural motives for supernatural ones would cause "considerable damage" to popular morality, but he thought eventually a "better order" would replace the "chaotic" and "unstable" civilization of the times.[79]

In explaining the radical transformation in his own views, Norton, like the genteel poets, gave major credit to Darwin. Darwin's recognition that nature was "clumsy, wasteful, blundering, low and horribly cruel" led Norton to believe that the moral process was no better.[80] "You expect less of men when you look at them not as a little lower than the angels, but as a little higher than the anthropoid apes."[81] He expected no comfort from a dead theology, but he was uneasy with the new cosmology.[82] Unlike the genteel poets, Norton seems genuinely to have wanted to accept life at it was. He could not always, however, resist the current pessimism. "The universe is unintelligible," he wrote in 1906. "We have no faculties for even forming rational theories concerning its nature, its origin or its purpose. Our words—"purpose,' for instance, have no significance in regard to it. Why should we, little atoms on a little atom, hope to account for our existence?"[83] He took grim comfort in recognizing "how absolutely insignificant and unimportant a part of the universe . . . is any individual life." In the teeth of the fact, he yet asserted that the aim of a good man should be "to make the best of himself for the service of others."[84] The sanctions for morality had collapsed, but men's needs allowed no argument.

Norton had been reared with deep respect for the New England tradition of public service. He was totally incapable of protesting the "despotism of citizenship" that so distressed the genteel poets. Although he would have substituted *Moral* for *Christian* he continued to believe, as Gilder put it in a speech in 1906, that whatever men "may believe or disbelieve in the realm of theology, [they] cannot doubt that bad citizenship is non-Christian."[85]

As a consequence, however, of relinquishing his belief in a fundamental moral law, Norton became all the more concerned with the immediate facts of American society, particularly American culture. In 1879 he wrote to an English friend that he felt "half starved" in America, but that he could be of more service there than in England.[86] By that time he had virtually given up any hope of improving American political or economic life, and he concentrated his efforts on raising the level of American culture. He thought that endeavor particularly important because he believed that culture was "the only real test of the spiritual qualities of a race, and the standard by which ultimately its share in the progress of humanity must be measured."[87] And in America more than elsewhere the arts were needed, "for nowhere in the civilized world are the practical concerns of life more engrossing; nowhere are the conditions of life more prosaic; nowhere is the poetic spirit less evident, and the love of beauty less diffused. The concern for beauty, as the highest end of work, and as the noblest expression of life, hardly exists among us, and forms no part of our character as a nation."[88] Norton emphasized that the tradition of culture had never been more than "weak" and "limited" in America.[89] But the decline of even that limited tradition after the Civil War led Norton to write to Ruskin that he wanted his Harvard students to realize that "we have in our days nothing to say, that silence befits us, that the arts of beauty are not for us to practice;—and seeing this to resolve so to live that another generation may begin to be happier than we."[90]

Norton did not doubt that the passage of time had made for some progress, but he questioned "whether the increase in knowledge and mastery of nature is to be counted as true progress.... Is there a moral advance at all in proportion to the material?"[91] He admitted that prosperity had made physical comfort more widespread but he felt that Americans tended to confuse the "free gift of nature" and the benefits of increased knowledge with personal talent and capacity. They claimed a "sense of mastery over the world and fate" that was not only optimistic, but fatalistic.[92]

And the spread of democracy, when added to prosperity, threatened to lower the moral standards of the republic "to the level of those whose moral sense is in their trowsers." Democracy did work, to be sure, but "ignobly, ignorantly, brutally," as well as in better ways.[93] In the short run, Norton did not hope for more, because he was deeply distrustful of democracy itself. When Cleveland's message on the Venezuelan boundary dispute was issued, Norton voiced his contempt for it in the course of a general broadside against democracy. "It is the rise of the uncivilized," he wrote to Leslie Stephen, "whom no school education can suffice to provide with intelligence and reason."[94] The American public was "becoming less open to any teaching but that of its own experience. The scorn of wisdom, the rejection of authority, are part and parcel of the process of development of the democracy.... It seems to me not unlikely that for a considerable time to come there will be an increase of lawlessness and of public folly."[95]

Technology and democracy had combined to widen the gulf between present and past, but Norton worried that no past was left at all.[96] It was the appalling newness of the modern world that overwhelmed him. It was no wonder, he thought, that the great majority of Americans were shallow, trivial, and materialistic. Too many Americans had come up in too short a time from the "lower orders of society" that were wholly oppressed, ignorant and servile.[97] Economic opportunity, as well as political and economic institutions, propelled the immigrant up the social ladder too rapidly for the good of the nation. Americans never got to feel the advantages and restraints of civilization, Norton complained; their virtues were not the civic virtues.

Norton did not look to the American educational system to remedy the shortcomings of American society. He believed it was only a fallacy to think that the schools could educate anyone; they could only give instruction. Without proper influence in the home and community, Norton expected the schools to do little.[98] He did approve of efforts to include cultural, as well as intellectual and moral, education within the curriculum.[99] He worried, despite his Positivism, that American education gave undue emphasis to mathematics and the physical sciences.[100]

Norton never stopped hoping that science might provide a direction for the future. Nevertheless, it is quite clear that the world of science, as it was developing in his day, repelled him. When a friend of his died in 1897, Norton wrote to E. L. Godkin, the editor of the *Nation*, that he considered himself "the solitary representative of a generation more interesting, and I cannot but think of far better breeding both intellectually and morally than that which takes it place. We have able and good men left, and perhaps they will do as good service as their predecessors, but they lack the breadth and charm of the elder generation. The old men represented the humanities, the young men stand for science so-called."[101] What Norton respected as science was the science of a man like John Stuart Mill, a man of wide reading and sensibility. He was notably unsympathetic to the professionalism that was establishing itself in American universities near the end of the century, whether that professionalism operated in science or in literature. He was frank to state his preference for the "old-fashioned literary culture" of the mid-nineteenth century.[102] He anticipated that posterity would look back to that time "as we look back to pre-Revolutionary times, as presenting a picture of delightful simplicity of manners and innocence of living."[103]

Unable by temperament to be enthusiastic about the Positivism to which he was intellectually committed, Norton nevertheless avoided the typical genteel extremes of self-pity and hypocrisy. Because he recognized and admitted the evisceration of the intellectual structure of genteel culture, he was left in the end with little to do but advocate the gentle civilizer, manners. He acknowledged the difficulty even of that limited endeavor, and could never have agreed with Gilder that gentility might cure not only the superficial ills of society, but its deeper evils.[104] Gilder, of course, continued to believe, or continued to wish to believe, in a fundamental moral law, whereas Norton did not. Without that reassuring frame, the enterprise of civilizing men could only be a hollow endeavor. Gentility, bereft of religion, could do little but amble to its own defense. Whatever vigor it once possessed, it finally forgot. There was no need to force genteel culture out of history; by 1910 it had no real resources left to contest the sentence of retirement.

Conclusion: A Genteel Endeavor

THE GENTEEL ENDEAVOR to create a unified culture for the enlightenment and civilization of America did not outlive its architects. The endeavor was, from the beginning, both too broad and too shallow to be sustained.

It was too broad in that the concept of culture from which it arose envisioned a comprehensive antidote for all the failings of American society. The gentleman-artist-scholar-statesman who exemplified that concept of culture belonged to a vanishing species, as the genteel group themselves admitted. Increasing specialization and professionalization—processes hastened, ironically enough, by the genteel journalists themselves—were already dissolving the links, once regarded as self-evident, that held the diverse ingredients of genteel culture together. The culture began to seem amorphous even to its spokesmen. It had its tendencies and its attitudes, but who could find its center or point to its dominant values? If Norton could not, no one could. Santayana tried, but his Genteel Tradition was more admirable as an intellectual construct than as a description of American culture. Nonetheless, Santayana's attempt was a near miss. Santayana was intellectually closer to Norton than has usually been thought. He wanted "the higher things of the mind" reinvigorated, but his commitment was definitely to them, not to the bustling lower world.

The genteel endeavor was as shallow as it was broad. Genteel culture was designed to dignify the upper classes and to elevate the middle classes; any effect on the rest of America would be incidental. The genteel writers firmly resisted attempts to extend their audience much beyond its size at mid-century. For them it was, among other things, a question of quality *versus* quantity. It is doubtful that they would have been able to attract large numbers of new readers even if they had tried. The new reading audience that developed at the turn of the century was interested in contemporary America, whereas genteel culture looked to the past. A new literature created for this audience not only undercut genteel culture, but robbed it of the chance to extend its influence.

Genteel culture was attacked on its home ground, too. A new generation of intellectuals plunged into new reform movements —Progressivism, the Social Gospel, woman suffrage, the creation of the modern American university—movements that were not hostile on principle, as the genteel reformers were, to the forces for change in nineteenth-century America: industrialization, urbanization, immigration. The genteel endeavor was consciously conservative in its principled hostility to the transformation of America. It was not this conservatism as such that caused potential adherents to fall away. Most significant contemporary reform movements were sympathetic with the conservative impulses of the genteel endeavor. Their leaders were not immune from the genteel anxieties about the instability of American society and its basic institutions. But they found a faith in science, in expertise, in bureaucracy, that the genteel writers could not find. And the genteel endeavor offered no persuasive alternative to the status quo—no means either of reversing the direction of social change or of moderating its effects. It offered none, simply, because it was unable to discover any stable institutions on which to base such an alternative. If from afar the genteel endeavor appeared arrogant in its certainty, from nearby it seemed vulnerable in its hollowness. In the institutions where intellectuals congregated, the enemies of genteel culture found their first foothold.

The charge of smugness so often leveled against genteel culture is a fair indictment only of its public face. Its private face was fear. Before the Civil War most of the genteel group sounded a youthfully optimistic note in their writings, but very soon they gave up any hope of effecting basic reforms in American culture. Thereafter their public role, the only role in which their critics knew them, was that of teacher and conserver. Disheartened even in this function, they narrowed the range of their attention to an increasingly trivial concern with manners, as their critics justly complained.

But the critics, as I have said, knew only the public face of genteel culture and did not suspect the extent to which public optimism functioned as a compensation for private pessimism. Letters and parts of letters were systematically excluded from authorized nineteenth-century biographies as much because they revealed moments of sadness and discontent as because they referred to sexual matters. With access to these letters, we can see the leaders of genteel culture more intimately than they ever intended to be seen. We find them a group of men deeply dissatisfied with American culture and with their own art, but unable or unwilling to understand the sources of their own dissatisfaction. America was, as they insisted, too new, too raw, too provincial, to offer a setting for a sophisticated culture. And the forces of industrial change after the Civil War offered little prospect for cultural improvement. But the genteel artists without exception failed to understand the degree to which their concept of culture was shaped by the conditions of their professions. It was the way they made their living, above all, that hampered their understanding.

Except for Boker (and he had his ties to the Philadelphia magazines) all of the men discussed in this book were influential in shaping and prospering from the golden age of American magazines. But they paid a higher price than they realized for the profit and prestige they enjoyed. As their own situation showed, the artist in America was moving into a new and not entirely desirable relationship with society. American society had no aristocracy to which the artist might look for financial support or for artistic encouragement. There were men of wealth in America, of course, but they seemed to be less interested in fostering art than at least part of the European aristocracy. Finding no other source of support, the American artist was obliged to write for a middle-class audience. In order to do otherwise, he would have had to expatriate himself. He often did. Since the genteel authors did not, they were obliged either to celebrate the values of middle-class society or to provide acceptable alternatives to them. The moralistic and sentimental domestic novel, typically written by women, illustrates the former alternative; the escapist literature of the genteel authors, the latter.

Because the genteel artists had neither the originality nor the courage to find their own way, they did not resist the profit and prestige that American magazines offered; they agreed to provide a literature for middle-class society. In private, however, the genteel authors nourished from the start a cult of poetry that was a protest against the rise of the middle classes to cultural power.[1] It was pathetic that the genteel artist should compensate for the declining quality of his audience by exalting himself and his poetry to virtually divine rank. Yet this is precisely what happened. Behind the literary idealism that united the genteel group lay their continued commitment to poetry as the noblest of arts. Aldrich's reputation rested on his fiction and Taylor's on his travel accounts, but they, like all the rest of the group, were proudest of their poetry. None of them was sympathetic to the realism that Howells, Twain, and James were developing into a new literary genre. They found Howells too much concerned with the dull commonplace, Twain too colloquial and racy, and James simply too depressing. They could accommodate Howells and moderate Twain, which they did, but they could not deal with James; they were always insensitive to the greatest American artist of their day.

In pursuit of their initial literary goal, art for art's sake, they tried only to introduce into America an already dated English romanticism. Because this derivative verse prospered, they had no incentive for innovation either in art or in publishing. Their imitative poetry was little more than ornament. Untouched by life, it could be threatened only by a challenge to its traditionally favored position in literature. The rise of realism and the realistic novel offered just such a challenge. Realism was hotly debated not so much because the novel jeopardized the popularity of poetry, but because the novelist, by his use of realism, deflated the traditional image of the artist, and thus of poetry as the noblest of the arts. His pretensions to divine genius had consoled the genteel artist for having to write for an inferior audience. Stripped of those pretensions, he had nothing but his talent on which to base his self-esteem. Rather than face the limitations of that talent, he retired from the present and looked back to a day when things were otherwise.

In its social thought as well as its literature and criticism, gentility represented a withdrawal from contemporary life. The genteel group were not disinterested in politics *per se*, but even when they were active as reformers, they exhibited a marked disdain for the political life. They especially liked the rather unpolitical notion of the scholar in politics, applying to particular circumstances a code of unchanging morals.

This belief in the existence of an eternal moral law deprived the genteel reformers of an incentive to develop a specific body of political principles. The genteel writers had plenty of principles (they aspired to them in all things), but their thought was often unsystematic and disorderly. To the extent, however, that they did share any basic political idea, it was the idea of an organic society. They believed that society grew and was not formed, that its members, whatever their rights as individuals, were bound to each other by mutual responsibility, and that under ordinary circumstances the government had a positive obligation to provide for the public welfare.

Of the two competing political theories in late-nineteenth-century America, Spencerian laissez-faire and the regulatory state, the genteel group subscribed to neither, but was closer to the latter than to the former. Its own tradition of positive government was an older one, and can be traced back to Whiggery, and from there back through the Federalists to the Puritans. Histories of American political theory so frequently center on liberalism and individualism that it is interesting to find at least a minority tradition supporting paternalistic, centralized government.

The origins of genteel literature were almost identical with the origins of American individualistic romanticism, but this individualism is not incompatible with genteel political theory. The major impulse of the American romantic revolt (as it is reflected in genteel literature) was to assert that human nature could not be measured, weighed, and fenced in the ways that Puritan theology and Transcendental reformism had attempted. The romantic revolt, although it aimed in a broad sense at liberating the human spirit, cannot be called a liberal revolt in any political sense; its concern was too exclusively with the spirit, and not the body, for that. It was essentially Emersonian, with all of Emerson's ambiguities toward liberalism and conservatism. As time passed, its vision of the free soul did not entirely disappear, but was transformed into a pragmatic bias and a dislike for systematic theologies, philosophies, and politics. At no period in their lives can the genteel authors, except for Norton, be viewed as men who saw human nature as an abstraction subject to scientific laws. Human nature, for them, remained something ultimately undefinable and subject only to moral laws.[2]

American intellectuals have often been charged with shallow and unsystematic thinking, and the genteel intellectuals are no exception. The avoidance of dogmatism that is a virtue in Emerson becomes in genteel thought a definite vice, one that did not go unremarked in its own day. In their own defense, the genteel authors pled the difficulty of maintaining a consistent belief system in the face of constant change. Stedman spoke for the group when he summed up their age as an age of transition, a transition induced by industrialism. When the genteel authors became aware of the enormity of the changes going on around them, then the organic element in their social thought became most evident. When, for instance, they saw capitalism rupturing traditional social bonds and its spokesmen producing a theory to justify the disintegration of what remained of the organic state, the genteel authors turned back to theories appropriate to that vanishing state. In the world of John Quincy Adams they found their social ideals of homogeneity and cooperation.

The deep sense of alienation that marked *The Education of Henry Adams* was also, if not in the same way, characteristic of Adams's genteel contemporaries. It was only when they were young that they were full of confidence in the future of their nation. Then, even the Civil War, instead of being a shock to them, became a symbol of the moral superiority of the American nation. They did not mean by their emphasis on the uniqueness of America to deny that universal moral principles existed. On the contrary, they saw the Civil War as an attempt to assert, for the first time in history, a universal moral law. In the disillusioning aftermath of the War, the genteel group abandoned its belief in the uniqueness and superiority of America. But second thoughts about America did not invalidate the universal moral law; they merely meant that it must be more conservatively applied. A cautious attitude toward experience became the hallmark of the genteel mind.

It is ironic that the moralism so marked in the mature genteel mind was characteristic of the theological tradition against which the youthful genteel romantics had struggled. But the shadow of New England was a long one and the romantic revolt too short. From the New England theology came a world view that provided the genteel group with the necessary basis for its moral optimism. When the influence of science on religion cut away that structure, they were forced to salvage whatever standards they could.

In their youth the genteel writers accepted the view that philosophies were unnecessary in America because the future would invalidate them. They rejected the systems of Puritanism and Transcendentalism because they fixed man's nature, and the nature of man could not really be fixed in a still-fluid America. When the course of events set them to looking for answers to questions they had spurned before, they were in a hopeless position. They could not turn back to religion because they had almost forgotten it. And in ridding themselves of theology, they had given up the only tools they knew how to use for grappling with the modern world. Had they been able to reassert the theology of Puritanism and to combine it with Transcendentalism as Santayana thought Josiah Royce did, then they might have found in philosophical idealism a new set of sanctions for traditional values. But they did not make the step, and Santayana erred in suggesting that they did. Santayana's error was at least a logical one; if the genteel group were not philosophical ideal-

ists, they should have been. They were able to use Emerson and
James against the harshness of Calvinist theology, but they
could never have had any genuine affinities, except in despair,
with the relativisms of the modern world.

As the genteel authors drifted into a kind of agnosticism from
which they seemed incapable of emancipating themselves, their
intellectual discomfort became acute. Unable either to reassert
traditional cosmologies or to adopt newer ones, they tried to
discover in culture some basis for a defense of traditional values.
But culture could never answer fundamental questions, and to
expect that it could was an admission of intellectual bankruptcy.
Culture alone could never be an adequate justification for a set
of morals religious in origin. Theology had to be readmitted to
intellectual respectability if values were to be more than opinions. But with no acceptable rejuvenated theology in sight the
genteel writers lost faith in the rightness of their personal vision,
and their attention fell back on rectitude of conduct.

The genteel authors' eventual pervasive emphasis on manners
was an index of their intellectual degeneration. Gilder put the
matter more bluntly than most, but his friends would not have
put it very differently. For the introspective conscience of Puritanism, Gilder substituted moral taste. The man who possessed
this faculty would by definition be a gentleman. He would in-
stinctively know the proper course of action in all spheres of
conduct. It was true that gentlemen would no longer be born
gentlemen, but that is where culture came in—it would train
them up in the ways of moral taste.[3]

The substitution of culture for theology was clearly intended
by the genteel writers as a defense of traditional moral values.
Romantic from the first, they recognized that the development
of nineteenth-century romanticism led logically to the languid
and sophisticated aestheticism that was later called the fin de
siècle. And however attractive that movement might appear, it
seemed to the Americans to manifest the modern heresies of
subjectivism and relativism. Against these the genteel authors
threw up the bulwark of culture. They were realistic enough,
however, to sense that they could not stem the tide of modernity.
Their own intellectual position was too precarious, too ambigu-

ous, to be satisfying. So they withdrew emotionally from the modern world, and lapsed into pessimism.

There were others, however, whose pessimism had more fiber. In the world of upper-class Boston sketched in John P. Marquand's *The Late George Apley*, the hero, a perfect type of the genteel businessman, held firmly to his ways until after World War I. His marriage and his profession did not satisfy him, but he did not waver in defense of the interests of his class. He saw the world being transformed around him, but he did not doubt the superiority of inherited wealth and old family to the characteristics of the newer class of businessmen who were unimpressed by anything but money. Fortified by intricate family relationships that elicited the highest loyalty, Apley's world had to the end a fixed quality that, even if it was illusory, had more dignity than the world of the genteel writers. Outside his family Apley offered a proper face for the public, but he was no hypocrite. He knew what he stood for and why he stood for it. He could have been accused of confusing the interests of his family and his class with those of the public, but he knew that his accomplishments were tangible.

The world of nineteenth-century business was never so pure and genteel as Marquand imagined it. Even when disciplined by tradition, American capitalism was too vigorous to be confined for long by hereditary wealth and family ties. American culture, in contrast to American business, was too often a product of its own fears. In the hands of its genteel custodians, it was at best an endeavor, a genteel endeavor, to spread culture among the middle and upper classes. The attempt was earnest, but no more vigorous than politeness would permit. For all its pretensions to aristocracy, however, the world of genteel culture was further from it than the world of genteel business. Without either the money or the family ties of an Apley, the genteel writers were from the beginning creatures of a middle-class culture they half despised. They had considerable difficulty in persuading themselves that they were not serving an audience without taste. They talked of elevating their audience, but doing so would have meant elevating themselves. Had they been secure in their self-esteem, their pursuit of culture might not have been so pure and lofty—in their minds, prestigious—an undertaking. But because they knew well how they had engineered their own success, their pride could not have gone deep. The genteel authors did not lead or innovate; but they did not intend to. They merely controlled, for a time. They were significant because they were the architects of a culture that embodied conservatism in a threatening age.

Notes

Notes

Following is a list of the abbreviations that are used in the Notes. Authors' full names, complete titles, and publication data for all works appearing in short form in the Notes will be found in the Bibliography, pp. 221–27.

BPL   Boston Public Library
CUL   Columbia University Library
HLH   Houghton Library, Harvard University
LAAAL Library of the American Academy of Arts and Letters
NYPL   New York Public Library
PUL   Princeton University Library
YCAL   Yale Collection of American Literature

Chapter One

1. Wilson, pp. 39–40.

2. *Ibid.*, p. 73.

3. Noah Webster, *An American Dictionary of the English Language* (Springfield, Massachusetts: 1851); *The Century Dictionary and Cyclopedia* (New York: 1911); Eric Partridge, *A Dictionary of Slang and Unconventional English* (New York: 1938); *A New English Dictionary on Historical Principles* (Oxford: 1901).

4. Taylor, *At Home,* 1st Ser., p. 450.

5. Mark Van Doren, ed., *The Portable Walt Whitman* (New York: 1962), p. 422.

6. *Ibid.*, p. 446.

7. Brooks, *Coming-of-Age, passim.*

8. "Puritanism as a Literary Force," *A Book of Prefaces,* pp. 197–283.

9. *Main Currents in American Thought, passim.*

10. Sinclair Lewis, *Address before the Swedish Academy* (New York: 1930).

11. Pp. 239–47.

12. Pp. 455–58.

13. Malcolm Cowley, *After the Genteel Tradition* (Carbondale, Ill.: 1965), p. 10.

14. *Ibid.*, p. 15.   15. Samuels, p. 33.

16. Johnson, p. 125.   17. Winter, p. 105.

18. James D. Hart, *The Popular Book* (New York: 1950), pp. 92, 127.

19. Hansen-Taylor and Scudder, II, 703.

20. Winter, p. 81.

21. Sinclair Lewis, *Address before the Swedish Academy* (New York: 1930), pp. 20–21.

22. Praise for Aldrich and Boker can be found in Samuels and in Bradley.

23. Samuels, p. 128.   24. *Ibid.*, p. 129.

25. *Ibid.*, Preface.   26. Beatty, p. 61.

27. Stoddard, *Recollections*, p. 187.

28. Bradley, pp. 62–67; Beatty, p. 62.

29. Bradley, p. 44.

30. Stoddard, *Recollections*, pp. 248, 253.

31. Bradley, pp. 66–67, 174.

32. Greenslet, p. 32.

33. Mrs. Thomas Bailey Aldrich, *Crowding Memories* (Boston and New York: 1920), p. 15.

34. Greenslet, pp. 38–42; Samuels, pp. 35–38.

35. Winter, p. 140.   36. Beatty, pp. 252–53.

37. Stedman and Gould, I, 204.   38. *Ibid.*, 204–6.

39. *Ibid.*, 107.

40. Stoddard, *Recollections*, p. 264.

41. Stedman and Gould, II, 92.

42. *Ibid.*, 203.

43. Richard Cary, p. 11.

44. Rosamond Gilder, pp. 39, 44, 47.

45. Stedman and Gould, I, 460.

46. Rosamond Gilder, pp. 66, 80–82.

47. *Ibid.*, p. 69.

48. For the elder Norton's theology, see Vanderbilt, pp. 15–20.

49. Milne, p. 51.   50. *Ibid.*, p. 54.

51. Milne, pp. 132–35.   52. Norton and Howe, II, 90.

53. Milne, p. 176.   54. *Ibid.*, p. 87.

55. Jackson, *passim.*   56. Holt, p. 110.

57. Milne, p. 235.   58. Rosamond Gilder, p. 396.

59. Ziff, p. 41.   60. Mott, II, 26; III, 17–18.

61. Rosamond Gilder, p. 50

62. The discussion of magazines, except where cited otherwise, is based upon Mott, II–IV. See also Wood.

63. Mott, II, 34.

64. *Ibid.*, III, 16–17.

65. *Ibid.*, IV, 38.

66. *Ibid.*, IV, 35.

67. Holt, p. 105.

68. Rosamond Gilder, p. 203.

69. Putnam, p. 383.

70. Holt, pp. 97–98.

71. Fields, *passim.*

72. Rosamond Gilder, p. 357.

73. The following discussion of nineteenth-century publishing is based on Sheehan.

74. Fields, pp. 53–55.

75. Stoddard, *Recollections*, p. 87.

76. Greenslet, p. 147.

77. Gilder and Gilder, p. 5.

78. Samuels, pp. 29, 31.

79. Gilder and Gilder, *passim.*

80. The decline in status of the man of letters is discussed in Gross, *passim.*

81. Winter, p. 108.

82. Ziff, pp. 129–30.

83. Duberman, p. 192.

84. Norton and Howe, I, 272.

Chapter Two

1. For an account of Taylor's life, see Beatty.

2. After an unsuccessful partnership in 1846 in the Phoenixville, Pennsylvania, *Gazette*, Taylor eagerly accepted an assistant editorship on Horace Greeley's *New York Tribune*, then a nursery for aspiring authors. Beatty, pp. 48–56. The following summary of Taylor's career is based on Hansen-Taylor and Scudder, I, 262, 271, 273, 132, and 275, Chapter 15, 355; II, 437, 432, 515, and 541.

3. *Ibid.*, II, 515; Beatty, pp. 267–68.

4. Hansen-Taylor and Scudder, I, 240.

5. Schultz, p. vii.

6. Hansen-Taylor and Scudder, II, 530.

7. *Ibid.*, 559.

8. *Ibid.*

9. Schultz, p. 168.

10. Hansen-Taylor and Scudder, II, 465–66.

11. *Ibid.*, 540.

12. Pochmann, p. 455.

13. Beatty, p. 275.

14. *Ibid.*, p. 271.

15. Hansen-Taylor and Scudder, II, 680, 686ff.

16. This estimate by the literary historian Fred Lewis Pattee is quoted in Beatty, p. 344.

17. Schultz, p. 205.

18. Beatty, pp. 259–60.

19. Taylor, *Poems of the Orient*, pp. 186–92.

20. Taylor to Mrs. Bayard Taylor, Dec. 9, 1860, HLH.

21. Taylor to Mrs. Rebecca Taylor, June 17, 1853, HLH. See also Taylor's *Central Africa*, p. 380; *Visit to India*, pp. 113, 244; *Northern Travel*, pp. 157–58.

22. Taylor, *At Home*, 1st Ser., p. 403.

23. Stoddard to Mrs. Kinney, May 23, 1867, HLH; Boker to Stoddard, August 12, 1850, PUL.

24. Taylor said he had no doubt that any intelligent reformer would admit there were "excrescences" in the movement; Schultz, pp. 73–74.

25. Norton and Howe, I, 112–13.

26. Cooke, pp. 154–59.

27. Curtis, "Hawthorne and Brook Farm," *Easy Chair*, 3rd Ser., pp. 1–19.

28. *The Poet's Journal*, pp. 164–65. See also "Proem" to *Home Pastorals* in *Poetical Works of Bayard Taylor*, pp. 249–50, for a sharp attack on the self-righteousness and drabness of the Quakers.

29. Taylor, *Beauty and the Beast*, pp. 200, 212, 224–28, 238.

30. Stoddard, *Songs of Summer*, pp. 56–74.

31. Taylor, *At Home*, I, 492–500; "The American People," unpublished lecture summarized in Beatty, pp. 154–58.

32. Stedman and Gould, I, 376–80.

33. March 15, 1851, HLH.

34. Stedman and Gould, II, 368.

35. Boker to Stoddard, Jan. 7, 1850, PUL.

36. Curtis, *Lotus-Eating*, pp. 138–40.

37. Beatty, p. 212.

38. Taylor, *Travels in Greece*, pp. 356–58.

39. Taylor, *Central Africa*, p. 325.

40. *Ibid.*, pp. 396–97.

41. Taylor, *Northern Travel*, p. 74.

42. *Ibid.*

43. Taylor, *At Home*, II, 168.

44. Taylor, *At Home*, I, 450.

45. Taylor, *Lands of the Saracen*, pp. 310–11.

46. Taylor, *Central Africa*, pp. 209, 309; *Visit to India*, pp. 178–79; Hansen-Taylor and Scudder, I, 232.

47. Schultz, p. 31.

48. Taylor, *Central Africa*, p. 86.

49. Taylor, *Poetical Works*, pp. 160–64.

50. Curtis, *Nile Notes*, p. 306.

51. Taylor, *Poetical Works*, pp. 9–10.

52. Stoddard, *Poems*, p. 19.

53. Taylor, *Lands of the Saracen*.

54. Taylor, *Lands of the Saracen*, p. 133. In the Orient Taylor sampled opium; *Visit to India*, pp. 493–94.

55. Schultz, pp. 68–69. Speaking through the character of Maxwell Woodbury, Taylor admits to being "something of an Epicurean in my philosophy" (*Hannah Thurston*, p. 100).

56. Hansen-Taylor and Scudder, I, 129.

57. *Ibid.*, 260.

58. Taylor, *Eldorado*, pp. 310–13.

59. Beatty, pp. 149–52.

60. *Ibid.*, p. 207.

61. Taylor, *At Home*, II, 200–201.

62. Taylor, *Central Africa*, p. 327; *Visit to India*, p. 273. But he hated the Irish: "All the scum of New-York is on the surface today, and such vile Irish brutal figures I never beheld," he wrote his wife in reference to a riot in which twenty Irishmen were killed. He commented that "there ought to be 20,000 (killed) in order to purify the city." To Marie Taylor, Dec. 12, 1871, HLH.

63. Hansen-Taylor and Scudder, I, 354.

64. *Ibid.*, 111.

65. *Ibid.*, 123.

66. Stedman and Gould, I, 83–84.

67. Taylor, *At Home*, I, 392.

68. Hansen-Taylor and Scudder, I, 404.

69. Taylor, *Rhymes of Travel*, p. 61.

70. Taylor to Stedman in Hansen-Taylor and Scudder, II, 434.

71. Curtis to O'Connor, Nov. 16, 1854, HLH.

Chapter Three

1. Tyack, *passim*.

2. Vanderbilt, p. 134. For general biographical information on Norton see this volume, *passim*.

3. Norton and Howe, I, 97, 116–17, 119, 178.

4. Ruskin, I, 28.

5. For a general discussion of the nineteenth-century preoccupation with universal laws, see May, Part I. The reaction against *a priori* thought in the early twentieth century is treated in White, *passim*.

6. Ruskin, II, 163.

7. Quoted from *Praeterita* in Norton and Howe, I, 137.

8. For American literary criticism in the early nineteenth century, see Pritchard, *Criticism*; Charvat; Stovall; Clark; Pritchard, *Wise Men*; and Stein, of particular interest because of the significance of Norton's relationship with Ruskin.

9. Norton, "Dante," 509–29.

10. Norton, "Muntz's *Life of Raphael*," 208–9; *Notes of Travel*, pp. 62, 108.

11. Norton, *Notes of Travel*, pp. 102–6; Vanderbilt, pp. 129–32.

12. Norton, *Notes of Travel*, pp. 107–8.

13. *Ibid.*, pp. 109–10, 126–27.

14. Ruskin, II, 129 (italics mine).

15. "The Greek Play at Harvard," *Atlantic Monthly*, XLVIII (1881), 106–10; Vanderbilt, pp. 127–28.

16. Vanderbilt, pp. 229–31.

17. *Ibid.*, pp. 133–34.

18. Stein, pp. 255–60.

19. Stoddard to Stedman, Dec. 19, 1862, CUL; Boker to Stoddard,

204   *Notes to Pages 59–72*

March 3, 1869, NYPL; Stoddard, *Poems*, pp. 283–88; Stoddard, *Recollections*, p. 254.

20. Norton and Howe, I, 222–23, 224.

21. Edward Cary, pp. 127–28, 130–32, 134–35.

22. Bradley, pp. 193, 206.

23. *Ibid.*, pp. 193, 225; Boker, *Poems of the War*, pp. 166–67.

24. Boker, *Königsmark*, pp. 213–23.

25. See Taylor, *Poetical Works*, pp. 135–37, 331–35.

26. Greenslet, pp. 54–63.

27. August 20, 1864, HLH. The offer to pay for a substitute is contained in an undated fragment in the file of Aldrich letters for 1864 at the Houghton Library.

28. Hansen-Taylor and Scudder, I, 373–76.

29. *Ibid.*, 384, 395–403, 414.

30. Stedman and Gould, I, 226, 229, 233–35.

31. *Ibid.*, 241–42, 247, 254, 321, 345.

32. Rosamond Gilder, pp. 22–28, 31, 34.

33. Fredrickson, Chap. 5.

34. Curtis, *Orations*, pp. 1, 3–35, 39–59, 65–93, 97–122.

35. Norton took a copy of Mill's *Political Economy* with him on his trip to India in 1849; Norton and Howe, I, 31.

36. Throughout his life, Norton was friendly to Mill. He repeatedly expressed his agreement with Mill's principles. The discussion that follows is based on the essays in Himmelfarb's edition of Mill's *Essays on Politics and Culture*.

37. Norton's discussions of Positivism insist that man is morally free despite the forces of history. See "Goldwin Smith," 523–39; review of *Thoughts on the Future Civil Policy of America*, 407–9; Norton and Howe, I, 193–94.

38. Norton and Howe, I, 110–11, 121–22, 123, 126–27.

39. Norton to Aubrey de Vere, February 24, 1861, HLH.

40. Norton, review of *The Laws of Race*, 252–54.

41. Norton, "The Advantages of Defeat," 360–65.

42. Norton, "Goldwin Smith," 523–29; "America and England," 331–46; "American Political Ideas," 550–65.

43. Ruskin, I, 146.

44. E. T. Cook and Alexander Wedderburn, eds., *The Works of John Ruskin*, 39 vols., (London: 1903–12), XXXVI, 504.

45. Norton, "Goldwin Smith," 523–29.

46. Norton, "American Political Ideas," 550–65.

47. Norton to Aubrey de Vere, March 29, 1868, HLH.

48. Norton, "Our Soldiers," 172–204.

49. Norton, "American Political Ideas," 550–65; "America and England," 331–46; Curtis, *Orations*, I, 39–59, 177.

50. As political editor for *Harper's Weekly* Curtis repeatedly expressed

his support for Reconstruction. For Norton's views, see Norton and Howe, I, 286–88; Norton to Frederick Law Olmstead, Sept. 16, 1866, HLH; "The President's Message," 250–66.

51. *The Nation*, a journal Norton helped found in 1865 and which he continued to support, illustrates the trend toward Northern disinterest in the Negro problem. See also Grimes, *passim*.

52. Curtis, *Orations*, I, 151–77; III, 35–58; Norton to Curtis, June 10, 1868, HLH; Norton and Howe, I, 285–86, 296–97.

Chapter Four

1. *The Century*, XXXIX (1900–1901), 473–74.

2. To Godkin, Jan. 17, 1900, HLH; to J. B. Harrison, May 17, 1902, HLH; to Goldwin Smith, Jan. 31, 1905, HLH.

3. Rosamond Gilder, pp. 254–73.

4. Bell, p. 50.

5. Curtis to Benjamin Paul Blood, Dec. 15, 1882, HLH.

6. *Harper's Weekly*, April 8, 1871, p. 306; May 4, 1872, p. 342; July 15, 1876, p. 570; to Charles Eliot Norton, June 30, 1872, HLH.

7. Timothy L. Smith, *passim*.

8. Edward Cary, pp. 207–208. This book details Curtis's political activities.

9. Rosamond Gilder, pp. 127–30, 142, 165, 224–25, 228, 235, 237, 245.

10. To George F. Parker, Aug. 10, 1892, LAAAL.

11. *The Century*, I (1881–82), 778–79. This and all subsequent references to *The Century* are to the editorial section, "Topics of the Time." According to an unpublished list in the New York Public Library, Gilder actually wrote very few editorials for the magazine. But *The Century's* assistant editor, Robert Underwood Johnson (*Remembered Yesterdays*, Boston: 1923), described Gilder's supervision of the editorial pages as very close. There is reason to believe, therefore, that the magazine's editorial viewpoint is Gilder's own. To George E. Woodberry, Dec. 26, 1895, HLH; Rosamond Gilder, p. 312; *The Century*, XXXIV (1898), 633; XXXV (1898–99), 314; XXXIX (1900–1901), 793–94.

12. Norton and Howe, II, 236, 458–59; to E. L. Godkin, Dec. 31, 1901, HLH.

13. Aldrich, *Prose Works*, IV, 13; Aldrich, *Poems*, pp. 275–76; *Prose Works*, IV, 60–61, 64, 100, 138–39, 166–67; VII, 39; III, 35; to George E. Woodberry, Sept. 27, 1894, HLH; to Woodberry, May 15, 1894, HLH; to Francis Bartlett, April 20, 1902, HLH.

14. Curtis, *Orations*, III, 62–83; *The Century*, XXIV (1893), 151–55; *The Century*, XXVI (1894), 951–52.

15. To Meta Gaskell, July 12, 1870; to Sir John Simon, Nov. 22, 1870 and Aug. 13, 1883; to Howells, March 26, 1902, HLH.

16. *Harper's Weekly*, May 30, 1891, p. 398; Curtis, *Easy Chair*, 3rd Ser., pp. 224–31.

17. Aldrich, *Prose Works*, III, 35.

18. Otherwise unidentified public letter, NYPL.

19. The following discussion of the civil service reform movement is based upon Hoogenboom, *passim.* See also his "Civil Service Reform and Public Morality," in Morgan, pp. 77–95.

20. Edward Cary, p. 269.

21. Morgan, pp. 87–88; Geoffrey Blodgett, "Reform Thought and the Genteel Tradition," in Morgan, pp. 55–76.

22. Curtis's speeches on civil service reform are collected in *Orations,* II.

23. To Isaac Hecker, Nov. 16, 1844, HLH.

24. Curtis, *Orations,* I, 7–8.   25. *Ibid.,* II, 331–33, 335–36.

26. *Ibid.,* I, 8.   27. *Ibid.,* II, 386–87.

28. *Ibid.,* I, 272–73, 277.

29. *Harper's Weekly,* July 15, 1865, p. 431; Norton and Howe, I, 372–73.

30. *Harper's Weekly,* Jan. 6, 1883, p. 2; Norton to Curtis, Mar. 5, 1883, HLH.

31. *Orations,* I, 277–78.

32. *Harper's Weekly,* Aug. 23, 1879, p. 662.

33. To George E. Woodberry, Oct. 15, 1874, Dec. 25, 1890, HLH.

Chapter Five

1. "Dwellings and Schools for the Poor," *North American Review,* LXXIV (1852), 464–89.

2. Curtis, "Charles Sumner," (1874), *Orations,* III, 201–50.

3. *Harper's Weekly,* Nov. 7, 1885, p. 723; Feb. 17, 1883, p. 99; Sept. 8, 1883, p. 562; Sept. 22, 1883, p. 595; June 21, 1891, p. 454; "Herbert Spencer on the Yankee," *Easy Chair,* 3rd Ser., 56–64; Curtis to ?, March 21, 1849, HLH.

4. Curtis, "Easy Does It, Guvner," *Easy Chair,* 2nd Ser., 203–7; "The Lounger," *Harper's Weekly,* Dec. 12, 1863, p. 787.

5. Curtis, "James Russell Lowell," (1892), *Orations,* III, 367–98; "Party and Patronage," (1892), *Ibid.,* II, 479–508.

6. Hartz, *passim.*

7. To Charles Eliot Norton, July 20, 1864, HLH; *Harper's Weekly,* Dec. 10, 1864, p. 787.

8. *Harper's Weekly,* Aug. 9, 1879, p. 622.

9. "Education and Local Patriotism," *Orations,* I, 455–82; *Harper's Weekly,* Nov. 29, 1873, p. 1059.

10. Norton, *Recent Social Theories,* Chaps. 1–2.

11. Norton to J. B. Harrison, July 7, 1878, HLH.

12. "The International Congress of Peace and Liberty," *Nation,* IX (1869), 313–15; "The Congress of Peace and Liberty at Lausanne," *Nation,* IX (1869), 336–37.

13. "The Lack of Old Homes in America," *Scribner's Magazine*, V (1889), 336–40.

14. "American Political Ideas," *North American Review*, CI (1865), 550–65.

15. "Dwellings and Schools for the Poor," *North American Review*, LXXIV (1852), 464–89.

16. *Ibid.*

17. Norton and Howe, I, 251–53.

18. To James Russell Lowell, Aug. 30, 1868, HLH.

19. To John Stuart Mill, Sept. 26, 1868, HLH.

20. "The Poverty of England," *North American Review*, CIX (1869), 122–54.

21. *Harper's Weekly*, March 31, 1866, p. 194; May 5, 1866, p. 274; Sept. 15, 1866, p. 578.

22. *Ibid.*, May 5, 1866, p. 274. 23. *Ibid.*, Dec. 30, 1871, p. 1219.

24. *Ibid.*, Aug. 11, 1877, p. 618. 25. *Ibid.*, Aug. 16, 1879, p. 643.

26. *Ibid.*, Sept. 13, 1879, p. 722; Aug. 24, 1878, p. 667.

27. *Ibid.*, Aug. 11, 1883, p. 498.

28. *Ibid.*, April 10, 1886, p. 226; April 17, 1886, p. 242.

29. *Ibid.*, May 8, 1886, p. 290.

30. *Ibid.*, May 15, 1886, p. 306; Jan. 1, 1887, p. 2.

31. *Ibid.*, May 22, 1886, p. 322.

32. *The Century*, IV (1883), 470–71.

33. *Ibid.*, V (1883–84), 624–25; Norton and Howe, II, 81.

34. *The Century*, VI (1884), 142–43.

35. To William Dean Howells, Feb. 18, 1885, HLH. Dynamiting was *"not the American way." The Century*, VII (1884–85), 953.

36. *The Century*, X (1886), 957–58; XI (1886–87), 148–49.

37. *Ibid.*, XXIV (1893), 151–52.

38. *Ibid.*, XXVI (1894), 951–52.

39. *Ibid.*, XIX (1890–91), 471–72.

40. Rosamond Gilder, pp. 205–8; "The Kindergarten," an address delivered by Gilder before the NEA in Boston, July 10, 1903, NYPL.

41. *The Century*, VII (1884–85), 311–12.

42. *Ibid.*, VIII (1885), 803–4.

43. *Harper's Weekly*, Sept. 21, 1889, p. 755.

44. *The Century*, XI (1886–87), 967–68.

45. *Ibid.*, XIII (1887–88), 963–64.

46. *Harper's Weekly*, Jan. 21, 1888, p. 37; Dec. 3, 1887, p. 875.

47. *The Century*, XIV (1888), 634–35.

48. *Ibid.*, XXXVIII (1900), 143–49, 152–53.

49. *Ibid.*, XL (1901), 315–16.

50. To Maria Lansdale, Jan. 25, 1908, March 5, 1908, PUL.

51. *The Century*, XLIII (1902–3), *passim*; XLVI (1904), 954–59.

52. *Harper's Weekly*, April 1, 1865, p. 194; Feb. 9, 1867, p. 83; May 2,

1868, p. 275; Feb. 22, 1873, pp. 146–47; May 17, 1873, p. 410; March 22, 1879, p. 223; March 29, 1879, p. 243; Feb. 11, 1882, p. 82; Jan. 27, 1883, p. 50.

53. *Ibid.*, Sept. 10, 1870, p. 579.

54. *Ibid.*, Dec. 18, 1880, p. 807; April 19, 1884, p. 247; Feb. 27, 1886, p. 131.

55. *Ibid.*, Jan. 21, 1888, p. 38.

56. Rosamond Gilder, pp. 172–73; *The Century*, III (1882–83), 615–16, 787.

57. *Harper's Weekly*, April 14, 1868, p. 243.

58. *Ibid.*, Jan. 23, 1869, p. 50.

59. *Ibid.*, May 6, 1872, p. 267; Dec. 24, 1872, p. 995; Feb. 19, 1881, p. 114.

60. *Ibid.*, July 8, 1865, p. 419; July 2, 1866, p. 418; Dec. 23, 1871, p. 1194; Dec. 10, 1881, pp. 818–19; July 28, 1888, p. 546; Sept. 15, 1888, p. 687.

61. *Ibid.*, Aug. 23, 1873, p. 738.   62. *Ibid.*, Feb. 12, 1881, p. 98.

63. *Ibid.*, March 24, 1883, p. 178.   64. *Ibid.*, Aug. 4, 1883, p. 482.

65. *Ibid.*, April 11, 1868, p. 227.   66. *Ibid.*, March 8, 1873, p. 186.

67. *Ibid.*, March 29, 1873, pp. 242–43; April 5, 1873, p. 266; Jan. 3, 1891, p. 2; Jan. 31, 1891, p. 83; June 6, 1891, p. 418.

68. *Ibid.*, May 10, 1873, p. 386.

69. *Ibid.*, June 21, 1873, p. 522; July 12, 1873, p. 594; Aug. 9, 1873, p. 691; Aug. 16, 1873, p. 715; Sept. 20, 1873, pp. 818–19.

70. *Ibid.*, Dec. 12, 1874, p. 1014.

71. *Ibid.*, Nov. 11, 1882, p. 706.

72. *Ibid.*, April 24, 1886, p. 259.

73. *Ibid.*, Jan. 29, 1887, p. 70; April 2, 1887, p. 235; Dec. 29, 1888, p. 998.

74. See, for example, Theodore Roosevelt, "Phases of State Legislation," *The Century*, VII (1884–85), 820–31; editorial comment on the article appears on 953.

75. *The Century*, IX (1885–86), 51–59, 737–49; XVII (1889–90), 938–51.

76. *Ibid.*, IX (1885–86), 475–76.

Chapter Six

1. *The New York Times*, Jan. 25, 1908.

2. Stedman and Gould, II, 568.

3. Stedman and Gould, II, Chap. 27.

4. *The Springfield Republican*, Jan. 19, 1908.

5. *The New York Times*, Jan. 25, 1908.

6. Stedman and Gould, I, 183–94.

7. *Ibid.*, I, 562, 568.

8. *Ibid.*, I, 118. The letter dates from 1857 but it could have been written thirty years later as well.

9. *Ibid.*, I, 452–54, 604.   10. *Ibid.*, II, 308.

11. *Ibid.*, II, 503.   12. *Ibid.*, II, 569.

13. *Genius, and other Essays*, p. 39.

14. "Persia," *Songs of Summer*, p. 174.

15. Stedman, *Victorian Poets*, p. 4.

16. Stedman, *Nature and Elements*, p. 187.

17. Stedman, *Victorian Poets*, p. 4.

18. Stedman, *Nature and Elements*, pp. 129–31.

19. *Ibid.*, p. 262; Stedman, *Victorian Poets*, p. 394.

20. Stedman, *Victorian Poets*, p. 382.

21. Stedman, *Nature and Elements*, p. 124.

22. Stedman, *Poets of America*, p. xii.

23. *Ibid.*, pp. 121, 222.

24. The objective–subjective dichotomy was developed in German romantic thought in the 1790's and brought to America after 1820; Abrams, p. 242.

25. Stedman, *Nature and Elements*, pp. 76–91, 139–45.

26. Stedman, *Victorian Poets*, p. 92.   27. *Ibid.*, p. 95.

28. *Ibid.*, pp. 95–96.   29. *Ibid.*, p. 442.

30. Stedman and Gould, I, 485.

31. Stedman, *Poets of America*, pp. 1–25.

32. Charles Duffy, "An Unpublished Letter: Stedman to Howells," *American Literature*, XXX (Nov. 1958), 367–70.

33. Stedman, *Victorian Poets*, pp. 23–24; *Nature and Elements*, pp. 121, 265.

34. Stedman and Gould, II, 68–69.

35. Stedman to Horace E. Scudder, May 2, 1894, HLH.

36. Winter, p. 25.   37. Beer, p. 216.

38. Mott, III, 20.   39. Milne, pp. 67–68.

40. Rosamond Gilder, pp. 398–99.

41. Stallman, p. 67; Van Wyck Brooks, *Confident Years*, p. 303n.

42. Stallman, p. 91.   43. Stedman and Gould, I, 401.

44. *Ibid.*, II, 371.   45. Sheehan, Chap. 5.

46. Johnson, p. 125.

47. Gilder to Robert Grant, June 4, 1883, HLH; Gilder to George Washington Cable, February 1, 1882, NYPL.

48. Ziff, pp. 131–35.

49. Stedman and Gould, II, 320.

50. *Ibid.*, II, 20–21.

51. See the introductions to Stedman's *Victorian Poets* and *Poets of America*.

52. Stedman, *Poets of America*, p. 27.

53. Stedman, *Victorian Poets*, pp. 11–13. See also Stedman's "Fin de Siècle" in *Poems*, pp. 456–58.

54. Stedman, *Nature and Elements*, pp. xiii–xiv.

55. *Ibid.*, p. xv.

56. *Ibid.*, p. 151.

57. *Ibid.*, p. 5.

58. Stedman and Gould, I, 138–39.

59. Stedman, *Nature and Elements*, p. 3.

60. *Ibid.*, p. 43.

61. *Ibid.*, pp. 6–8.

62. *Ibid.*, pp. 44, 50–51.

63. *Ibid.*, pp. 52–55.

64. *Ibid.*, p. 21.

65. *Ibid.*, p. 28.

66. *Ibid.*, pp. 28, 33.

67. Abrams, p. 313.

68. Stedman, *Poets of America*, p. 27.

69. Stedman, *Victorian Poets*, p. 17; *Nature and Elements*, p. 39. Stedman held that Whitman agreed with him (*Nature and Elements*, p. 38).

70. Stedman, *Nature and Elements*, p. 95; *Victorian Poets*, pp. 30, 95, 247, 448.

71. Stedman and Gould, II, 299.

72. Stedman, *Nature and Elements*, p. 149; Stedman and Gould, II, 586.

73. Stedman, *Nature and Elements*, pp. 148–49.

74. *Ibid.*, p. 45.

75. Stedman and Gould, II, 299. Stedman said Whittier and the Quakers had taken up his "Corda Concordia" as an expression of their doctrine (*Nature and Elements*, p. 45).

76. Stedman, *Nature and Elements*, p. 45.

77. For Stedman's fullest presentation of his theory of genius, see "Genius," in *Genius, and other Essays*, pp. 1–37. See also *The Nature and Elements of Poetry*, pp. 46, 278–89; *Victorian Poets*, p. 24; *Poets of America*, p. 3.

78. Stedman, *Poets of America*, p. 369.

79. *Ibid.*, p. 368.

80. Stedman, *Nature and Elements*, p. 197.

81. *Ibid.*, p. 198.

82. Stedman, *Poets of America*, p. 69.

83. Stedman, *Nature and Elements*, p. 199.

84. Stedman, *Genius*, pp. 29–30.

85. Stedman and Gould, II, 373, 350, 580.

86. *Ibid.*, II, 548; Stedman, *Nature and Elements*, pp. 190–92.

87. Stedman and Gould, II, 370–72.

88. *Ibid.*, 338.

89. Stedman, *Genius*, pp. 155–56, 269, 272.

90. Stedman, *Nature and Elements*, p. 168.

91. *Ibid.*, pp. 155–56.

92. Bate, p. 184.

93. Stedman, *Nature and Elements*, p. 188.

94. *Ibid.*, p. 146.

95. *Ibid.*, p. 151. Stedman disliked Poe's preoccupation with the bizarre. Art, like nature, "must be fantastic, not in her frequent, but in her exceptional moods"; *Poets of America*, p. 258.

96. Stedman and Gould, I, 201.

97. Stedman, *Poets of America*, p. 219.

98. Abrams, p. 328.

99. Stedman and Gould, I, 143.

100. Foerster, Chaps. 1 and 2.

101. Stedman, *Nature and Elements*, pp. 187–88, 211, 213, 216.

102. *Ibid.*, pp. 231–33.   103. *Ibid.*, p. 233.

104. *Ibid.*, p. 5.   105. *Ibid.*, pp. 261–65.

106. *Ibid.*, pp. 271–75.   107. *Ibid.*, pp. 116–19, 173.

108. Stedman, *Victorian Poets*, p. 3.

109. Stedman, *Nature and Elements*, pp. 10–11.

110. *Ibid.*, p. 201.

111. *Ibid.*, p. 220.

112. He said that the period of French neoclassicism had lacked a "soul"; *Nature and Elements*, pp. 18, 116–19, 173.

113. *Ibid.*, p. xv.

114. *Ibid.*, p. 11.

115. *Ibid.*, p. 48.

116. Stedman and Gould, I, 143; Stedman, *Victorian Poets*, p. 183.

117. Stedman, *Nature and Elements*, p. 26; Stedman, *Poets of America*, p. 239.

118. Stedman, *Poets of America*, p. 249.

119. Stedman, *Nature and Elements*, pp. 121–22.

120. Stedman, *Poets of America*, p. 64; for examples of Stedman's use of the term *health*, see *Victorian Poets*, pp. 250, 262, 267, 284, 442, and *Poets of America*, pp. xi, 306, 317, 341.

121. Stedman, *Victorian Poets*, p. 88.

Chapter Seven

1. There is no biography of Stoddard; see his *Recollections*.

2. See Greenslet; Samuels.

3. See Bradley.

4. Boker to Stoddard, Jan. 7, 1850, PUL.

5. Boker, *Königsmark*, pp. 199–202.

6. *Ibid.*, pp. 199–201.

7. *Ibid.*, p. 200.

8. Stoddard, *Songs of Summer*, p. 203.

9. Bradley, pp. 34, 185–89, 295.

10. To Stedman, Dec. 7, 1867, CUL. See also Sonnet 244 in *Königsmark*; Boker, *Plays and Poems*, II, 278–91.

11. Aldrich to Francis Bartlett, April 20, 1902, HLH.

12. Aldrich, *Prose Works*, VII, 18.

13. *Ibid.*, 4.

14. To George E. Woodberry, May 12, 1899, HLH.

15. To Silas Weir Mitchell, May 3, 1898; to Francis Bartlett, July 17, 1898, HLH; to William Young, July 7, 1898, YCAL; to Lawrence Hutton, June 15, 1899, PUL.

16. *Prose Works*, III, 35.

17. To George E. Woodberry, Sept. 27, 1894, HLH.

18. To Woodberry, May 15, 1894, HLH.

19. To Francis Bartlett, April 20, 1902, HLH.

20. Stoddard, *Recollections*, p. 64.

21. April 26, 1851, PUL.

22. Stoddard, *Lion's Cub*, pp. 112–14.

23. Boker to Stoddard, May 21, 1852, PUL.

24. Aldrich, *Poems*, p. 399.

25. Boker to Stoddard, May 21, 1852, PUL.

26. Aldrich, *Poems*, pp. 14–16. This idea is especially strong in Taylor's *The Picture of St. John.*

27. Bradley, pp. 78, 97–98, 165–68.

28. April 26, 1851, PUL.

29. To Stoddard, Sept. 4, 1854, June 11, 1855, PUL.

30. Bradley, p. 168.

31. See, for example, Aldrich's *Poems*, pp. 25–27, 63–64.

32. To Stedman, Oct. 30, 1873, CUL; also Aldrich to James Ripley Osgood, Dec. 21, 1874, HLH.

33. Aldrich, *Poems*, p. 40. In "The World's Way," in *Poems*, pp. 62–63, Aldrich pictured an Arab court poet who was beheaded the first time he failed to produce verse on demand.

34. Boker to Stoddard, Dec. 26, 1852, March 23, 1854, and Oct. 3, 1865, PUL. Italics mine.

35. To Frank D. Sherman, Feb. 19, 1880, HLH.

36. Aldrich, *Poems*, pp. 138–40.

37. To Stedman, Dec. 25, 1882, CUL. Italics mine.

38. Aldrich to James Russell Lowell, Dec. 4, 1868, Feb. 14, 1873, and May 27, 1874, HLH. Aldrich to Henry Wadsworth Longfellow, eleven letters, 1866–82, HLH.

39. Aldrich to George E. Woodberry, Oct. 21, 1885, HLH.

40. To William Dean Howells, May 12, 1880, HLH.

41. To Stoddard, March 2, 1864, PUL.

42. Stoddard, *Recollections*, pp. 95–96, 100, 201.

43. Aldrich to Stedman, Sept. 4, 1885, YCAL.

44. Pattee, *passim.*

45. Aldrich, *Poems*, pp. 3–7.

46. Aldrich, *Prose Works*, V, 240–45.

47. Stedman thought Bryant was not realistic enough; *Poets of America*, Chap. 3.

48. Aldrich, *Prose Works*, VII, 32; *Poems*, pp. 45, 297–99; to George E. Woodberry, June 12, 1899, HLH.

49. To Oliver Wendell Holmes, March 20, 1890; to Francis Bartlett, Aug. 5, 1895, HLH.

50. To "Mr. Thayer," Feb. 27, 1889, YCAL.

51. To Frank D. Sherman, Dec. 31, 1896, BPL.

52. Probably because of his didacticism, Wordsworth did not appeal to Boker; Boker to Stoddard, May 6, 1852, PUL.

53. Stoddard, *Recollections*, pp. 56, 150; Aldrich, *Poems*, pp. 283–85, 301–2; Boker to Stoddard, Oct. 6, 1850, PUL.
54. To Francis Bartlett, Dec. 24, 1903, HLH.
55. To Frederick Locker-Lampson, May 1, 1882, HLH.
56. Kindilien, *passim*.
57. More, *Shelburne Essays*, pp. 138–49.
58. Pearson, p. 79.   59. Wilde, p. 57.
60. Pearson, pp. 86, 159.   61. *Ibid.*, p. 81.
62. *Ibid.*, pp. 264–65.   63. Aldrich, *Poems*, pp. 130–33.
64. Stoddard, *Songs of Summer*, pp. 56–79; *Poems*, p. 33.
65. Stoddard, *Poems*, pp. 3–11.
66. *Ibid.*, p. 368.
67. Aldrich, *Poems*, pp. 142–45.
68. Taylor, *Poetical Works*, pp. 149–50.
69. "Son of Earth," *Plays and Poems*, II, 278–91.
70. To William Winter, (1855), HLH.
71. To William Winter, July 17, 1855, HLH.
72. To Lillian, (1863), HLH.
73. To Lillian, June 17, 1863 and Oct. 20, 1863, HLH.
74. To Lillian, Dec. 11, Dec. 12, Dec. 15, 1863, HLH.
75. To Lillian, Oct. 3, Oct. 5, 1864, HLH.
76. To Lillian, Nov. 17, 1863, HLH. Heroes who love sick females figure in both *A Stillwater Tragedy* and *The Queen of Sheba*.
77. To Lillian (1863), HLH.
78. Stedman and Gould, I, 29, 36, 39, 57, 63–64.
79. *Ibid.*, 16, 61.   80. *Ibid.*, 66–67.
81. *Ibid.*, II, 503–10.   82. *Ibid.*, I, 17, 29, 56.
83. *Ibid.*, 66–67.   84. *Ibid.*, 101–2.
85. Stedman, *Victorian Poets*, pp. 134–38, 148.
86. Stedman and Gould, II, 518.   87. June 21, 1865, CUL.
88. May 3, 1860, HLH.   89. Beatty, p. 345.
90. Richard Cary, pp. 28–32. For Mrs. Stoddard's viewpoint, see her letters to Stedman, CUL. Aldrich to Lillian, July 7, 1863, and December 15, 1863, HLH.
91. Bradley, pp. 21–23, 326. See also Beatty, p. 257.
92. Introduction to Boker's *Sonnets*; Boker to Stoddard, Feb. 11, 1856, PUL. Bradley is incorrect in saying that Boker's first affair began in 1857. Boker mentioned a mistress or mistresses as early as 1852. Boker to Stoddard, Oct. 12, 1852, and Dec. 26, 1852, PUL.
93. In *Francesca da Rimini* Boker sidestepped the moral implications of his position by attaching tragic consequences to the guiltless love of Paolo and Francesca; Bradley, pp. 125–28; *Sonnets*, 144.
94. Boker, *Sonnets*, p. 69.   95. *Ibid.*, p. 55.
96. *Ibid.*, p. 52.   97. *Ibid.*, pp. 52–53.
98. Boker to Stoddard, Feb. 11, 1856, PUL.
99. June 15, 1850, PUL.

100. Boker to Stoddard, Sept. 28, 1868, in Richard Cary, p. 34. The novel, *A Year's Letters*, was published in America in 1901.

101. Oct. 21, 1868, PUL.

102. N.d., CUL.

103. For some examples see Taylor's *Poetical Works*, pp. 106–9, 124–25; *Poems of the Orient*, p. 124; *Central Africa*, p. 196; *Egypt and Iceland*, pp. 102–3.

104. Taylor, "Twin Love," pp. 167–97, *Beauty and the Beast*.

105. The quotation is from a letter by Taylor to Mrs. Rebecca W. Taylor, Dec. 19, 1851, HLH. It is cut from the letter published in Hansen-Taylor and Scudder, I, 224. For the details of Taylor's relationship with Bufleb and of his second marriage, see *Ibid.*, 222, 224, 307, 333, 336.

106. Taylor's first wife Mary Agnew died of "pulmonary attacks" in 1850 after two months of marriage. Taylor married her knowing that her disease was fatal; *Ibid.*, 22, 81, 190, 197.

107. See Kraditor, *passim*.

108. Taylor, *Hannah Thurston*, pp. 254–56.

109. Taylor, *At Home*, II, 321–22.

110. Taylor, *Hannah Thurston*, p. 215.

111. *Ibid.*, pp. 275–76.

112. Taylor thought the celibate Shakers had a "singularly dry, starved, hungry, lonely look." For him the purest life was wedded life; *At Home*, II, 334–35.

113. Taylor, *Critical Essays*, pp. 369–70.

114. Taylor, *Hannah Thurston*, p. 62.

115. Dec. 4, 1908, NYPL.

116. To William O'Connor, Sept. 7, 1855, HLH.

117. "The Right of Suffrage," (1867), *Orations*, I, 183–213.

118. "Fair Play for Women," (1870), *Ibid.*, 217–38; "The Higher Education of Women," *Ibid.*, (1890), 401–25.

119. *Ibid.*, 201.

Chapter Eight

1. Aldrich, *Prose Works*, V, 66–70.

2. Stoddard, *Recollections*, p. 6.

3. *Ibid.*, pp. 32–33.

4. To Woodberry, March 5, 1893, HLH.

5. To Lillian Aldrich, Oct. 21, 1863, Oct. 28, 1963, April 4, 1863, Aug. 4, 1864, and Aug. 5, 1864, HLH.

6. To Lillian Aldrich, Aug. 17, 1864, HLH. See also Stoddard, *Songs of Summer*, p. 104; Aldrich, *Poems*, pp. 55–56.

7. Aldrich, *Poems*, pp. 881–89; Stoddard, *Poems*, pp. 382–85.

8. To Stedman, Nov. 16, 1876, CUL.

9. To Mrs. Kinney, May 23, 1867, CUL.

10. Boker to Stoddard, Aug. 12, 1850, PUL.

11. Bradley, pp. 15–17.

12. Boker to Stoddard, March 3, 1869, NYPL. See Stoddard, *Poems*, pp. 288–90.

13. Boker, *Sonnets, passim.*

14. Taylor, *At Home*, I, 216–17.

15. Taylor, *Lands of the Saracen*, pp. 84–85.

16. Schultz, pp. 140–41.

17. Taylor, *Dramatic Works*, pp. 173, 183, 188–89.

18. *Ibid.*, pp. 1–164.

19. Hansen-Taylor and Scudder, II, 635, 664–65.

20. Taylor considered this the key to his play; Taylor to Marie Taylor, Dec. 4, 1874, HLH.

21. Mrs. Taylor's notes to the play make it clear that Taylor's major argument was directed at religious literalism; *Dramatic Works*, pp. 323–45.

22. Taylor, *Dramatic Works*, pp. 203, 210, 220.

23. *Ibid.*, pp. 227, 230, 233–35, 250.

24. *Ibid.*, pp. 267, 274, 268–69, 286–87.

25. *Ibid.*, pp. 287, 299.

26. Hansen-Taylor and Scudder, II, 716–17.

27. To Richard Grant White, Sept. 14, 1883, HLH.

28. June 19, 1882, HLH.

29. To "Dear Sir," May 7, 1886, YCAL.

30. To William Dean Howells, May 12, 1902, HLH.

31. Stoddard, *Poems*, pp. 91–92.

32. Aldrich, *Poems*, pp. 19–21, 404.

33. To Francis Bartlett, Feb. 23, 1903, HLH.

34. To Alexander V. Stout Anthony, May 1, 1899, HLH.

35. Aldrich, *Poems*, p. 378.

36. Rosamond Gilder, p. 476; see also pp. 436–37.

37. *Ibid.*, p. 356.   38. Gilder, *Poems*, pp. 247–49.

39. *The Century*, II (1882), 790–92.   40. Gilder, *Poems*, p. 265.

41. *Ibid.*, pp. 247–49.   42. *Ibid.*, p. 245.

43. *Ibid.*, pp. 177–79.   44. *Ibid.*

45. *The Century*, III (1882–83), 460–62.

46. Gilder, *Poems*, pp. 239–42.

47. *Ibid.*, pp. 68–69.

48. *Ibid.*, pp. 181–85; Rosamond Gilder, pp. 423–24.

49. Rosamond Gilder, p. 425.

50. Stoddard, *Songs of Summer*, pp. 56–79.

51. To Stedman, June 15, 1870, CUL.

52. See his later praise of nature in *Poems*, pp. 302–4, 317–18, 492–94.

53. *Ibid.*, pp. 492–94.

54. Stedman, *Nature and Elements*, pp. 102–3.

55. Stedman and Gould, II, 584.

56. *Ibid.*, 581.

57. The following discussion of Stoddard's concept of transience is

based on *Songs of Summer*, pp. 5, 7, 20, 30, 40, 45, 48, 56, 87–88, 91, 116, 117, 145–46; *Poems*, pp. 18, 42–44, 48, 305–6, 306–7, 311, 315–16, 319, 323–34, 336–51, 491, 498; *Lion's Cub*, 32–34.

58. "The Dead Master," *Poems*, p. 491.

59. Stoddard, "The Morals of Marcus Aurelius," in *Lion's Cub*, pp. 27–32.

60. *Poems*, pp. 392–93; See also pp. 390–91, 395–96.

61. To Francis Bartlett, Jan. 2, 1904, HLH.

62. To Lillian, (1863), HLH.

63. Stoddard, *Poems*, pp. 191–92. Aldrich spoke of sleep as a rest from that "sweet bitter world we know by day"; *Poems*, p. 394.

64. *Prose Works*, VII, 99.

65. N.d., CUL.

66. *The Century*, IV (1883), 633–34; V (1883–84), 784–85; IX (1885–86), 51–59, 737–49; XVII (1889–90), 89–90, 938–40.

67. Norton and Howe, II, 356.

68. *Ibid.*, 412. Norton's letters to William James in HLH were all written after 1900; they are friendly, but skeptical of all philosophy.

69. Norton and Howe, I, 294–96.

70. "Religious Liberty," *North American Review*, CIV (1867), 586–97.

71. "The Church and Religion," *North American Review*, CVI (1868), 376–96.

72. Norton and Howe, II, 53–54.

73. To John Ruskin, Oct. 8, 1869, HLH. Italics mine.

74. Norton and Howe, II, 248–49. Italics mine.

75. "Goldwin Smith," *North American Review*, XCIX (1864), 523–39; *Nation*, I (1865), 407–9.

76. To George E. Woodberry, Sept. 27, 1878, HLH.

77. To J. B. Harrison, Nov. 17, 1902, HLH.

78. Norton and Howe, II, 182–83.

79. *Ibid.*, 347.   80. *Ibid.*, 335–36.

81. *Ibid.*, 167–68.   82. *Ibid.*, 304–5.

83. To Samuel Gray Ward, Nov. 20, 1906, HLH.

84. To J. B. Harrison, Nov. 17, 1902, HLH.

85. "On Citizenship," Address to Presbyterian Social Union of Philadelphia, Feb. 26, 1906, NYPL.

86. Norton and Howe, II, 91–92.

87. *Forum*, VII (1889), 30–40, 89.

88. Norton and Howe, II, 8–9.

89. *Ibid.*, 401.

90. Feb. 10, 1874, HLH. The passage is omitted from Norton and Howe II, 34. In 1905 Norton wrote that he had been reluctant to join the American Academy of Arts and Letters because he thought the situation of American art and the nature of the national character would prevent the Academy from being of real service. To Robert Underwood Johnson, Nov. 14, 1905, LAAAL.

91. Norton and Howe, II, 297–98.

92. "Some Aspects of Civilization in America," *Forum*, XX (1896), 641–51.

93. Norton and Howe, II, 165–66.

94. *Ibid.*, 236–37.

95. *Ibid.*, 243–44.

96. To Samuel Gray Ward, March 3, 1904, HLH.

97. To J. B. Harrison, March 13, 1894, HLH.

98. "Some Aspects of Civilization in America," *Forum*, XX (1896), pp. 641–51.

99. "Educational Value of the History of the Fine Arts," *Educational Review*, IX (1895), 343–48.

100. "Education at the Great English Public Schools," *Nation*, I (1865), 149–50.

101. Jan. 3, 1897, HLH.

102. Norton and Howe, II, 401.

103. "Waste," *Nation*, II (1866), 301–2.

104. *The Century*, XXXVI (1899), 322–23.

Chapter Nine

1. For a discussion of this same phenomenon in England, see Williams, *passim*.

2. A characterization of nineteenth-century American thought that does not fit the genteel group is offered in White, *passim*.

3. Rosamond Gilder, pp. 378–79; *The Century*, II (1882), 297–98, XXXVI (1899), 322–23.

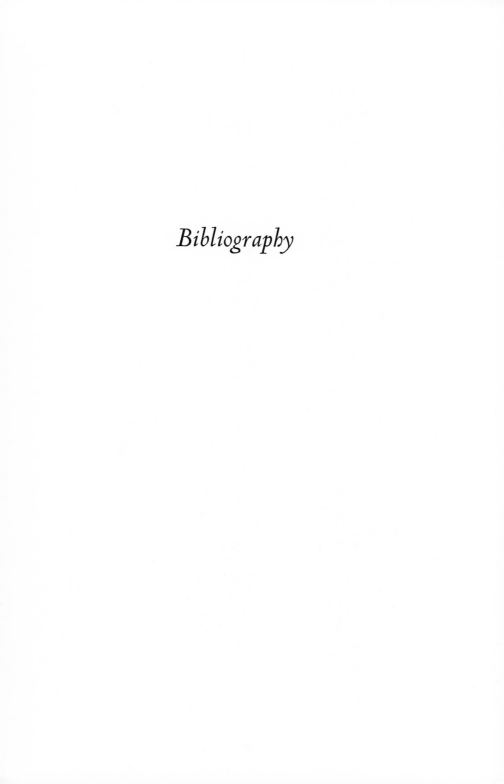

Bibliography

Bibliography

Abrams, M. H. *The Mirror and the Lamp.* New York, 1953.
Aldrich, Thomas Bailey. *Poems of Thomas Bailey Aldrich,* Boston, 1897.
————. *The Prose Works of Thomas Bailey Aldrich,* 7 vols. Boston and New York, 1907.
Armstrong, William M. E. L. *Godkin and American Foreign Policy, 1865–1900.* New York, 1957.
Bate, Walter Jackson. *From Classic to Romantic.* Cambridge, Mass., 1956.
Beatty, Richmond Croom. *Bayard Taylor; Laureate of the Gilded Age.* Norman, Okla., 1936.
————. *James Russell Lowell.* Nashville, Tenn., 1942.
Beer, Thomas. *The Mauve Decade.* New York, 1926.
Bell, Daniel, ed. *The Radical Right.* New York, 1963.
Blodgett, Geoffrey. *The Gentle Reformers: Massachusetts Democrats in the Cleveland Era.* Cambridge, Mass., 1966.
Boker, George Henry. *Königsmark, the Legend of the hounds and other poems.* Philadelphia, 1869.
————. *Plays and Poems,* 2 vols. Boston, 1869.
————. *Poems of the War.* Philadelphia, 1864.
————. *Sonnets; A Sequence on Profane Love.* Philadelphia, 1929.
Bradley, Edward S. *George Henry Boker.* Philadelphia, 1927.
Brooks, Van Wyck. *America's Coming-of-Age.* New York, 1913.
————. *The Confident Years: 1885–1915.* New York, 1952.
————. *New England: Indian Summer, 1865–1915.* New York, 1940.
Buckley, Jerome Hamilton. *The Victorian Temper.* Cambridge, Mass., 1951.
Cady, Edwin H. *The Gentleman in America.* Syracuse, N.Y., 1949.
Cary, Edward. *George William Curtis.* Boston and New York, 1894.
Cary, Richard. *The Genteel Circle.* Ithaca, 1954.
The Century Magazine. Editorials, 1880–1910.
Charvat, William. *The Origins of American Critical Thought, 1810–1835.* London, 1936.

Clark, Harry Hayden, ed. *Transitions in American Literature*. Durham, N.C., 1953.

Cooke, George Willis, ed. *Early Letters of George William Curtis to John S. Dwight*. New York and London, 1898.

Curtis, George William. *Early Letters of George William Curtis to John S. Dwight*. Ed. George Willis Cooke. New York and London, 1898.

——. *From the Easy Chair*, 1st, 2nd, 3rd Ser., 3 vols. New York, 1894.

——. *The Howadji in Syria*. New York, 1857.

——. *Literary and Social Essays*. New York, 1894.

——. *Lotus-Eating*. New York, 1856.

——. "The Lounger," *Harper's Weekly*, Dec. 12, 1863, p. 787.

——. *Nile Notes of a Howadji*. New York, 1851.

——. *Orations and Addresses of George William Curtis*. Ed. Charles Eliot Norton, 3 vols. New York, 1894.

——. *Potiphar Papers*. New York, 1856.

——. *Prue and I*. New York, 1873.

——. *Trumps*. New York, 1861.

DeMille, George E. *Literary Criticism in America*. New York, 1931.

Dickason, David H. *The Daring Young Men*. Bloomington, Ind., 1953.

Ditzion, Sidney H. *Marriage, Morals and Sex in America*. New York, 1953.

Duberman, Martin. *James Russell Lowell*. Boston, 1966.

Duffy, Charles. "An Unpublished Letter: Stedman to Howells," *American Literature*, XXX (1958), 367–70.

Fields, Annie Adams. *James T. Fields*. Cambridge, Mass., 1882.

Foerster, Norman. *American Criticism*. Boston and New York, 1928.

Fredrickson, George M. *The Inner Civil War*. New York, 1965.

Gilder, Jeanette Leonard, and Joseph B. Gilder, eds. *Authors at Home*. New York, 1888.

Gilder, Richard Watson. *Grover Cleveland: A Record of Friendship*. New York, 1910.

——. "The Kindergarten." Address to Boston N.E.A., 1903. New York Public Library.

——. *Letters of Richard Watson Gilder*. Ed. Rosamond Gilder. Boston and New York, 1916.

——. "On Citizenship." Address to Presbyterian Social Union of Philadelphia, 1906. New York Public Library.

——. *The Poems of Richard Watson Gilder*. Boston and New York, 1908.

Gilder, Rosamond, ed. *Letters of Richard Watson Gilder*. Boston and New York, 1916.

Greenslet, Ferris. *The Life of Thomas Bailey Aldrich*. Boston and New York, 1908.

Grimes, Alan Pendleton. *The Political Liberalism of the New York 'Nation,' 1865–1932*. Chapel Hill, N.C., 1953.

Gross, John. *The Rise and Fall of the Man of Letters*. New York, 1969.

Hansen-Taylor, Marie, and Horace E. Scudder, eds. *Life and Letters of Bayard Taylor,* 2 vols. Boston, 1895.

Harper's Weekly. Editorials, 1863–1892.

Hartz, Louis. *The Liberal Tradition in America.* New York, 1955.

Hofstadter, Richard. *Age of Reform.* New York, 1955.

———. *Social Darwinism in American Thought.* Boston, 1955.

Holt, Henry. *Garrulities of an Octogenarian Editor.* Boston and New York, 1923.

Hoogenboom, Ari. *Outlawing the Spoils.* Urbana, Ill., 1961.

Houghton, Walter. *The Victorian Frame of Mind.* New Haven, 1957.

Jackson, Isabel Hooper. Nineteenth Century American Literary Societies. Unpublished M.A. Thesis. University of California, Berkeley, 1934.

Jaher, Frederic Cople, ed. *The Age of Industrialism in America; Essays in Social Structure and Cultural Values.* New York, 1968.

Johnson, Robert Underwood. *Remembered Yesterdays.* Boston, 1923.

Kindilien, Carlin T. *American Poetry in the 1890's.* Providence, R.I., 1956.

Kolko, Gabriel. *Railroads and Regulation, 1877–1916.* Princeton, N.J., 1965.

———. *The Triumph of Conservatism; A Re-interpretation of American History, 1900–1916.* Glencoe, Ill., 1963.

Kraditor, Eileen S. *The Ideas of the Woman Suffrage Movement, 1890–1920.* New York, 1965.

Lippincott, Benjamin. *Victorian Critics of Democracy.* Minneapolis, 1938.

Marcus, Steven. *The Other Victorians; A Study of Sexuality and Pornography in Mid-Nineteenth Century England.* New York, 1966.

Matthiessen, F. O. *American Renaissance.* New York, 1941.

May, Henry. *The End of American Innocence.* New York, 1959.

McCloskey, Robert. *American Conservatism in the Age of Enterprise.* Cambridge, Mass., 1951.

Mencken, H. L. *A Book of Prefaces.* New York, 1917.

Merriam, Charles E. *American Political Ideas.* New York, 1923.

Mill, John Stuart. *Essays on Politics and Culture.* Ed. Gertrude Himmelfarb. New York, 1963.

Milne, Gordon. *George William Curtis and the Genteel Tradition.* Bloomington, Ind., 1956.

More, Paul Elmer. *Shelburne Essays,* 7th Ser. New York and London, 1910.

Morgan, H. Wayne, ed. *The Gilded Age.* Syracuse, N.Y., 1970.

Mott, Frank Luther. *A History of American Magazines,* 5 vols. New York and Cambridge, Mass., 1930–68.

Mowry, George Edwin. *The California Progressives.* Berkeley, 1951.

Nevins, Allan. *The 'Evening Post.'* New York, 1922.

Norton, Charles Eliot. "Abraham Lincoln," *North American Review,* C (1865), 1–21.

———. "The Advantages of Defeat," *Atlantic Monthly,* VIII (1861), 360–65.

————. "America and England," *North American Review*, C (1865), 331–46.

————. "American Political Ideas," *North American Review*, CI (1865), 550–65.

————. "Arthur Hugh Clough," *North American Review*, CV (1867), 434–77.

————. "The Church and Religion," *North American Review*, CVI (1868), 376–96.

————. "The Congress of Peace and Liberty at Lausanne," *Nation*, IX (1869), 336–37.

————. *Considerations on Some Recent Social Theories*. Boston, 1853.

————. "Dante and his Latest English Translators," *North American Review*, CII (1866), 509–29.

————. "A Definition of the Fine Arts," *Forum*, VII (1889), 30–40.

————. "Dwellings and Schools for the Poor," *North American Review*, LXXIV (1852), 464–89.

————. "Education at the Great English Public Schools," *Nation*, I (1865), 149–50.

————. "The Educational Value of the History of the Fine Arts," *Educational Review*, IX (1895), 343–48.

————. "Feminine Poetry," *Nation*, XXII (1876), 132–34.

————. "Goldwin Smith," *North American Review*, XCIX (1864), 523–39.

————. "Good Manners," *Nation*, II (1866), 571.

————. "The Greek Play at Harvard," *Atlantic Monthly*, XLVIII (1881), 106–10.

————. *Historical Studies of Church-Building in the Middle Ages: Venice, Siena, Florence*. New York, 1880.

————. "The International Congress of Peace and Liberty at Lausanne," *Nation*, IX (1869), 313–15.

————. "James Russell Lowell," *Harper's Monthly*, LXXXVI (1893), 846–57.

————. "The Lack of Old Homes in America," *Scribner's Magazine*, V (1889), 336–40.

————. "The Launching of the Magazine," *Atlantic Monthly*, C (1907), 579–81.

————. Review of *The Laws of Race* by W. P. Hazard, *Atlantic Monthly*, VII (1861), 252–54.

————. *The Letters of Charles Eliot Norton*. Eds. Sara Norton and Mark A. DeWolf Howe, 2 vols. Boston and New York, 1913.

————. "The Life and Death of Jason," *Nation*, V (1867), 146–47.

————. "The Life of George Ticknor," *Nation*, XXII (1876), 148–49.

————. "Matthew Arnold," *Proceedings of the American Academy of Arts and Sciences*, XXIII (1887–8), 349–53.

————. "Muntz's *Life of Raphael*," *Nation*, XXXII (1881), 208–9.

————. "Notes," *Nation*, XX (1875), 190–92.

————. "Notes," *Nation*, XXI (1875), 7–9.

————. *Notes of Travel and Study in Italy*, Boston, 1859.

————. "Our Soldiers," *North American Review*, XCIX (1864), 172–204.

————. "The Paradise of Mediocrities," *Nation*, I (1865), 43–44.

————. "The Poetry of Rudyard Kipling," *Atlantic Monthly*, LXXIX (1897), 111–15.

————. "The Poverty of England," *North American Review*, CIX (1869), 122–54.

————. "The President's Message," *North American Review*, CII (1866), 250–66.

————. "Religious Liberty," *North American Review*, CIV (1867), 586–97.

————. "Some Aspects of Civilization in America," *Forum*, XX (1896), 641–51.

————. "Stedman's *Victorian Poets*," *Nation*, XXII (1876), 117–18.

————. Review of *Thoughts on the Future Civil Policy of America* by John William Draper. *Nation*, I (1865), 407–9.

————. "Waste," *Nation*, II (1866), 301–2.

————. "Whitman's *Leaves of Grass*," *Putnam's Monthly*, VI, (1855), 321–23.

————, ed. *Addresses and Orations of George William Curtis*, 3 vols. New York, 1894.

Norton, Sara, and Mark A. De Wolf Howe, eds. *The Letters of Charles Eliot Norton*. Boston and New York, 1913.

Ogden, Rollo. *Life and Letters of E. L. Godkin*, 2 vols. New York, 1907.

Parrington, Vernon L. *Main Currents in American Thought*, 3 vols. New York, 1927–30.

Pattee, Fred Lewis. *The Feminine Fifties*. New York, 1940.

Pearson, Hesketh. *The Life of Oscar Wilde*. London, 1954.

Pochmann, Henry A. *German Culture in America*. Madison, Wis., 1957.

Pritchard, John. *Criticism in America*. Norman, Okla., 1956.

————. *Literary Wise Men of Gotham*. Baton Rouge, La., 1963.

————. *Return to the Fountains*. Durham, N.C., 1942.

Putnam, George Haven. *Memories of a Publisher, 1865–1915*. New York and London, 1915.

Raleigh, John H. *Matthew Arnold and American Culture*. Berkeley, Calif., 1957.

Ross, Danforth, The Genteel Tradition, University of Minnesota, 1954. University Microfilms, Ann Arbor, Michigan.

Rossiter, Clinton. *Conservatism in America*. New York, 1955.

Ruskin, John. *Letters to Charles Eliot Norton*, 2 vols. Boston and New York, 1913.

Samuels, Charles. *Thomas Bailey Aldrich*. New York, 1965.

Santayana, George. *The Genteel Tradition at Bay*. New York, 1931.

———. *Winds of Doctrine.* New York, 1913.

Schultz, John Richie. *The Unpublished Letters of Bayard Taylor in the Huntington Library.* San Marino, Calif., 1937.

Schurz, Carl. *Reminiscences of Carl Schurz,* 3 vols. New York, 1907–8.

Sheehan, Donald. *This Was Publishing; A Chronicle of the Book Trade in the Gilded Age.* Bloomington, Ind., 1952.

Smith, Bernard. *Forces in American Literary Criticism.* New York, 1939.

Smith, Timothy L. *Revivalism and Social Reform in Mid-Nineteenth Century America.* New York, 1957.

Spiller, Robert, *et al. Literary History of the United States.* New York, 1959.

Sproat, John G. *The Best Men; Liberal Reformers in the Gilded Age.* New York, 1968.

Stallman, R. W. *Stephen Crane: A Biography.* New York, 1968.

Stedman, Edmund Clarence. *Genius, and other Essays.* New York, 1911.

———. *The Life and Letters of Edmund Clarence Stedman.* Eds. Laura Stedman and George M. Gould, 2 vols. New York, 1910.

———. *The Nature and Elements of Poetry.* Boston and New York, 1892.

———. *The Poems of Edmund Clarence Stedman.* New York, 1908.

———. *Poets of America.* Boston and New York, 1885.

———. *Victorian Poets.* New York, 1917.

Stedman, Laura, and George M. Gould, eds. *The Life and Letters of Edmund Clarence Stedman,* 2 vols. New York, 1910.

Stein, Roger. *John Ruskin and Aesthetic Thought in America, 1840–1900.* Cambridge, Mass., 1967.

Stoddard, Richard Henry. *The Lion's Cub, with Other Verse.* New York, 1890.

———. *Poems of Richard Henry Stoddard.* New York, 1880.

———. *Recollections Personal and Literary.* New York, 1903.

———. *Songs of Summer.* Boston, 1857.

Stovall, Floyd. *The Development of American Literary Criticism.* Chapel Hill, N.C., 1955.

Swinburne, Algernon Charles. *A Year's Letters.* Portland, Maine, 1901. Orig. pub. in *The Tatler,* Aug. 25–Dec. 29, 1877, under the pseudonym, Mrs. Horace Manners.

Taylor, Bayard. *At Home and Abroad,* 1st, 2nd Ser. New York, 1902.

———. *Beauty and the Beast.* New York, 1893.

———. *Boys of Other Countries.* New York, 1876.

———. *Critical Essays and Literary Notes.* New York, 1880.

———. *Diversions of the Echo Club.* London, 1877.

———. *Dramatic Works of Bayard Taylor.* Boston, 1880.

———. *Egypt and Iceland in the Year 1874.* New York, 1880.

———. *Eldorado.* New York, 1879.

———. *Hannah Thurston.* New York, 1903.

———. *Home Pastorals, Ballads, and Lyrics.* Boston, 1875.

———. *John Godfrey's Fortunes.* New York, 1899.

———. *Joseph and His Friend*. New York, 1893.
———. *Journey to Central Africa*. New York, 1879.
———. *Lands of the Saracen*. New York, 1880.
———. *Lars, a Pastoral of Norway*. Boston, 1873.
———. *Life and Letters of Bayard Taylor*. Eds. Marie Hansen-Taylor and Horace E. Scudder, 2 vols. Boston, 1895.
———. *Northern Travel*. New York, 1880.
———. *The Picture of St. John*. Boston, 1866.
———. *Poems of the Orient*. Boston, 1857.
———. *The Poetical Works of Bayard Taylor*. Boston, 1880.
———. *The Poet's Journal*. Boston, 1862.
———. *Rhymes of Travel, Ballads and Poems*. New York, 1848.
———. *The Story of Kennett*. New York, 1866.
———. *Studies in German Literature*. New York, 1879.
———. *Travels in Greece and Russia*. New York, 1880.
———. *Views Afoot*. New York, 1846.
———. *A Visit to India, China and Japan in the Year 1853*. New York, 1880.
Trilling, Lionel. *Matthew Arnold*. New York, 1939.
Tyack, David B. *George Ticknor and the Boston Brahmins*. Cambridge, Mass., 1967.
Vanderbilt, Kermit. *Charles Eliot Norton; Apostle of Culture in a Democracy*. Cambridge, Mass., 1959.
Walcutt, Charles C. *American Literary Naturalism, a Divided Stream*. Minneapolis, Minn., 1956.
White, Morton. *Social Thought in America, the Revolt Against Formalism*. New York, 1949.
Wiebe, Robert H. *The Search for Order, 1877–1920*. New York, 1967.
Wilde, Oscar. *De Profundis*. New York, 1964.
Williams, Raymond. *Culture and Society, 1780–1850*. New York, 1958.
Wilson, Douglas L., ed. *The Genteel Tradition; Nine Essays by George Santayana*. Cambridge, Mass., 1967.
Winter, William. *Old Friends*. New York, 1909.
Wood, James Playsted. *Magazines in the United States*. New York, 1956.
Ziff, Larzer. *The American 1890's*. New York, 1966.

Index

Index